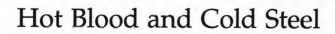

Hot Blood and Cold Steel

HOT BLOOD AND COLD STEEL
Life and Death in the Trenches of the First World War

Edited and compiled by Andy Simpson

Tom Donovan
London

First published in 1993 by

Tom Donovan Publishing Ltd.
52 Willow Road
Hampstead
London NW3 1TP

ISBN: 1-871085-12-8

Desk-top typeset by Tom Donovan Publishing Ltd.

Printed in the United States of America

Contents

Twenty-eight photographs will be found between pages 108-109
Numbers 3, 5, 6, 9-16, 18, 19, 22-28 are reproduced by kind permission of the
Trustees of the Imperial War Museum, London.

Maps

Acknowledgements

The editor and publishers would like most gratefully to thank the following individuals for their contributions to this book. Emma Jane Brooks, for her sterling efforts in typing the manuscript, deciphering the author's handwriting and unfailing good humour. Brian Turner for allowing us to draw on his extensive Great War library. Andrew Read for his contributions to the photographs. Donald Simpson and Mike Calnan for so kindly proof-reading the text and for their other useful suggestions; any mistakes remaining in the book are ours and not theirs. Peter T. Scott for encouragement and much useful advice. Richard Duke and Stuart Hobbs for their technical support and advice.

Foreword

This book is an attempt to capture, in their own words, the experience of British front line soldiers on the Western Front in the Great War. It is fair to say that this conflict was, for the men of this country at least, uniquely ghastly; more died than in any other in our history and the scars left on the survivors, both physical and mental can only be guessed at. The statistics speak for themselves. Twenty years after the end of the war disability pensions were being paid (amongst many others) to 11,600 men with amputated limbs and to 10,000 who had been blinded; a further 3,200 were confined in mental asylums; and in 1980 27,000 Great War disability pensions were still being paid.

These figures can only partially reflect the scale of the suffering. Only the voices of those who took part can perhaps convey its quality. And yet it is a distortion of the truth to concentrate solely on this aspect of the war; for many men other qualities counterbalanced the more unpalatable aspects of their experience, such as adventure, fellowship, responsibility beyond their years (in the case of many young officers), and freedom from the yoke of the frequently appalling industrial working conditions in Great Britain.

In addition, one should not overlook the fact that these were men of a different era, many of whom were idealistic fighters for 'poor little Belgium' or motivated by a sense of duty to their country and empire perceived differently than today. Much of the seemingly meaningless sacrifice was cheerfully accepted by its victims, intent on 'doing their bit' and inculcated with the team spirit at school or church. Many were even able to laugh in the face of the horror; a great number of them were boys of nineteen or twenty who delighted in childish horse-play. Perhaps youthful resilience helped them in adapting to the conditions they faced and to the peculiarities of service life. One anecdote - which is set too far behind the lines to qualify for this book - nevertheless conveys well the extreme youth and naivety of its author and his colleagues. It is of the first court-martial in which the distinguished writer Guy Chapman took part:

At Barly, too, came my first experience of that admirable fountain of justice, the court-martial. The accused was the elderly pioneer sergeant of the 60th; the charge, 'drunk in trenches'. He was duly found guilty. As he was marched out, I hurriedly turned the pages of the Manual of Military Law, and found to my horror that the punishment was death, tout court. So when Major the Hon. George Keppel turned to me as junior member of the court and demanded my sentence, I replied, "Oh, death, sir, I suppose." Major Keppel blenched and turned to my opposite number, Gwinnell. Gwinnell, who was as young and unlearned in expedience as myself, answered, as I had, "Death, I suppose." Our good president looked at us from the top of his six feet and groaned: "But, my boys, my boys, you can't do it."

"But, sir," we protested in unison, anxious to justify ourselves, "it says so here."

To return, however, to the purpose of this book, it is necessary to lay out the criteria used in selecting the anecdotes. These are: firstly, that the anecdote is of a first hand experience; secondly, that it should have taken place in the trenches (or other front line situation); thirdly, that it be British or Empire in origin; fourthly, that it be set on the Western Front.

These are laid out without any intention of denigrating the experiences of other nations, or of British troops in other theatres of war. But to include them in this book would render it unmanageably large, and for the general reader the trenches of the Western Front are surely synonymous with the Great War. And despite the not infrequent inclusion of humorous anecdotes, one should always bear in mind the words of one veteran in his introduction to his account of his own experiences, published in 1934:

> After my discharge from the Army on the 25th March, 1919, I made up my mind to write a book on my experiences, as the havoc, desolation, and destruction in the Great War so appalled me. Added to these was the torment of the vermin, the continual fear of death, the suffering and hardships. It all appeared to me as a thing that should never be. Surely human beings were never intended to go through such harrowing experiences.

> This book was written with the intention of doing good, of educating people who were not engaged in the Great War to understand what war is; not as some people would have us believe, but as it really is, and if it will make people realize the awfulness and uselessness of war in settling International disputes, it will have achieved the object with which it was written. [Henry Gregory]

Like the writer of that piece many survivors found a need to record and publish their experiences. The first appeared while the war was still being fought, often in the form of memorials to fallen sons, and not a year has passed since 1918 without a new account appearing in print. The first great tranche was a cycle of self-justification or soul purging, this, loosely, from the mid-1920s to the outbreak of the Second World War. In the 1960s and '70s many, now aged, veterans felt, quite rightly, that they had something valid to say, and alongside their considerable output more and more letters home and contemporary diaries have been discovered and published. Given the official policy that all letters should be censored, it may seem surprising that so much valuable material can be found in them. Nearly all letters were, however, censored by a man's own officers, and they often were not especially rigorous.

> The censor's stamp does not mean that all my letters get read but merely that we are rather proud of our censor's stamp and like playing with it; so somebody has just leant over my shoulder and stamped this and various other things. [R.C.Hopkins, RE]

In addition to the system of censorship within a unit, there was also the 'green envelope' system; these envelopes were liable to censorship at the Base, but only a small proportion was opened. It was essentially a system based on trust, which enabled the writers to record details of a more initimate nature which they would have been reluctant to let their immediate superiors read.

It is largely from this mass of material that the editor and publishers of this anthology have selected extracts which present an all-encompassing portrayal of what it was like to live, fight, suffer and die in the trenches of the Western Front.

It is the human story of the front line, drawn from hundreds of published and unpublished sources, some well-known, most not so. Some classics are included (although there are notable exceptions), but to get to the terrible realities of that grisly, seemingly endless, lifestyle in all its facets the editor has consciously set out to draw on more obscure contemporary letters and diaries which will be unfamiliar to the vast majority of readers.

Historical Overview

The Great War on the Western Front was entered into by Britain, Belgium, France and Germany on a tide of optimism and misconception. The vast majority of people in all four countries were convinced that - as is so often quoted - 'it will all be over by Christmas', and they were joined in this view by the majority of soldiers. The British Expeditionary Force was sent to France 100,000 strong, with a vague brief to keep in touch with the French left flank, but no other, more specific objectives were defined. In fact, the initiative very swiftly passed to the Germans. The French Plan XVII ground to a bloody halt as their attacks all along their front from the Ardennes to the Swiss border met with stiff German resistance and the German right wing swept through Belgium and into northern France. Their object, as defined in the famous Schleiffen Plan, was to envelop Paris and crush the French army against the Franco-German border in the east. But they were too successful; the French armies in the east were not drawn into the trap (ironically, as a result of their own lack of success in the attack) and the situation to the west looked good enough for two corps to be taken away from the crucial right wing of the attack and sent against the Russians on the eastern front.

Having retreated almost constantly after making first contact with the Germans, and administering two bloody checks to them at Mons and le Cateau, the British Expeditionary Force and French forces were able to counter-attack at the Marne, where a combination of over-optimism, bad communications and simple ineptitude had left the German 1st Army, which formed the extreme right of their attack, comparatively isolated from its fellows.

After the Marne, the Germans having fallen back and then held the attacking Allies at the Aisne, wherever the two sides were in contact stalemate now arose. The only way to keep a mobile war going, and with it a quick end to hostilities, was to outflank the other side. This led to the 'race for the sea', as each attempted to get around the other's western flank, pushing the line of battle further and further until it reached the Channel coast. Neither succeeded, and the front was established as it would remain - with minor changes - until March 1918. In the process the old British regular army had effectively ceased to exist, its demise being hastened at the First Battle of Ypres, where a German breakthrough was narrowly averted.

Britain had entered the war unprepared for a conflict on that scale. Her army was small and composed of long-service volunteers whose quality was excellent; the speed and accuracy of their rifle fire has become legendary for misleading the Germans in 1914 into thinking that the British Expeditionary Force had twice as many machine-guns as in fact it had. British industry was likewise unready to produce the guns, ammunition and other matériel required for all-out modern war; the Territorial Forces sent to reinforce the overstretched BEF being armed with obsolete rifles and artillery until 1915.

As soon as war broke out there was a rush of men to the colours, as Lord Kitchener, the Minister of War, announced the formation of a 'New Army' (later to be a nominal five New Armies). These men and the later conscripts formed the first citizen army in British history and contributed the bulk of the memoirs and reminiscences gathered together in this book. Most are concerned with life in the trenches, for by the close of 1914 both sides sat facing one another in a solid line of field fortifications, protected by barbed wire, from Switzerland to the sea. It is important to bear in mind that these positions were frequently sited in such a way as to increase the danger and hardship suffered by the men facing the German army, who all too often held the higher ground. It was politically unthinkable for any more French or Belgian soil to be surrendered to the enemy so the British and French remained in less than ideal positions, under observation that made any movement above ground in daylight even more dangerous as well as giving the Germans greater artillery accuracy. In themselves, the low-lying Allied trenches were all the less bearable to live in as a result of rain water and effluent from the German lines draining into them.

The Germans made another attempt to break through the British defences in April 1915, again at Ypres where the British and French front line protruded eastwards in a salient - known as The Salient - which offered to the Germans a chance to pinch it off from each side. In the event, and at the cost of 35,000 men to themselves and 70,000 to the French and British, they succeeded only in shrinking it to a size whereby their artillery, facing it on three sides, could reach anywhere within it. It acquired a justifiably bad reputation among the British and Empire troops called upon to serve there, as the place name of one particularly dangerous crossroads on the Menin Road illustrates - Hellfire Corner.

Given the size of the British contribution to the war in 1914, and the massive scale of their own (generally unsuccessful) attacks, it is hardly surprising that the French were not convinced that their allies were serious in the prosecution of the war. In order to alleviate this the attack at Neuve Chapelle, took place on 10 March 1915; after a promising start it turned into a bloody shambles. This was followed in May by the attack on Aubers Ridge and in September the battle of Loos. All that was achieved was the slaughter of the remaining regulars, Territorial Forces in France and reservists, who could have been used to train the raw recruits of the New Armies. Instead, the latter had to learn from their mistakes; but in war mistakes are all too often fatal. And the commanders of the BEF learned the wrong lessons. Like their men, they were unaccustomed to this style of warfare, and like their men they had to learn to cope with it. It is unfair and inaccurate to say that they 'should' have broken through in 1915 or 1916. For if the German army - greater in numbers of men and guns, better trained and holding the strategic initiative until late 1916 - could not succeed, it hardly seems likely that the British could. Both sides had to adapt to the unthinkable. The British thought the solution to the impasse was 'guns, guns and more guns'.

As a result, comparatively little thought was given to the employment of the infantry, who were there just to mop-up after the artillery barrage. It took some time to realise that guns on their own, no matter how destructive their fire, could not win the war.

One result of this way of thinking was the first day of the Battle of the Somme, 1st July 1916. Originally conceived as a joint effort with the French, German pressure on the latter at Verdun greatly reduced their participation and it became principally a British and Empire affair. The attack was preceded by a week-long barrage, in which 1.6 million shells were expended. This was designed to annihilate the Germans in the front line and cut their wire; the infantry attack was expected by virtually everyone to be a literal walkover, and much of the infantry (laden, on average, with 60lbs of kit) was ordered to attack in line, at walking pace. There would be no opposition. However, not all the wire was cut and the Germans had 20 foot deep dugouts which even a barrage the magnitude of that employed could not destroy. The result was carnage; 20,000 British dead and 40,000 wounded in one day. As soon as the barrage had lifted, the Germans clambered out of their dugouts and manned their trenches and machine-gun posts. Where the German front line was reached and captured, the attackers were ultimately killed, taken prisoner or forced to retreat through the German counter-barrage sweeping no man's land and preventing reinforcements getting through. The New Army men in the attack had a brutal 'baptism of fire'; of 32 battalions suffering more than 500 casualties, 20 were New Army.

Despite this, some limited success on the southern flank of the attack was deemed to hold promise for the long-awaited breakthrough which would permit the cavalry to get into the open country behind the German lines and re-establish mobile warfare. Consequently, the battle dragged on until November, when it was finally realised that the impetus of the offensive was lost, not least as a result of the effect of shelling on the battlefield - which, coupled with the worsening weather, churned the land into a morass of mud negotiable only with difficulty.

It is, however, not inconceivable that the Battle of the Somme might have been permitted to carry on through the winter of 1916-17 had success seemed achievable. But the strength of the British and Empire troops had to be restored and conserved for attacks in 1917 which held a greater prospect of defeating the Germans, in concert with attacks by the French and on other fronts, the Italians and Russians. The first 1917 attack in the west was to be made jointly between the British and Empire troops near Arras and the French, on each side of the old Somme battleground. This was dislocated even before it began by a major German withdrawal to a new defensive line - known to the Allies as the Hindenburg line - from Arras to Royon, which gave them strong, well thought out defensive positions and freed manpower by shortening their line. Despite the strength of the Hindenburg Line, the fact that the German withdrawal rendered their original plan pointless and that the Germans had detailed intelligence of it, the French nevertheless insisted that they should attack in Champagne.

In order to draw German reserves away from the latter, the British and Colonial troops attacked at Arras. As was so often the case, a promising start was left as just that, the offensive bogging down against stiffening resistance in terrain worsened by the attackers' own artillery. Nevertheless, the attack was deemed a success, and compared to the

French effort a week later, on April 16th, it was. Their commander, Nivelle, had predicted a six mile advance on the first day; 600 yards were gained. By the end of the second, the French had advanced some two miles and had lost just under 120,000 men. German losses were about 40,000, with 20,000 prisoners in French hands. This was the final straw for a large proportion (the full details have yet to be established, 75 years on) of the French army. Sixteen army corps mutinied, refusing to join any attack even though they were prepared to enter the trenches. Fortuitously, the Germans did not discover this until too late, after the mutinies had been suppressed by General Pétain. But the onus of keeping up the pressure on the Germans was left to Britain and her Empire.

For some 18 months, since early 1916, the British C-in-C, Sir Douglas Haig, had wished to launch an offensive to break out of the Ypres Salient (firstly capturing the ridges surrounding it) and join the French and Belgian armies holding the line in the Salient to the coast. Capturing that part of the Belgian coast line held by the Germans would deprive them of submarine bases and threaten their communications in Belgium. This plan had the further advantage of removing the Germans from the vicinity of Ypres, where they were inflicting 7,000 casualties per week on the troops holding it for no gain in return whatsoever. The fundamental weakness of the plan was, however, its initial phase of capturing the ridges round the Salient. This essentially reduced it to another brutal, frontal attack on a strong defensive position.

The Third Battle of Ypres, also known as Passchendaele, began on the 31st July 1917 after the successful capture of the Messines Ridge on 7th June by the dramatic expedient of blowing 19 mines (which could be heard in London) under the German lines. Sadly, the attack guaranteed its own miserable and bloody outcome. The water table in that part of Flanders is only two feet below ground level and so a complex drainage system is necessary to prevent large areas becoming bogs. The barrage preceding the British attack was the most concentrated of the war to date and devastated the drainage system of the area; this was exacerbated by the heaviest rainfall for many years. Mud, a serious problem in early offensives, was the worst experienced in the war and to leave the few tracks across the battlefield (themselves constant targets for German artillery) was to invite death by drowning. Trench lines at times ceased to exist, being replaced by chains of shell holes, half-filled with water from which attacks and counter-attacks were launched with increasing losses, and resulting in, at best, snail-like progress against a strong, deep defensive position designed by the Germans to minimise the effect of British artillery. One position changed hands 18 times, exemplifying the image of two exhausted men struggling not just to hurt one another, but to stand up at all. On 12th November the campaign was closed down; along the line, the average gain of ground was about four miles - which according to plan should have been in British hands by about 4th August.

After the Passchendaele offensive was brought to its more or less unsatisfactory conclusion another battle was commenced at Cambrai. Using tanks in large numbers for the first time a major break was achieved in the German line, but, as had so often proved the case, the Germans came back with a vengeance and this battle also tailed off to no gain as winter set in. Two new salients had been created but less than half of the Passchendaele-Messines ridge was in British hands. And the cost was some 250,000 casualties at Third Ypres and over 44,000 at Cambrai.

The strategic position in early 1918 was the most unfavourable to Britain and her allies since August 1914. The French army was still comparatively weak; like France, Britain was short of front line troops and nearing exhaustion after the haemorrhage of over three years of war; America was only just beginning to put her war machine into operation; Italy was still reeling from her defeats in 1917, and the Russian revolution had put paid to that country's war effort. While for Germany and her allies, who had been greatly weakened in the at times unintentionally attritional battles of 1916 and 1917, Russia's collapse had freed very experienced men from the Eastern Front for action in the West. A series of attacks, using new tactics of sudden 'hurricane' bombardment and infiltration of the British front line by élite teams of heavily-armed storm troops seemed to be all that was required to put the European Allies out of the war before the Americans arrived in strength.

The blow fell on 21st March, against the weakest part of the British line; in just over two weeks the Germans created a 40 mile deep salient, compelling the abandonment of the hard-won gains of 1916. Unlike the British High Command, the German General Staff on this occasion had the military acumen to break off their offensive at the point when it ceased to yield useful results (although they nevertheless committed more troops than they ultimately could afford). Further, similar attacks followed on the River Lys in Flanders in April and against the French on the Aisne and elsewhere in May, June and July. The Allied position seemed desperate, and it was under this stress that the generals finally accepted the creation of an overall Allied commander - General Foch. It was at this point that the stubbornness and refusal to panic of men like Foch and Haig, which had cost their countries so dear earlier in the war, bore fruit. Even when the picture seemed blackest, their minds turned to the counter-offensive. On 8th August, a major counter-attack at Amiens, using similar tactics to those of the Germans, but combining them with tank and air support, pushed the Germans back up to seven miles on a twelve mile front. That day was described by Ludendorff, their effective Commander in Chief, as 'the black day of the German Army.' The attack was broken off after a week since it seemed no longer likely to bear fruit as German resistance hardened, but from then until the end of the war constant pressure on the Germans was kept up, each attack being broken off when it had done as much as it could and a new blow swiftly falling elsewhere. Haig - unlike his masters in London - recognised that the war could be won in 1918 and acted accordingly; Foch agreed, and co-ordinated American and French attacks with those of the British, denying the German army any respite from the pressure. It is noteworthy that the British army, by far the junior partners of the French in 1914, captured in the last 100 days of 1918 almost as much ground, men and guns than their Belgian, French and American allies combined.

The German High Command had recognised as early as 10th August that defeat was inevitable, but held out for an improvement in the military situation in order to gain more favourable peace terms. None was forthcoming and the army's morale was beginning to fail; this was matched by serious unrest amongst the civilian population and mutiny by part of the Navy at Kiel. Armistice negotiations began on 8th November 1918; the Kaiser abdicated on the 9th; the Armistice was signed at 5.10am on the 11th and came into effect at 11am that day.

Structure

This book is not laid out chronologically; instead, a thematic approach has been adopted. Each chapter relates to a specific aspect of front line life, with the first acting as a general introduction to the trenches. Chapter 14, on offensive operations, relates only to the Battle of the Somme. This is for a number of reasons; firstly, that battle was a watershed since it was the first large-scale British offensive and marks the 'blooding' of the New Armies; and secondly, it laid the foundations, in terms of lessons learned and absorbed, of the attacks in 1917 and 1918. It was not the war-winning battle (arguably, Amiens in 1918) or the most costly in terms of casualties (Third Ypres, 1917), but for subsequent generations it has become synonymous with the struggle on the Western Front. And lastly, while this book does not purport to be a full operational history of the Great War, it is essential to portray the experience of battle.

At the end of the book are two appendices, one outlining the structure of the British army in the Great War and the other explaining abbreviations and technical terms used in the text.

The extracts from diaries, letters and memoirs used in the text are printed in their original style, and so the reader will notice inconsistencies between them and the linking text; for example, the latter refers to 'No-Man's-Land,' while the extracts vary between 'no-man's-land,' 'No Mans Land' and sundry other permutations. It was felt that the text of the originals should be left intact as far as possible, however, and so such variations have been retained.

1
The Trenches

A man's first introduction to war is a unique landmark in his life. Is it better to approach it by easy stages, gradually accustoming oneself to the scent of danger in the air, or be faced at once with the full aroma?

The 14th Light Division had no choice. We were flung in at the deep end and within a few weeks of arrival in Flanders were charged with the defence of part of the Ypres Salient. It was already a place of ill-omen. Here was not only the scent of danger but the all-pervading odour of death, the sickly 'perfume of the battlefield', as the Germans elegantly called it. Even in the early summer of 1915, as we dug in just behind the front line, 'freezing' when the flares went up, it was not so much the sudden scream of a shell or the whipcrack of a bullet which was unnerving as the fact that nowhere could one dig for more than a few feet without plunging one's spade into the spongy putrescence of a corpse.

Moving up to take over the line, we were marching as a battalion through Poperinghe, singing cheerfully, when, out of nowhere, a high-velocity shell screamed into the street. I was riding near the Colonel and it burst just behind us on the *pavé*, in the middle of a platoon. Five or six were killed, a dozen wounded. For the first time we heard the mournful raven's cry of 'Stretcher-bear-ers!'

That night, after the relief, I was going round my trenches in front of 'Y' Wood and stopped in a fire bay to speak to a corporal who had been with us in C Company since the early days in Blenheim Barracks. He was wearing round his chest a sort of lifebelt of yellow 'lemon' bombs. When it was time to move on, I made the excuse that I did not like the way he was dressed. I preferred people who did not wear waistcoats of bombs. We all laughed.

As I turned the traverse, a whizz-bang burst on the parapet. A splinter must have struck him, for there was a dull roar. Back in the fire bay, my torch at first showed nothing - except the limbless trunk of the corporal on the ground. It seemed to be still moving. Then I saw that the fragments of the other three men were plastered round the walls. Company-Sergeant-Major Kent and I scraped them off with shovels and

carried them behind the trench into 'Y' Wood, itself a skeleton. The
flares curved up, the odd shell lumbered over, occasionally a
machine-gun chattered: it was a quiet night on the Western Front.'

So wrote the author Desmond Young, then a young officer in the
King's Royal Rifle Corps, recalling his introduction to the front line in
Flanders in 1915.

The complex system of trenches, of which Young was entering one
small part, varied considerably. Whilst always unpleasant and
dangerous (even in so-called 'quiet' sectors) conditions necessarily
differed according to locality, season and the proximity of the German
front line. In the Salient, where Desmond Young met his baptism of
fire, the trenches were more often than not waterlogged and the
infamous Flanders mud, together with the closeness of the two
opposing lines imposed their own unique way of life. But in the chalky
ground of the Somme region, where the trenches were often some
hundreds of yards apart, trench life and fighting bore different
characteristics; even the mud itself was not the same.

When the 48th Division was moved from the Ypres Salient to the
Ancre Valley in July 1915, such differences were evident to Pte.
H.Raymond Smith of the 1/8th Worcesters:

> These trenches were very different from those we had been occupying in
> the 'Plugstreet' Sector. In that particular part of the line, where the
> ground for the most part was very flat, they were composed of sandbag
> breastworks, and our line and that of the enemy ran close together.
> Never much more than 300 yards separated our front parapet from
> theirs, while in places they were as close together as thirty yards. In the
> Hébuterne Sector all this was changed. Here we were in the valley of the
> Ancre, part of the Valley of the Somme. All around us were rolling
> plains, with villages dotted about here and there. Much of it was
> undulating park land, with Gommecourt Wood on our left, behind the
> enemy lines. Up till recently these trenches had been part of the long
> line held by our French allies. At Hébuterne, which must have been a
> flourishing village or small market town, but which was then in
> complete ruins, the trenches ran directly out of the village. That is to say
> the two main communication trenches commenced at the top of the
> village street, and wended their tortuous way through ruined gardens
> and apple orchards to the support line and the front dug-outs were of a
> superior and more permanent type than any we had hitherto seen.

> At Hébuterne, so far as danger was concerned, exactly the reverse
> conditions prevailed compared with those we had experienced in the
> 'Plugstreet' Sector. There the opposing trenches had been so close that
> they were seldom shelled, as the artillery on either side were afraid of

hitting their own men but the sniping was deadly. Here, on the other hand, a valley, about seven hundred yards wide, separated friend from foe, and the consequence was that we were frequently shelled, and suffered casualties from this, but there was, at first, little rifle fire. There was a strange, though false air of peacefulness about these trenches in the Valley of the Ancre.

The 48th Division was fortunate to be transferred to what at the time was one of the most peaceful sectors of the British line; most British troops were rarely so lucky. The physical features which dictated the nature of the front line were not always created by Nature. The La Bassée sector was a heavily industrialised area, which gave it unusual perils:

> In November of this year [1916] the corps, to vary the picture, took over the Cuinchy sector on the right of Givenchy and immediately south of the La Bassée Canal. It was a unique and damnable sector, in which a company of my men were set to dig tunnels from the reserve to the support and front trenches.
>
> It was unique by reason of the brick-stacks, and damnable by reason of the Minenwerfer and the Railway Triangle. Our line ran in and out of a dozen or so brick-stacks, enormous maroon cubes of solid brick that withstood both shell and mine. Some we held and some the enemy held. Inside them tiny staircases were made, and camouflaged snipers, impossible to detect, made life miserable. Occasionally we tried to take each other's brickstacks, but these attempts were unsuccessful, and we settled down, each as uncomfortable as he well could be. And in this sector the enemy employed minenwerfer with the utmost enterprise. Our trenches were literally blown to pieces. In the daytime we ran about like disturbed ants, ever listening for the little thud of the "minnie's" discharge and then looking upwards for the black speck by day or the glow of it by night. [Major W.H.L. Watson]

When Pte. A.O.Pollard of the Honourable Artillery Company entered the line near Ypres for the first time in November 1914, only the season was the same; conditions were much different:

> Winter was upon us and it was bitterly cold. From Kemmel village we left the road and proceeded across country. Part of the way traversed a turnip field. I had been detailed to help carry ammunition for the Vickers guns. Two heavy boxes in addition to my rifle and ordinary equipment. Every time I stepped on a turnip, I slipped. Stray bullets from the German line hummed through the air. Once, whilst crossing a ditch, I fell. My outflung hand came in contact with a slimy something that gave to the touch. It was the face of a Frenchman who had been lying dead for some months. It was my first experience of death. I

wondered whether it would ever be my fate to lie like that uncared for and uncaring.

The trench, when we reached it, was half full of mud and water. We set to work to try and drain it. Our efforts were hampered by the fact that the French, who had first occupied it, had buried their dead in the bottom and sides. Every stroke of the pick encountered a body. The smell! Ugh!

The cold was terrible. Standing in water as we were, it was impossible to keep warm. I kept beating my feet against the parapet to keep them from going to sleep. We lived for the rum ration which was all too meagre. I was in a traverse of the trench with the Trinity and 'Scully' Hull. We swore that when we got out we would have a roast goose and a jolly good tuck in.

Whilst Pollard was new to the line, an old soldier, (Cpl. Henry Gregory, serving with 119th Machine Gun Company) returning to the line during the appalling winter of 1917, found the conditions as, if not more distasteful:

During this winter, after hard frosty weather, the ground was frozen as hard as a brick. It suddenly turned to rain, and kept it up for weeks on end. This was the winter when the trenches gave way and fell in. What a state they were in; they were two and three feet deep in water and mud. In some places it came above our thighs, and when going up the line you had to keep on the move or you were done. It was certainly not safe to go up alone.

It was hard work going up the trenches while they were in this condition, the water swishing above your knees, and your boots slipping about in the slime underneath. We used to get on top of the parapet when we got the chance, as it was slow moving down in the water and mud, but the order came through that no one was to walk on top of the parapet. This they made a crime.

It was hard work ploughing through all this muck with full fighting kit on your back, and although it was bitterly cold we used to sweat at the exertion we had to use to get along. It was a heart-breaking job to get forward at all.

When we had arrived at the positions we were to occupy, we had to get our clothes dried as best we could. We were always soaked well above the knees, and plastered in mud. We had to sleep and stand about all day in this condition. The discomforts at this time were terrible, and can hardly be realized by those who were not there.

Mud on occasion provided indignities even greater than the discomfort that Cpl. Gregory described. Towards the end of the Battle of the

Somme an officer of the King's Shropshire Light Infantry encountered an unusual spectacle:

> On leaving the trench we saw a man stuck in a shell hole. "Give us a hand, mate. I can't move in this — mud." he shouted.
> It took two of us, one on each arm, to move him at all.
> "Something's caught," he yelled.
> Just then he came away from the mud causing us to fall over.
> We roared with laughter. Poor devil. He had left his breeches, pants, and everything else in the mud; he stood in his shirt.
> "What are you going to do now?" laughed the sergeant-major.
> "Don't you worry about me, Sir," he replied. I shall get back to billets if I have to crawl the whole — way!" [Capt. Geoffrey Dugdale]

Curiously, mud was not invariably viewed unfavourably. Lt. Bernard Pitt of the Border Regiment, wrote home on Christmas day 1915 that:

> This is an unfortunate region, and consists entirely of mud, a form of matter which has, however, been unfairly despised. I am prepared to take my oath that mud is warm and a friend to man. Mud is affectionate and clinging; mud has no pride; mud is soft to fall on; mud is not unpleasant to the taste, and does not greatly interfere with the hearing; and, finally, mud is warm.

A fortnight later, however, his enthusiasm for mud seems to have evaporated, to be replaced by a fascination with the nightly firework display:

> What is life like in the trenches, well, muddy, and cramped, and filthy. Everything gets covered with mud; you can't wash, for water has to be fetched for a mile. There is no room, and if you walk upright in many of the trenches, you run grave risks; and you sleep, huddled together, unable to stretch. Of course one gets greasy and smutty, and the place smells bad, as you can imagine. All day long shells and rifle bullets go banging and whistling, and from dark to midnight the Huns fire rifle-grenades and machine-guns at us. In our dug-out we can hear the bullets coming whop against the roof and against the sand-bags round it. But nobody minds that; nobody is one penny the worse. If you show a light, over come their little shells, 'whiz-bangs' or 'pip-squeaks,' as they are called from the sound they make. All night long they send up lights, greenish yellow and very bright, ours are purplish, and nowhere near as good, and we let them do the fireworks. The French, on our right, send up a reddish rocket which emits a great, green ball of flame, which slowly drifts down to earth. In the day-time our battery sends them a few presents, but up to now we have not found our targets with great accuracy. That will come when we are quite sure which of the many low moulds [sic] of chalk on our front, left, and right are real German trenches; for the Hun is an industrious swine, and makes line

after line of dummy trenches. All this part of the line is full of relics of the last great attack. We have a safer job. You can't get guns weighing 285lbs., and bombs weighing 64lbs. over the top of the parapet in an advance, so we just help the artillery to bombard and prepare for attacks [Pitt was a trench mortar officer at this time]. But there is little doing, though one of these days the Hun will blow up a bit of our line and try to take it. War is subterranean here now, and the German miners are indefatigable.

The spectacle was widely admired:

I had my first real experience of a bombardment last night in an observation-post just opposite Havrincourt. 'Minenwerfer' and whizzbangs were dropping all round me, bursting redly in the long grass and crashing on the sunless road beneath. The characteristic of a whizzbang is its speed: the victim has not time to estimate his chances before the shell is on him. It travels as swift as sound, with the result that the bang of the gun coincides with the explosion. I was wondering which one would get me next, but the enemy found it impossible to get anything like a direct hit. One, however, covered me with dirt and gave me a nice hour's work shaking shirt and trousers clear.

If you are in a mood for fireworks and artificial illumination, the scene last night would have satisfied your wildest expectations. The brigade to the right of us put over liquid-fire and shell-gas. I was dreaming comfortably at my post, watching thistle-heads bob up and down and rats trip lightly over the sandbags when a sudden flare on the opposite ridge wakened me to reality. A long, low bank of white smoke became visible in front of a yellow starlight thrown up from the enemy lines; then it swelled out, rose on end, trailed off in long tails, and at last rolled across in an overwhelming wave, burning like slag fresh from the furnace. Meanwhile green lights were rising to the right and left, showers of stars trailed in a long arc and fell into the white wave, flying darts rose and flickered, and occasionally a red light showed that the enemy craved the help of artillery.

The volume of smoke increased and blotted out even the highest Very lights, so that the illumination appeared to come from behind instead of within: to the left a broad yellow flare shone dimly, like an October moon rising from mist on the fields. Rising and falling, the great wave swept over Cambrai and beyond, forming of sky, valley, hill, a strangely gradated monotone in every shade of green - green of the first leaf and green of the deepest pool.

The noise was terrific: gas-shells, trench-mortars, 'flying-pigs', 'minenwerfers' 9.2's, 18-pounders, whizzbangs - all crashing together; machine-guns kept rattling away from both lines. Strange to say, the German artillery did not reply until an hour afterwards, when the bombardment I have mentioned began. Even in the darkness the bank of gas gleamed obscurely for miles, like a cloud lying along the horizon.

The effect appeared the most magnificent I have ever seen, even in imagination: the idea that so many lives perished in the smoke added a certain solemnity to the picture, not perhaps in the wave itself, nor in the flash and flare of light, but in the colouring thought. Even the slightest thing that tells of human struggle or pain becomes ennobled in self, and perhaps more sublime. That is my idea of last night.

While that writer, Hugh Quigley of the 12th Royal Scots, found the 'show' inspired him to the lyrical description above, the second in command of the 13th Royal Fusiliers adopted a more scientific approach:

It was not always pleasant to stroll with the second-in-command. He had become an amateur of shells and noted new varieties with all the enthusiasm of a naturalist. At recent excavations, ominous of further gifts, he would pause and prod hopefully with a stick, oblivious of the urgent tapping of his companion's foot. So, too, he would thrust his head over the parapet as a shattering detonation rent the air, and gaze mildly at whirring clods, barbed wire and garbage. 'By Jove, that's a funny one,' he would remark: 'I haven't seen one burst like that before'; and vainly attempt to persuade my own craven soul to share his hobby. [Guy Chapman]

The function of shellfire was not, of course, to provide entertainment for eccentric officers, as the following extract from the diary of Lt. Edwin Campion Vaughan during the Arras offensive shows:

Well, all was quiet now, and it was 6pm. We had only an hour before our relief was due, so Holmes sent Browne [his soldier servant] along to the neighbouring dugout to fetch Sergeant Phillips for his orders, whilst Watkins and I commenced to plug up the gaping hole in our roof with sandbags, to prevent the light shining through. It was now quite dark.

After a few minutes Browne returned, rather white in the face, saying that he could not find the NCO's dugout. This was only ten yards away, and consisted of an unfinished shaft of a few steps leading to a tiny excavation in which there was just room for three or four men to sit. Holmes guessed that Browne was shaken up by the shelling, so he laughed and said, 'Come on then, I'll help you to search for it, perhaps someone's pinched it.' And they set off together down the muddy trench.

I was just finishing off the roof, when Browne came tumbling in moaning and laughing hysterically. He stared at me screaming 'Oh God! It is. It is.' Then we slung him in a chair, gave him a tot of rum, and ran off down the trench to the mine shaft which had been occupied by

Sergeant Phillips, Sergeant Bennett, Corporal Everett and Corporal Hollins.

The last of the shells had obviously burst inside the shaft, for the entrance was completely blocked, and the top of the shelter was lying across the trench. In the faint light that still remained we saw the sandbags and pieces of timber half buried in the mud. Holmes stooped to raise one of these short beams, then let it go, with a shuddering exclamation, for he had bent back an arm with Sergeant's stripes. There was a narrow gap through the blockage and we shouted down through it, but our voices sank into the wet earth, and there was no sound from below.

So we returned to the cellar to discuss the matter and found Browne, gibbering and chattering like a monkey. First of all we wired off the casualties to Anstey in code, and then we went for the next senior NCO of each platoon. We explained to them what had happened and instructed them to take charge of their platoons and carry out the relief without letting the men know about the casualties. These NCO's were very badly shaken by the news, and particularly by the deaths of the two brothers Bennett in succeeding days; there is a third brother in the Company who is due back from leave tomorrow.

We started at once to pull away the wreckage of the entrance, and had just come to Sergeant Phillips, when Jerry started his 'blue pigeon' strafe. Amidst their flashes and crumps we pulled him out and laid him behind the parapet. He had been killed by the dugout falling in as he ran up the steps, for there was no wound on his body but his head was crushed by the weight of sand-bags and timber from the roof. Two men started to bury him while we returned to the more horrible task of excavation.

As we worked down the sides, we realized (in the darkness) that the beams and sides were splashed with blood and flesh. The stench of lyddite and fresh blood was ghastly, and the foulness of our groping in the dark cannot be described. At last we could stand it no longer, and regardless of consequences, we lit a candle and commenced working by its shaded light. This evoked a shower of 'pineapples' and bullets which continued to fall until we had cleared the shaft.

Of Corporal Everett we found no trace; he must have been struck by the shell and blown to atoms. Bennett was badly shattered and most of his head was gone, whilst Hollins, who had been sitting with his rifle between his knees was unrecognizable and the twisted rifle was buried in the front of his body.

While it may seem from this that shellfire was a constant danger, there were occasions when shelling was actually impossible, owing to the proximity of the opposing front lines. This brought with it its own disadvantages. In June 1915, near Ypres, Pte. H.S. Clapham noted these:

> We got shots from all sides but one, and so far as I can tell, we were near the point of a small triangle, with the Huns on two sides of us. On the third night we moved into the point itself. The wood tapers out, and from the end we passed up the side of a water-logged communication trench into what appeared to be the neck of a bottle. Two trenches run out a short distance apart, but they do not actually join at the end. One stops near the stables at the Château, and they are only fifteen yards from the end of the trench. The stables are falling to pieces, but what is left of the Château is a big square fort of stone with sandbagged windows. The Huns are all around us, on five sides out of six, and bullets and trench-mortar shells can come from any of those five sides. We ourselves can fire at them, both in front and at the back, but luckily they dare not shell us, as they would probably get hurt themselves.

> We had one man posted in the stable as a guard, and he was in full view of my traverse. Some joker amongst the Huns was amusing himself by firing at the top of the wall above his head, and while I watched he succeeded in dislodging half a dozen bricks, the pieces of which fell all about the guard. The latter could not move far without showing himself.

As is apparent from this general introduction to the trenches the life of the fighting soldier in France and Flanders was one of deep discomfort punctuated by moments of horror. In the following chapters, the daily and nightly round of trench life is explored in more detail.

2
Domestic Life in the Line

The routine of the front-line soldier was essentially an ordered affair. Units would typically spend a 'tour' in the front line which varied from a few days to (in extreme cases) a period of several weeks. This would alternate with commensurate periods in support trenches or in 'rest' further behind the line. Irrespective of their location, troops were rarely idle. In the front line, there was constant defensive work to be carried out, as well as the day-to-day necessities of providing themselves with food and shelter. In support, too, there was always work to be done, while 'rest' was a misnomer, for regiments underwent constant training, drill and even at times labouring work (such as building roads and moving stores).

Day-to-day life in the line had its own routine, of which the following is a typical example:

> A Company had two platoons in the front line trench 41, some 100 yards from the enemy, and two platoons in a support line called '41 support.' The trenches themselves were well built and revetted with sand bags, and dry enough even during the wettest weather. We had in these days only small shelters - the deep dugout was unknown. The three subalterns in A Company took turns at duty in the trenches, four hours on and eight hours off, night and day. The duty consisted chiefly of visiting the sentries every hour, and keeping a general look-out, and seeing that the trench rules were obeyed. A good deal of rifle fire went on at night. Sentries on either side would exchange shots, and an occasional machine-gun would open out. At close range the bullets make a curious crack as they pass overhead. Being tall and having been warned of the efficiency of the German sniper, I had to walk in most of the trenches with a bend in the back, which soon became tiring.

This was the experience of Francis Buckley (7th Northumberland Fusiliers) in January 1916; the pattern, though not invariably the same, did not really change until the resumption of open warfare in 1918. For the benefit of his family, Capt. Geoffrey Bowen delineated a typical day with the 2nd Battalion Lancashire Fusiliers, in this case September 3rd, 1917:

8 p.m. Started.
9.30 p.m. Arrived.
11 p.m. Company arrived.

11 p.m.-3 a.m. Round the line.
3.15 a.m.-4.15 a.m. Sleep.
4.15 a.m.-6 a.m. Stand to.
6 a.m.-6.30 Reports
6.30 a.m.-9. Sleep
9 a.m.-9.30 Breakfast: bacon, eggs, tinned sausage
9.30 a.m.-10.10. Round line.
10.10 a.m.-12. Reports, etc.
12.30 p.m. Lunch: Steak, potatoes, beans, sweet omelette.
1.45 p.m.-2.15. Daylight patrol.
2.15 p.m.-2.30. Sleep.
2.30 p.m.-3.40. Gup[1] with C.O.
4 p.m. Tea, bread, jam.
4.30 p.m.-4.35. Sleep
4.35 p.m.-5.10. Entertain 'Bowes'
5.10 p.m.-5.15. Sleep.
5.15 p.m.-5.25. Trench Mortar Officer reports.
5.25 p.m.-6.15. Sleep
6.15 p.m.-6.35. Entertain Brain and Padre.
6.35 p.m.-7.30. Sleep.
7.30 p.m.-8. Round line.
8 p.m.-8.15. Dinner: steak, potatoes, tinned fruit and custard.
8.15 p.m.-9. Round line.
11.30 p.m.-12.30 a.m. Sleep.
12.30-2.30 a.m. Intensive sniping.
2.30-5 a.m. Sleep.

Much time was devoted to maintaining and improving the defences. The major part of these were the barbed-wire entanglements (reaching a maximum width of hundreds of yards as part of the Hindenburg line) which sprang up in front of both the Allied and German trenches as soon as the front line stabilised in late 1914. They were an extremely effective barrier, designed to impede movement towards the trench they guarded. Because of their complexity, and ability to trap a man by snagging his clothes and flesh, it was essential before any offensive operation to cut the opposing wire by any means available - from gunfire to the issuing of wire cutters to attacking troops (these were not always available, and the army issue was greatly maligned, even to the extent that officers went to the length of acquiring their own from home). Given its vulnerability to the constant shell and mortar fire, this

---

[1] From the Hindi *gap*; idle gossip.

vital component of the defences always required attention. Repairs were generally undertaken at night, for obvious reasons:

> At night we do watches of two hours in turn, and when we are not on duty there are always working parties to be attended to. Thank God, wire is about done for the present. The other night I was as usual up to my neck in barbed wire, and I saw a party of men strolling along, and shouted 'What platoon are you?' - thinking they were some fatigue party or other.

> They were the General staff! The Brigadier was awfully amused, and actually went and got tied up in my wire to test it. He seemed quite pleased with it. I took them all round the place and answered all their questions. I tried to get them to come to my dug-out and drink rum, but they declined with thanks. I then went and woke up Murphy, and he carried on. I finished off my wire and went to bed. We've had some — attached to learn things and see life... The men were a poor lot compared with, say, the Artists, and had to be watched to see that they sat up and took notice on post duty. They were an awful nuisance, as my platoon had to clear out of a bit of trench at 4 in the morning, and occupy another bit for 24 hours, and then move in again at 4 in the morning. But the others never co-operated in any way to make our work easier.... We've got a goodish trench now, though the fellows who take over from us do their best to spoil it every time. [2nd Lt. D.O. Barnett, 2nd Battalion Leinster Regiment]

Even the cover of darkness did not always mean that wiring parties escaped the unwelcome attentions of the Germans. Lt. Barnett wrote, in February 1915:

> Last night we had to do wire again. There was a brilliant moon, and they put the machine gun on to us! I had a stream handy and fell in gracefully. I sat in it for some time and improved the shining hour by winding barbed wire all in and about it. Then I sent the section back and carried on with two sergeants, but they all turned out and fired volleys at us, so we solemnly crawled home on all fours. Later it got a bit cloudy and I went out with the captain, and we worked till 5 in the morning and got lots done. They did not snipe at us very much. We had a little panic about a German patrol, but it soon blew over. Slept late this morning. Shelling and sniping pretty heavy to-day, but former not on this trench. I'm very well and happy.

> Last night we had to work at the wire again, but it was not a bit exciting, as the moon was clouded over. We could hear Johnnie German doing the same 350 yards off, knocking in posts and fixing up (as we can see this morning) a most awful fence. I don't think stray cattle will break through their hedge or ours either. They seem a very cheery lot opposite. They are always singing and doing 'milk-o' calls, especially

when we fire volleys in the night. Once they held a light up when we had fired on them, a thing I wouldn't have done for anything. We had some hand grenades sent up yesterday. I am in charge of the company bomb-throwers, and it is a most inspiring job.

In the quiet sectors, where the fighting was not at such close quarters, conditions were more relaxed. In October 1917, in the then relatively peaceful Havrincourt sector, near Cambrai, there appeared to be an unofficial policy of 'live and let live' with regard to work in No-Man's-Land, which permitted Capt. Dugdale to adopt decidedly unorthodox wiring techniques:

Time passed very peacefully, as the Germans were very quiet. My battalion snipers had the time of their lives; never before had they been given such targets. We literally kept a game book of hits for the first three days; after that the Germans did not show themselves so much; also they started to retaliate.

Wiring was carried out nearly every night, but not in the style we were accustomed to in the days of the Somme. Our men did not creep through the wire carrying coils of wire, stakes, etc.; instead, a general service wagon was driven into No Man's Land with materials on board, which were dumped out when required. At first we expected bursts of machine gun fire every minute, but nothing happened. It must have become a well-established custom, as the enemy did the same thing themselves; we did not interfere.

This passage mentions the use of stakes; these were to secure the wire firmly in place. The importance of this precaution is clearly revealed in the next anecdote, where Major R.T.Rees (8th Loyal North Lancs.) relates taking over a section of line from inexperienced troops:

Battalion and Company Commanders paid a visit to the line the day before the relief was to take place, in order to learn all necessary details about the condition of the trenches and the wire, the positions of listening posts, snipers' posts and so on. The Company Commander who received Clarke and myself told us that he had done a great deal to strengthen the wire, and invited us to look through a periscope, saying that we should easily distinguish the new wire from the old. So we did, and saw the new wire clearly, but in front of the German trench! Our friends who had been holding the line had merely produced a number of ready-made pieces of concertina wire and rolled them over the top, without troubling to fasten them down; and the wily foe, realising that he had green horns to deal with, had come over during the night, abstracted the concertina wire, and fastened it firmly in front of his own trench.

As already noted, working parties in No-Man's-Land were, if possible, disrupted by the Germans, whose machine-guns and offensive patrols made it essential to send out covering troops. Needless to say, this was a hazardous duty:

> Old Aitken was shot through the leg two nights ago. We miss him very much. He was the best platoon officer I've ever had. He was hit during a very sticky job my company had to do. The whole company had to be covering party to a huge working party. Directly it was dark I had to take the company out into No Man's Land and post my groups, about 600 yards in some cases from our own trenches and 150 to 200 yards from Brother Boche. I had posted eight of my groups when Aitken's group came in contact with a Boche patrol, and then there were crumps from bombs and a lot of rifle fire. We had to lie as flat as pancakes, praying hard while those infernal bullets zipped, buzzed, and ricochetted all round. I began to think that No Man's Land was no place for a staid old company commander.
>
> Once a Boche challenged in a very high-pitched and obviously frightened voice *'Wer da'* three times. One could hear him as plainly as talking to him.
>
> We were out all night, withdrawing just before dawn. The Boches brought into action one or two machine guns which were an infernal nuisance and made me lie flat on several occasions. One burst of fire killed an Aylesbury man called Fall and wounded one of my best Lance-Corporals, also an Aylesbury man. His name is Whipps. He was hit in the head and also in the side, but is not seriously hurt. He was a rum sight, his face smothered in blood, but cheery as anything and said: 'I don't think I shall be back with you for a little while, sir,' and sent a message back to me from the dressing-station asking me not to write to his people.
>
> The Boche shelled occasionally, but the darned idiot fired on his night lines and the shells fell well behind the working party and hurt no one. One of my men went off his chump. I had an awful job getting him in.
>
> Brother Boche was evidently much startled next morning when he saw what had happened during the night, and chattered away again like a packet of monkeys. [Captain Lionel Crouch, Bucks. Battalion]

The maintenance of silence was the best way to avoid detection. Early in the war, wooden stakes were used to support the wire (as mentioned above); these had to be hammered into the ground, and even when the mallets used were muffled with sandbags, it was a noisy business. After some time, metal corkscrew stakes were employed, which could be wound silently into the ground.

The need for quiet was ignored by men working in No-Man's-Land at not only their peril, but that of their comrades:

> One night, when we were in the front line on this same front, a carrying party was working in front of our trenches. They were a noisy crowd, shouting and bawling all over the place, One man would shout an order, then another would shout and ask what he had said. This went on for some time, and we did not like it.
>
> We thought that the enemy would not allow this to go on for long, and all at once he opened out with his whiz bangs. These were terrible things, and as quick as lightning. They had no sooner left the gun that they were on top of you. One had to find cover quickly when these were flying about.
>
> He peppered us for all he was worth. Shells were bursting in all directions, throwing up clouds of earth as they exploded with a deafening roar.
>
> Not long elapsed before the cry went up for stretcher bearers; some poor fellows had paid the price for other men's folly. [Henry Gregory]

Needless to say, in the harassment of working parties, the Germans did not always have things their own way:

> Sometime about eleven o'clock I could distinctly hear the noise made apparently by the hammering in of metal stakes at a point in the enemy line just opposite where I was stationed on guard with the machine gun beside me. Acting on my orders, I gripped the traversing handles, pressed the double button, and immediately the gun poured its stream of bullets into 'no-man's-land.' I fired about half a belt (125 rounds) before releasing the double button, and did not get a single jam. When the last echoes of my devil's tattoo had died away I listened for the hammering noise, but it had ceased, and instead there was a sound of shouting from the direction of the German working party - probably someone shouting for stretcher-bearers. I hoped then, as I hope now, that I had not killed anybody. I think one always hoped that on these occasions, and the one consolation about this night firing was that you could not tell whether or not you had actually been responsible for some fellow human being's death. [H. Raymond Smith]

Another important, and peculiarly lonely duty in No-Man's-Land, was that of manning a listening post, in order to monitor German activity and warn of any potential raid or patrol by them:

> Right in the middle of No Man's Land, in a disused trench, we had a listening and bombing post. I did twenty-four hours there in charge of a party of six. We had our rifles and several bags of bombs, but none of

my men was a bomber, and I doubt if we could have used the bombs very effectively.

It was a really ghastly spot, particularly in the moonlight. On two sides of us, but some distance away, were the woods, or what had been woods. One is now a forest of masts, without branches or leaves, and many of them broken in half and blackened by fire. All around us were abandoned trenches - many of them filled with the dead - underground passages, and shell-craters. Close beside us was a crater fifteen feet deep, with a pool of water at the bottom, and scattered about in the water and around I saw a box of bombs, spades, a shovel, broken rifles, and a human head without a body.

Just to our rear, about four yards away, was a row of graves, Hun-made apparently, for they were mere mounds of earth, and, from one, another head protruded.

Throughout the night hundreds of rats scuffled about, and at intervals we heard the sounds of patrols and burial parties. Half the night, against the skyline on the ridge, we could see the burial parties at work, cast into sharp relief by the light of the star-shells. We could hear the noise made by the Hun transport quite plainly, and from the sounds I should think they were working in their trenches. I could hear voices and a good deal of banging and hammering.

There were two other posts, some distance from ours, but these were not used in the daytime at all. We were practically isolated, and after going in at night, could not move for twenty-four hours. The daytime was most unpleasant. The heat was terrific and there was absolutely no shelter. We had nothing to do but to lie still as low as possible, in order to evade observation by the planes, which hovered over us all day long. [H.S. Clapham]

An integral defensive feature of the trenches themselves and of all the associated excavations, such as dugouts and machine-gun posts was the ubiquitous sandbag. Sandbags (which were actually filled with earth) formed the parapet of the trench and provided overhead protection for shelters. Filling and positioning them was just one of the many 'fatigues' faced by the men in the line:

On our second day in this sector I had to take part in a very uncomfortable fatigue consisting of filling sandbags behind a low parapet. A German sniper could evidently hear us, for he kept firing at us. It was, of course, comparatively safe if you kept your head down, but filling sandbags in a crouching position, with the knowledge that if you stood upright for a moment you would get a bullet through the head, is not the most pleasant of occupations. It was during this tour of trench duty that we had our first serious crop of casualties. One of our men was killed, and several, including 'Joe' S—, of our machine gun section, were wounded. 'Joe' was wounded in a rather unusual manner. He was sitting on the fire-step on Sunday afternoon, when a bullet from the German trenches went right through his shoulder, having previously passed through the parapet - probably through a chink in the breastwork of sandbags. [H. Raymond Smith]

Early in the war, material of all kinds tended to be in short supply; Guy Chapman's battalion were the fortunate recipients of gifts from the home front:

> Even sandbags were scarce, and an order was promulgated that they were not to be used for personal requirements. This order became more stringent when some admirable ladies in England formed a sandbag club for our benefit, and their first contribution began to arrive. For these sandbags were obviously too good to be put to such humdrum uses as parapets or traverses. Beautifully stitched - hand-stitched - of materials which Patou would not disdain to handle; of colours which the doting Joseph might have dyed for Benjamin, they were too splendid to have mere clay thrust into them. To be sure, some barbarians in No. 4 Company did roof a dugout with their share, a stately pyramid which lay conspicuously above the surrounding country. But the other companies found better use. A really charming black pair kept my boots from soiling my head, while a nattier blue affair held my washing tackle. Batty-Smith, our machine-gun officer, who shared my dug-out, had a preference for green in varying tinges. We blessed our unknown benefactresses.

Everything in the front line had to be carried there - food, water, ammunition; wire, stakes and sandbags for defences; wood for revetting the trench wall, duckboards for the trench floor, corrugated iron for dugout roofs and tools of all kinds. And everything not needed there had to be carried out, such as casualties and the mails. Ration boxes did not have to be carried out of the line again. Being made of wood, they could be used for firewood or to revet the trench or as dugout furniture.

The working parties who carried all these necessities of trench warfare were mostly found from those troops supposedly at rest. In fact, real rest was a scarce commodity since supplying the needs of the front line was a nightly chore. Rations were the most important thing to be brought up, so far as most men were concerned, and their safe arrival in the line was a priority:

> During the late autumn and winter months the work of carrying up rations to the front line trenches was difficult and dangerous. The rations were usually deposited at the entrance to a communication

trench, and one or two of us would go and fetch them from there, and distribute them to the machine gunners at the various posts. On one occasion our mid-day meal (it was to have been stew) was very late, and we had become exceptionally hungry. At last the ration orderly arrived, but alas, in coming up the communication trench he had trodden on a loose duckboard, which had sprung up and tipped him into a few feet of icy water. The dixie containing the stew was also upset, and all that was rescued were a few carrots and a little gravy!

One pitch dark winter night I was detailed to fetch the rations, and accompanied by Oliver G—, set off down the communication trench, at this point about a mile from our machine gun post. We met the cook's orderly and took the sacks or dry rations from him, and also the rum jar. We had gone about a quarter of the way back when Oliver exclaimed 'Good heavens, R—, we've forgotten the rum!' It was only too true. Somehow we had put the jar down near the entrance to the communication trench, and failed to pick it up again. I don't know what our punishment would have been for such gross carelessness, but I am sure we should have been the most unpopular members of the 8th Worcesters for many a week! There was nothing for it but to go back, so we retraced our steps, but with little hope in our hearts of finding the precious jar. Eventually we arrived at the place where we had picked up the rations, and started to search round in the dark. In a few seconds I found the jar, covered in mud, and lying on its side, but with the cork still in, and the contents untouched! During our absence a whole company, or working party, had passed up the trench, and someone had actually kicked the jar over, and left it, not realising it was full. We were indeed thankful, and Oliver suggested we should for once break a rule and celebrate the occasion, by each taking a nip of rum, which we did. [H. Raymond Smith]

An unusual load which Anthony Eden and his men were employed to transport on one occasion in the Spring of 1916 brought with it its own special hardships:

The bane of our life was working parties, usually at night. For these unwelcome chores men had to be constantly provided. The worst assignment that summer was to carry gas cylinders up communication trenches and to instal them in our front line. This took many weary and exhausting hours. The most disagreeable part of the business was that we had to wear gas masks rolled up on the top of our heads under our tin hats all the time. These masks, effective only against chlorine, were damp and impregnated with some unpleasant-smelling stuff which, as we were soon to learn, could bring out an ugly and itching rash on the forehead. The masks had to be at the ready in this way for fear that a chance shell or even machine-gun fire might puncture a cylinder, which did not add to the attractions of the whole exercise. Then it rained and the slippery duckboards, slithering cylinders, traversed trenches, stinking masks and stumbling, swearing men, added up to a long black night in C Company's memory.

Ration parties did not have to bring supplies all the way from the base dumps; it was deemed safe for battalion transport or ASC personnel to transport them by truck or horse-drawn wagon to the vicinity of the front line, where they were then picked up. As well as materiél, messages had to be taken up and down the line by hand; although wireless and telephone communications existed, they were not always reliable. The men doing this job were known as 'runners:'

I had now been taken off a gun team and appointed company runner, that is, to take dispatches from Head-quarters to the Officers in the line. Another part of this duty was to take rations, letters, and parcels to the men in the line. This running is dangerous, as a runner is always in open country, often with not a bit of cover and he had to have a very good memory for landmarks, so that he could find his way across open country at night time. Many were the shocks that a runner would get in the night, as each rustle of the trees made him think it was the enemy. He would strain his eyes and ears on those night runs to near bursting point, as every little sound in the night seemed to magnify itself many times over, and at every sound his hold on his rifle would tighten.

While we were on this front, we always went up the line with rations at night with a mule and a driver. These drivers, as a rule, were very 'windy.' They used to get the 'wind up' at the least thing that happened. On one night I was going up to a gun position on the main Arras-Cambrai road. At ration time every night the enemy used to play on the position with a machine gun, and he had the thing 'taped' so well that he used to put the bullets right into the entrance to the dug-out.

The driver I was going up with this night had not been there before, but some of the other drivers had told him what a dangerous place it was; in fact, all the drivers used to fight shy of it, but I had to go there every night.

I went to the place where we had met the ration party, we got loaded up, and set off on our journey. The driver seemed to be very talkative. He was evidently after information. He first asked me what sort of a place we were going to. I told him that it was all right if we used care. He then told me that the other drivers had told him they would not go there for a pension, if they could get out of it.

There was no doubt about it, he had got the 'wind up,' and badly. He asked me if I thought there was much danger. I told him that the only thing to do when the enemy opened out with his machine gun was to stand still, as generally the bullets landed on the ground where we had to unload the rations.

This information did not soothe him, but rather made him more 'windy' still. At last I asked him what the Hell had he to bother about? I had to go there every night, seven nights a week, and if he did as I told him he would be alright. I told him that on no account must he fall on the ground, or he would get the bullets in his head, but if he remained standing at the worst he would only get them in his legs.

All went quiet as we went up, and the driver remarked on this. But I knew only too well from experience that by the time we got to the place where we took the rations from the mule, the bullets would come whizzing all around us. I pacified him by telling him that Jerry must not be bothering to-night, and he settled down a bit: but sure enough, when we arrived at the road on the opposite side to the gun position, Jerry opened out with his machine gun as usual.

The mule pricked up its ears, and reared on its hind legs. The driver had a job to hold it. Bullets were now flying about us like wasps. The 'swish, swish,' as they flew past us was not nice to hear. I told the driver to throw the rations on the ground and clear. He did not need telling twice; the next minute he had the rations off, had jumped on to the mules' back, and they were both off, with not a thought about me. [Henry Gregory]

The pressure of not only being frequently exposed to 'hot spots' but also having to negotiate muddy, cramped and sometimes unfamiliar trench systems in pitch blackness, and all this while carrying a heavy load of rations, could prove too much for the temper even of a seasoned soldier like Gregory. Finding themselves lost, Gregory and a fellow-runner ended up arguing violently as to what direction to take:

We got to arguing, then to swearing. He called me all the names he could put his tongue to, and I retaliated in kind. We cursed one another that night, until I do not think that there was a swear word left that we had forgotten; we went through the whole list. These were the times that swearing came in as a safety valve; we had to swear or burst.

At last he told me I could clear off, as he would find it himself. This would be about 10 p.m. Before leaving him he said he would throw the sandbags of rations across the trench, and then get across himself. The first bag he threw landed short of the top of the other side and rolled down into the trench with a splash. The trench would now be about a foot deep in water. After this I left him to do the best he could.

But in the light of day, with no pressure upon them, the two men found it easy to let bygones be bygones:

Next morning I asked the other runner how he had got on the night before. He said that I was right, as the trench we could not make out had been dug after I had been up with the rations on the previous night. We shook hands, and thus patched up our differences of the night before.

Owing to the difficulty of communications, the regiments in the line not only had to provide runners, but also additional fatigue parties. While this duty was naturally seen as an extra burden by the men detailed to it, the officers for whom it was undertaken were simply glad of the manpower. Lt. R.C.Hopkinson, the signalling officer of 35th Brigade, felt himself especially fortunate in this regard:

> I have got a lot of wires out now, and shall have more before long. I have even got to the luxury of having separate wires carried on poles with nice little ohms insulators, reserved for when the Brigade Staff wishes to speak to Battalions. The only trouble about these is, they are very liable to get cut by shell-fire. All the other wires which we just use for buzzer work go along ditches. There used to be fearful grousing about the badness of my telephone service. They get very annoyed with the cross-talk, or when some wretched operator chimes in on their conversation with his buzzer. However, I have not heard so much of it lately.

> At present I am kept very busy burying cable up in the trenches, to keep it out of the way of shell-fire. To do this, I have infantry working-parties to do the digging for me. My Brigade is very good about working-parties, and I can always get as many men as I want, with the result that I am long way ahead of the other Brigades in the Division as regards buried cable. Sometimes it is very strenuous, as the working-parties often start at 6 A.M., and I can't get to bed much before 10.30 P.M. as a rule.

It should not be imagined that men engaged on digging fatigues were excavating virgin soil:

> Great excitement yesterday. The men were digging, and suddenly one came along awfully pleased: 'We've dug up a German.' I told him to dig him in again quick. I rather think he was a very dead German. [2nd Lt. J.S.Tatham, 9th King's Royal Rifle Corps]

In view of all the demands on their time and energy, it is hardly surprising that soldiers did their best to 'get away' with doing as little as they could, so long as it did not harm their immediate comrades. Old soldiers regarded it as a virtue to do the minimum unless in action. It seems that the view was that it was far more sensible to steal equipment from neighbours who had carried it up to the line than to carry it themselves. Major R.T.Rees described what he obviously viewed as a gem of a CSM:

Here I must introduce Company Sergt.-Major W. Pasquill, one of the
original members of the Company. He was an old regular soldier, not
over quick in the uptake, and inclined to some of the old soldier's
weaknesses. Such a man was never at his best in times of rest or
idleness. But in the trenches or in action he was worth his weight in
gold. He had a strong sense of humour, consistent loyalty, the courage
of a man to whom fear is quite unknown, and the men would follow
him anywhere. For these reasons I passed over various delinquencies,
while keeping a tight, though not always effective, hold of the rum
ration in the line. During the late fighting on the Somme the Company
had gained special distinction in an action at Stuff Redoubt, where they
had captured more than their own number of prisoners. On the evening
of that day old Pasquill had donned the overcoat of a captured German
officer, and filling the pockets with bombs, had strolled along No Man's
Land casting his missiles lavishly into the enemy trenches, under a
heavy fire from both sides! In the matter of stores, equipment, etc., he
had no scruples at all. His great pal was Sergt.-Major J.Anderson of 'B'
Company; but nothing gave him such keen pleasure as to have stolen
some of 'B' Company's property. He would come to me with a beaming
face to say, 'Ah've coom the dooble on old Joe, Sir. All his duck-boards
are safe where he won't find 'em.' Or with crestfallen mien, 'That there
old Joe's coom the dooble on me, Sir. He's pinched all my gas helmets.'

The rations brought up to the line had in most instances been prepared
in the rear and were transported in 'dixies,' ready to eat. But this was
not always the case. On occasion, cookhouses were set up in the
trenches, and these proved to be popular places to seek warmth and
scraps of food. Private A.S.Dolden, a company cook in the 1st London
Scottish recounted the unusual circumstances of producing Christmas
dinner in the front line:

25 December dawned - a perfect Christmas from the Christmas card
point of view, for the snow lay thickly everywhere, but, alas!, the last
thing we wanted was seasonable weather. We did our best as far as
possible, to keep the Feast. Our resources were sadly limited, for we had
a dugout eight feet by six feet by five feet, absolutely reeking with
smoke. The already small floor space was still further reduced by sacks
of fuel, tea and sugar. At every step we tripped over something, despite
the fact that we were always tidying up. Added to these problems were
the numerous cookhouse callers who pleaded to be able to sit by the fire
and, as it was freezing outside, we had not the heart to turn them away.
We received the usual Christmas greetings, but I regret to say that they
fell on deaf ears, for reference to goodwill seemed distinctly
inappropriate. We could not get much in the way of eatables, as the
canteen was practically sold out, so we made our Christmas dinner off
Christmas pudding out of a parcel, and custard. After this we sat round
with some of our pals, exhaling the fumes of cigars, also out of parcels.

We were quite happy considering the circumstances, and could have remained so if 'Fritz' had not thought fit to shell us at that particular moment. He sent some shells whistling over our heads. There was a crash, and a shower of dust as a shell landed about ten yards from our door, and we had to make a dart along the trench, and one fellow was wounded. Things became quieter after a bit, so we returned to the cookhouse. Fritz started his game again later, but luckily nothing came very near to us. Boxing Day was fairly uneventful. There was another heavy fall of snow, and towards the end of the day a sharp spell of frost. The enemy bumped us on and off all day, but our own artillery was to blame as they kept 'barking' at the Germans all day long.

Officers were generally better off for home comforts than their men, although at least one unfortunate had to spend Christmas Day 1914 acting as a FOO in a haystack. His senior officer regarded his plight with some amusement, as he wrote home:

I have finished the best meal I have had in France; the *pièce de résistance* was the most beautiful roast goose you ever saw, consequently 'bin satt.'

The farm we are now in is replete with every modern convenience except only spoons; the obvious inference we draw is that the Crown Prince's army is in the neighbourhood.[2]

When I was eating my roast goose this [Christmas] evening, the thought of poor Parsons sitting on his haystack, Hun-hunting in the rain, was too much for me; so I took my plate over to the telephone, rang him up and let him smell it. I should like to tell you what he said, but the Censor says 'NO'! besides I don't know how to spell most of the words...

...I go to my haystack again to-morrow. You will be glad to hear that I curdled Parsons' blood with tales of the sniper to such an extent that he took up sand-bags and made a miniature Maubeuge [i.e. a fortress] on the top of the stack.

The same correspondent, Major Graham, had already assured his family (writing home on October 19th 1914) that he and his colleagues in the officers' mess were well provided for:

I am sorry you should have had a wrong impression about the food; we have always had more than enough, both to eat and to drink. I give you a day's menu at random: *Breakfast* Bacon and tomatoes, bread, jam, and

---

2   One piece of propaganda early in the war was that the German Fifth Army, commanded by the Imperial Crown Prince, were notorious looters.

22222222

cocoa. *Lunch* Shepherd's pie, potted meat, potatoes, bread and jam. *Tea* Bread and jam. *Supper* Ox-tail soup, roast beef, whisky and soda, leeks, savoury, coffee. (Savoury alternates with rice pudding and stewed fruit.)

We have provided stores of groceries and Harrods have been ordered to send us out a weekly parcel. However, if you like to send us an occasional luxury it would be very welcome...

There are four chief events every day. They are: Breakfast, lunch, tea, dinner. Though I says it as shouldn't, being mess caterer, we are really feeding very well. I enclose to-nights menu - as under:

Soupe, queue de boeuf a la Harrods.

Roast Mutton a la Gouvernement.

Vegetables *ad lib.*

Apple tart à la Bailleul with cream.

Sausage roll à la chef (i.e. home-made).

Fromage, biscuits à la bain d'Oliver.

Confiture.

Dessert - Apples and Grapes.

Café.

The other ranks did not have the privilege of ordering food parcels from Harrods or Fortnum and Mason, and where they could, used other means to supplement their diet:

By the end of May we had got quite used to the trenches; it was wonderful how soon one accommodated one's self to the strangest of surroundings. My diary for May 31st records that T— and I crawled out from our support trench and picked gooseberries from bushes near the parapet in full view of the German lines. We moved with caution, and picked the gooseberries lying on our backs. Though the sun was shining at the time we were not fired on, and returned in safety. The gooseberries, stewed in a mess tin, made a welcome change.

There was a ruined farm house just behind our front line, and one occasion I remember, in a rash moment, volunteering to get some water from the pump in the yard of the farm, in order that we might make some tea. I walked to where the trench sloped up to the ground level, and there, some fifty yards in front of me, stood the pump close to a wall of the house. Crouching low, I ran with the dixie to the pump.

Good; no one had seen me, for not a shot was fired. I started to work the handle of the pump. To my horror it emitted a loud squeaking noise. In a moment German bullets were zipping round me and chipping bits out of the wall behind. I immediately fell flat and waited for a minute till all was quiet again. Then raising myself a little I began cautiously to work the pump handle once more. Immediately the firing started again, but by now I had filled the dixie. Then, waiting for several minutes to summon up my courage, I picked up my load and ran towards the shelter of the trench, I reached it in safety, though I spilt some of the water. However, there was more than enough to make tea for us all. [H. Raymond Smith]

Clearly, tea was of considerable importance; another bulwark of morale was the rum ration, a tot of which was issued in especially bad weather or before going over the top and during lulls in the subsequent fighting. Despite the rigorous control over its distribution, things on occasion went awry:

Mariott welcomed me cordially enough, and found me the dry corner of a bed, where I tried to get an hour's sleep, but with little success. After a time he came into the pill-box, grinning, to ask me to take away some men of mine who were creating a disturbance in his trench. I went out and found the ten ration-carriers of last night all roaring drunk. The poor devils had got lost, just like everyone else, had wandered all night, and finally decided that the company was annihilated. Not without good sense they decided not to starve. They did their best with a whole company's rations, but a whole company's rum defeated them. Hither they had wandered very happy and very sleepy, but rather inclined to sing themselves to sleep. We saved the rest of the food and rum, and sent over the remains, plenty for my handful of men. It was difficult to know what to do with these men. One or two were helpless and comatose, one or two were incurably cheerful, the others varied from one extreme to the other. To arrest them and send them down the line would bring shell-fire on them and their escort, besides weakening the outposts. I stormed at them in my severest manner, promising them all courts-martial and death sentences. Some understood me and sobered a little, but Bridgwater and two or three others only blinked and looked more amiable than ever. If I had had any laughter in me I should have burst out laughing, too. We brought most of them round to a condition soon where they could go back to the company.The hopeless cases we left to sleep it off. There were no shooting parties at dawn, after all, as a sequel to this episode. [Charles Edmonds]

A similar, if somewhat eccentric, attention to the welfare of his men was displayed by Lt. Col. E.P.Cawston:

My mind frequently dwelt on the perfect nature of a hard boiled ostrich egg as a nourishing ration for men in muddy trenches. Some years before 1914, I had managed for an uncle (who owned the Cawston Ostrich Farm in Los Angeles) an exhibition Ostrich farm of a score of birds at the Festival of Empire at the Crystal Palace, and we had sold eggs to Hatchetts of Piccadilly who introduced Ostrich Egg Omelettes; but the customers were not keen to pay a higher price than they paid for omelettes of the humble hen, for the tastes were identical. An Ostrich egg contains as much matter as 24 hen's eggs, and the best hens annual contribution is quite infrequent, without resort to fertility pills! The content of such an egg hard boiled (even if its shell had rolled in mud from Q.M. Stores to firing line) would arrive clean and intact. Cut like a melon into slices and served with a rasher of bacon to each slice would be considered a feast. Possibly the idea occurred to some enterprising Q.M. in Egypt!

This ingenious, but regrettably impractical idea was apparently never adopted by the authorities.

* * *

The 'dug-outs' in which the men in the line sheltered, varied from rough excavations in the trench wall - known as 'funk holes' - to reasonably well-appointed subterranean dwellings, at times consisting of several chambers. Whatever their size, life in them was never comfortable by civilian standards, but they provided a degree of protection from the weather, and most shellfire other than a direct hit. However well constructed (they were usually protected by sandbags above and were revetted with wood to prevent the sides from falling in), they required constant attention and their upkeep was a major preoccupation when their inhabitants were not otherwise busy. H.Raymond Smith's crude dugout at Armentières in December 1915 was not properly revetted:

> Our dug-out was a small one close to the gun emplacement. I had a nasty experience there one night. I awoke to see the clay wall of the trench above my head slowly collapsing on me! I had just presence of mind enough to pull my greatcoat over my face before I was completely buried under several hundredweights of earth. I found I was quite unable to move, and for one horrible moment thought I should be buried alive! I cannot describe my feelings when I heard the sound of digging, and presently felt hands tugging at my ankles. Two of my comrades dug me out, and I was none the worse. N— and F—, my rescuers, told me that one of them happened to enter the dug-out just as the wall of earth was falling.

Officers generally lived in greater comfort than other ranks, although the facilities were still rudimentary.

> We are up here now in a large dug-out behind the line - came up the night before last. The quarters are quite good and there is ample room for 4 of us, but it is rather a bore not being able to undress or take off one's boots. However, we can arrange to sleep moderately well. We are, I suppose, about 500 yards from the Boches, it may be less. Pat and his platoon are a little higher up in front, but he returns to us to-night, I believe. The men are hard at it all day, and there is plenty of work for them to do. Of course we have got our servants up here, and we get our food just the same as if we were back in billets. I always think porridge and eggs and bacon sound rather funny so close up. They send our mail up as well. There is not a great deal of opportunity for writing, but I have got a chance now.
>
> I have just had a prehistoric wash in a Huntley and Palmer's biscuit tin. It's wonderful what uses Mr. H. and P.'s biscuit tins can be put to. Our table is a trench floor-board nailed on to legs and covered with sandbags, and our chairs are disinfectant tins also upholstered with sandbags. [J.S.Tatham, at Boesinghe in January 1916]

Occupants of long-standing dug-outs were sometimes forcibly reminded that they were not the only inhabitants and that building materials did not consist only of wood and sandbags:

> February 16 [1917] This morning, carrying out a few improvements to our dugout, we started to level up the ground under our table which is very rickety. The earth was spongy, and we started digging with entrenching tools, but we struck an old blue tunic, and when we gave it a tug, the resistance - and an unpleasant smell - warned us that we had a guest, so we apologized and patted the earth back. As we replaced the table, a message was brought up by a signaller that I was to report to HQ at 6 p.m. to proceed on a course.
>
> So at 5 o'clock I filled my pack and set off with Dunham. The Battalion HQ dugout, being about 30 steps down, was very fuggy - no ventilation except the staircase which was screened by three blankets, a charcoal brazier glowing like a furnace, and 12 human beings living there. I stayed only long enough to get my papers and have a drink, but even then my head was throbbing when I climbed out with Thatcher of 'C' Company. [Lt. Edwin Campion Vaughan, 1/8th Battalion Warwicks]

Like Vaughan's battalion HQ, most German dugouts were renowned for their size and depth. But despite their apparent 'luxury' they were not always ideal:

I have just sat down on an extremely hard seat in a newly captured Bosche dug-out to indite these few lines, or perchance more, to you. We have had a terrific combat with the water, and even now I can hear (when the guns are quiet for a while) its sweet and gentle murmur as it flops down into the dug-out step by step. Eventually we managed to stop it coming down our stairway too quickly, by an ingenious arrangement of two mess tins and a petrol can with the one end knocked out. The trench is a sea of muddy water, with an underlying layer of watery mud, and if one ventured out without going along the much battered remnant of a parapet one would be literally up to the waist in mud before a hundred yards had been covered.

What it'll be like if the rain keeps on till morning I don't know (someone had upset the tin, and the water is rising rapidly), for it's simply pouring in now. Why did Tennyson write 'The Brook'? And why shouldn't I write a lyric to the 'River that runs into everyone's dug-out'?

I come from trenches deep in slime,
Soft slime so sweet and yellow,
And rumble down the steps in time
To souse "some shivering fellow."

I trickle in and trickle out
Of every nook and corner,
And, rushing like some waterspout,
Make many a rat a mourner.

I gather in from near and far
A thousand brooklets swelling,
And laugh aloud a great "Ha, ha!"
To flood poor Tommy's dwelling.

And so on and so on until I can't write more, because the water is up to my neck or eyes or some equally vulnerable part of my anatomy. [Lt. Harold Parry, 17th King's Royal Rifle Corps]

Rain always exacerbated the rigours of front-line life, and was not usually viewed in so humorous a vein. The problems it caused were all too real:

Oh, I've had the hell of a time, as the parrot said when the monkey had plucked him. Last night we had the worst time we've had since we've been out. A terrific thunderstorm broke out, the worst I've ever seen. Rain poured in torrents, and the trenches were rivers, up to one's knees in places and higher if one fell into a sump. Baby fell in one above his waist! It was pitch dark and all was murky in the extreme. The rifles all got choked with mud, through men falling down, so I instituted an armourer's shop in each dug-out, and the rifles were brought in one by one to be cleaned. A man worked in each dug-out all night. The rest sweated at baling with buckets. *Mon Dieu*, it was a night! Bits of the trench fell in. To cap it all, a thick mist arose at sunrise and we stood-to for five hours until it cleared! The mist, however, proved useful, and one could go out and inspect the wire in daylight. I had a wiring party out during the fog and they managed to do a lot of work. However, by 8 o'clock we managed to get the trenches fairly clear of water, but the mud was pretty bad.

I haven't got the palatial dug-out I occupied last time. I can't sleep in mine, as it is over-run with rats. Pullman slept here one morning and woke up to find one sitting on his face. I can't face that, so I share Newbery's dug-out for sleeping purposes. [Capt. L.W.Crouch, Bucks Battalion, August 1915]

Inextricably linked to rain was mud. Its principal effect (in addition to making men and equipment filthy) was to hinder mobility, making the daily routine all the more difficult:

We have taken over a bit of the line and words fail me to describe it. Never have I even heard of such a line. To start with, half of one of our companies in coming along a communication trench got stuck in the mud, and we had to send a fatigue party to pull them out. I went with them, and there we found this line of men down the trench with the mud over their knees, just standing there, unable to move forward or back. One really could not help laughing at them. To get them out we had to take off their equipment and greatcoats, and pass them along a line of men. We could not even get out of the trench, as it was about 10 feet deep. After we had got them all out, we had to get out three of the fatigue party who had stuck firmer than any of the original lot. It took about an hour to get the last three out. I lost a pair of thigh waders, and had to walk back along a mile of trench with bare feet. This morning it is snowing. [Capt. Geoffrey Bowen, MC, 2nd Battalion Lancashire Fusiliers]

The combination of rain, mud, previous occupants and the enemy's attentions frequently made a tour in the line a foul and dangerous experience:

The new trench ("F.2") was a rotten one, and as soon as we arrived we were warned to keep our heads down, as the parapet was low and weak in many places, and one or two spots were specially marked by snipers. As usual, we were in the low ground, and in many places the trench was a foot deep in water. Out of it opened little traverses which were not quite so wet, and most of them had a little shelter at each end, with a sort of thatch of wattle and straw.

They say this trench was originally a German one and was then held by the French, but whoever were the original owners, they were nasty people. When I arrived I was absolutely exhausted, and not being on guard, I crawled into one of the shelters. A few minutes' rest was what I wanted, but the place stank like a charnel-house, and I was very nearly sick before I could gather enough strength to crawl out again. Apparently the Huns used the bodies of the dead to form the nucleus of the parapet, and the resulting stench is horrible. In some places can be seen a foot or a hand sticking out of the trench wall, and one's hands stink from the mud which clings to them. My own are quite done in now. They get caked with this mud, and I can't wash, so the finger-tips fester and burst. It is painful to put my hands in my pocket.

We worked hard all night. A dozen yards at the back of the trench was a ruined cottage with unlimited supplies of brick-ends, and, unless I was actually doing my turn on guard, I filled sandbags with broken bricks and carried them into the trench to reinforce and raise the parapet. Brickends are not very suitable material, but for the moment, at any rate, the position was improved, and, in any case, the ground was too hard for digging.

The dawn came with a thick white mist, but in a short time a brilliant sun burst through. It rendered everything more slimy than ever, but things were quiet, and in the crisp air one felt it good to be alive.

My own little lot were having a very jolly meal of tea, tinned salmon, jam and biscuits, sitting round a brazier. X had his back to the parapet. We are always on the look-out for new sights, and some miles to the north, right up the trench, I saw a large captive balloon. We were all watching it, discussing if it were British or Hun, when there was a sudden crack, and X - who had risen to his feet - kicked the brazier over and fell back on to another man, who caught him in his arms. For a second one hardly realized what had happened, but the salmon on my biscuit was speckled red and white, and as we laid X down, we saw a furrow across the back of his head, from which the brains protruded. I don't think he could have felt anything at all, but he made inarticulate noises for three parts of an hour before he died. Poor K— who caught him as he fell, is very young and could do nothing but lean against the parapet and say 'Oh, God!' It was the first time I had seen death in war-time, and it was upsetting even to me. [H.S.Clapham, HAC Infantry, January 1915]

Both sides chose their best shots to carry out the duty of sniping; if the unwary or careless permitted themselves to be seen above the parapet, they stood a good chance of meeting a sniper's bullet. As early in the war as November 1914, Capt. the Hon. Julian Grenfell of 1st Royal Dragoons entered into the 'game' with evident relish (in curious contrast to the distaste he felt at the mowing down of large numbers of attacking Germans):

> The German trench [was] in some places 40 yards ahead... We had been worried by snipers all along, and I had always been asking for leave to go out and have a try myself. Well, on Tuesday the 16th, the day before yesterday, they gave me leave. Only after great difficulty. They told me to take a section with me, and I said I would sooner cut my throat and have done with it. So they let me go alone. Off I crawled through sodden clay and trenches, going about a yard a minute, and listening and looking as I thought it was not possible to look and to listen. I went out to the right of our lines, where the 10th were, and where the Germans were nearest. I took about 30 minutes to do 30 yards; then I saw the Hun trench, and I waited there a long time, but could see or hear nothing. It was about 10 yards from me. Then I heard some Germans talking, and saw one put his head up over some bushes, about 10 yards behind the trench. I could not get a shot at him, I was too low down, and of course I could not get up. So I crawled on again very slowly to the parapet of their trench. I peered through their loop-hole and saw nobody in the trench. Then the German behind me put up his head again. He was laughing and talking. I saw his teeth glistening against my foresight, and I pulled the trigger very slowly. He just grunted, and crumpled up... I went out again in the afternoon in front of our bit of the line. I waited there for an hour, but saw nobody...I reported the trench empty. The next day, just before dawn, I crawled out there again, and found it empty again. Then a single German came through the woods toward the trench. I saw him 50 yards off. He was coming along upright and careless, making a great noise. I heard him before I saw him. I let him get within 25 yards, and shot him in the heart. He never made a sound. Nothing for 10 minutes, and then there was a noise and talking, and a lot of them came along through the wood... I counted about 20, and there were more coming. They halted in front, and I picked out the one I thought was the officer, or sergeant. He stood facing the other way, and I had a steady shot at him behind the shoulder. He went down, and that was all I saw, I went back at a sort of galloping crawl to our lines, and sent a message to the 10th that the Germans were moving up their way in some numbers. Half an hour afterwards, they attacked the 10th and our right, in massed formation, advancing slowly to within 10 yards of the trenches. We simply mowed them down. It was rather horrible...

By 1916, sniping had become a more technical job for both sides, and the techniques employed, more sophisticated:

> I spent most of the day in the trenches, checking snipers' reports, sniping myself and watching the German line from behind a heavy iron loophole plate with a high-powered telescope. We often saw Germans moving about a mile or more away. It gave me a curious feeling to

watch them. Watching and reporting all movement was part of the sniper's job. I sent a report of what we had seen to Divisional Intelligence by runner every night. We looked for their snipers' posts and when we found them we tried to destroy them. There were no armour-piercing bullets then. So we used a heavy sporting rifle - a 600 Express. These heavy rifles had been donated to the army by British big-game hunters and when we hit a plate we stove it right in, into the German sniper's face. But it had to be fired from a standing or kneeling position to take up the recoil. The first man who fired it in the prone position had his collar-bone broken. I hit two Germans at long range - about four hundred yards - with telescopic sights, and fired at a good many others. My best sniper turned out, when his parents at last traced him, to be only fourteen years old. He was discharged as under age. He was the finest shot and the best little soldier I had. A very nice boy, always happy. I got him a military medal and when he went back to Blighty and, I suppose, to school, he had a credit of six Germans hit. He was big for his age and had lied about it when he enlisted under a false name, and then had had sufficient self-restraint to write to no one. I had noticed that he received no mail and wrote no letters but had never spoken to him about it. The snipers worked in pairs, one observer with a telescope and one with the rifle. They changed over every half hour as it is very tiring to use a telescope for a long period. In action the sniper's job was to work independently and try to pick off any enemy leaders he could see. That was what the Germans did to us and they had no difficulty as we wore officers' uniforms with long tunics, riding breeches, trench boots and Sam Browne belts. This was one reason why the officers' casualties were so high. The Germans had a further advantage in their sniping. With them it was done by their Jaeger battalions, picked sharpshooters who in peacetime had been gamekeepers and guides. They wore green uniforms insted of grey and were permanently stationed in one sector, so that they knew every blade of grass in front of them and spotted the slightest change; this gave them a big edge on us because we were moved quite often. [Lt. Stuart Cloete, 9th KOYLI]

In addition, German machine-gunners were often placed to play on exposed positions; and so again, to forget oneself could be fatal:

While in the line one evening just after tea, we were visited by Nobby Clark - everybody named Clark was nicknamed "Nobby." He was No. 1 on one of the gun teams of another section of our company, and had only returned from leave that evening. He had called at our gun position to see the Corporal. They were big pals. He sat on the top of the machine gun emplacement, telling of all the good times he had had at home while on leave. They were laughing and joking, when all at once the enemy opened out with his machine gun. A bullet caught Clark in the neck, and he fell over, blood running from the wound like a tap. A stretcher bearer was sent for, and he was taken down the line to the

Field Hospital in the rear. He was in a very bad way when they got him to hospital, through loss of blood and died shortly after arrival. The bullet which had hit him had severed his jugular vein, and he bled to death. This was a very unhappy ending to a pleasant leave at home. [Henry Gregory]

People found different ways of coping with this juxtaposition of near-normality and sudden, violent death:

To remain cheery under depressing circumstances is a necessity to the average mortal out here. The other thing has one ending only - lunacy. Of course, one does meet not infrequently pessimists of the darkest sort and grousers of the most complete equipment out here, but if one were to enquire closely into their antecedents one would inevitably find that in civil life they were the same. Their pessimism is their life blood. They do not lack cheeriness or humour - they seriously believe that pessimism is most exquisite wit - and use it as a balm and salve to all their ills and misfortunes. [Harold Parry]

To remain 'cheery' was a considerable challenge, to which Lt. Edwin Campion Vaughan rose with no little flair:

During dusk stand-to I was fooling about behind the trench where I found a dump of German stick bombs, close to where a hole in the ground acted as a ventilator to our dugout. I was prompted to perpetrate a little joke, and later, when Johnny Teague entered the dugout to talk to Ewing, I unscrewed the canister of a bomb, removed the detonator, then pulled the fuse and dropped the stick just inside the ventilator shaft. With a fizz the fuse burnt for five seconds, growing louder and ending in a sharp dull spurt.

Putting my ear to the hole I heard Ewing say 'Good God! That was a near one!' 'Blinking good job it was a dud', replied Johnny, whereupon I chuckled hugely and prepared half a dozen more. I waited a few minutes until they had settled down, then I dropped them in rapid succession. There was a faint groan from Ewing and I heard Johnny say in a puzzled tone, 'They can't all be duds.' Then I pictured Ewing's horrified face as he yelled 'They're GAS! Can ye no smell them?' I heard the rustle of their gas-masks and thought it was time to end the comedy, so I jumped into the trench just in time to meet them as they rushed out to warn the Company.

'Hallo!' I said. 'Have you joined the Ku Klux Klan? Or are you doing a little badly needed gas drill?' Ewing choked over his mouthpiece and gurgled 'Put on your helmet, ye fule! The air's a fog o gas!' And he coughed up what he imagined he had drawn into his lungs. I was quite at a loss as to how I should persuade them to unmask, when Chalk came along and stopped in blank amazement at the sight of the masked figures.

'Are the officers testing their masks, Sir?' he asked, 'because I wanted to speak to the Captain if I might.' Ewing knew that the 'Little Treasure' could not be wrong, so he pulled off his mask and asked, 'Is it a' clear now?' Chalk and I both denied having smelt any gas and after spitting all round the trench Ewing in bewilderment asked 'Did ye no' hear the shelling? They crashed wi'in a hundred yards, and the gas was strong.' Chalk declared that he had been standing in the trench for the last half hour and had heard no unusal sound, so they had perforce to abandon the matter and entered the dugout to discuss strength returns.

Little Teague, however, was not satisfied and when we entered, wondering at the phenomenon I saw his eyes wandering round the walls until they were arrested by the ventilation hole. Then they switched to my face in a searching scrutiny. However, he said nothing and a moment later Whitehouse and Mortimore came in and crowded into our beds demanding whisky. Whitehouse was in little drill shorts and his bare knees were plastered with earth owing to some heaven-inspired machine-gunner having caught him with a chance burst as he was coming across.

Ewing immediately told his exciting story, omitting the denials of SM Chalk and myself, whereupon Whitehouse in great alarm fished out his gas-mask and asked Mortimore to show him how it worked, as he had never looked at it. Mortimore thought it was 'rather strange. I heard nothing as we came over. Did you, Major?' 'No,' said Whitehouse, 'that blank machine gun took all my attention, and I'm blanked if I come round the line again if this is what we get.'

Johnny sat quietly with a slight grin on his face, then suddenly changed the conversation by producing a letter. 'I say, Major, I've had a letter today from a girl who asks me if Major Whitehouse is still with us. I don't know whether she means you or Willy. Her name is Miss Dash, do you know her?'

'No, er no. I'm afraid not. Is she very sweet?'

'Very!'

'Then tell her I am here; tell her I'm young and handsome, very rich but very rude - that's it! Just say 'rich but rude'.'

Then he remembered that he had called in with a definite purpose and after thinking hard for a few minutes he slapped his bare knee. 'I knew I had a message for you Ewing! The General is going round the line tonight and you have to meet him at your right post at nine o'clock. Moreover,' he added reproachfully, 'as it is now 8.45 you'll have to put your skates on me boy.'

Ewing jumped up in a panic and started to put on his equipment, while I slipped out to call his runner. As I stepped into the trench, my belt was grasped from behind and Johnny's voice over my shoulder said 'How did you work it, Vaughan?' 'Stick-bombs without detonators,' I gurgled and my pent-up mirth escaped in a shriek of laughter. We both leant against the trench side and howled at the memory of Ewing's stricken face.

A sense of humour was not confined solely to junior ranks; even battalion CO's were prepared to indulge in a certain amount of fun at their peers' expense:

> ...Lincoln & Bennett write that my helmet has been despatched, but I shall stick to the one I have borrowed until it comes, as I shall be up in the trenches pretty often. De Lisle is right with his order. The same exists here, but it is not obeyed by a certain proportion of officers. Which reminds me of a score I had off an old pal in my old regiment (Sussex), who commands a new army Sussex battalion in this vicinity. Knowing he was about, I spotted him walking along, so shouted out to him in a very commanding voice: 'Hi, you, officer; what are you doing without your trench helmet on? Come here, please!' So come he did, looking very uncomfortable up to within a few yards, where a deep trench stopped him. Then he began to make excuses, etc., which having heard, I shied mud at him, and loping the trench, smote him on the bosom, when only he spotted who I was. We haven't met for years. [Lt. Col. Frank Maxwell, VC]

Despite the unpleasantness of their surroundings it seems that many felt the need to explore them further, often souvenir-hunting as they went:

> Yesterday broke very misty and, as I went along the reserve trench, where I live, it occurred to me that the enemy could not see me. So I climbed into the field, which of course consists of shell holes, and had a look round. One is in an irregular bit of flat ground; across this stretches a line of demolished German barbed wire, and the whole is pitted with holes two feet to twenty feet across. Along by the high banks of the trenches thousands of tins are lying, bully beef, jam, soup, cigarette, sausage, etc. Bits of iron and bits of shell are everywhere, and here and there are the conical fuses, our own and the enemy's, since this ground was once in German hands. Well I collected some fuses and went off across the top to my men. I told them that the misty day would give us good opportunities for finding new gun emplacements, and that they were to clean all the guns, and not to go a-souvenir-ing on top.

> Then I went off, and souveniered all day. I found a dug-out that had got lost and took some crockery out of it. Corpses had been uncovered, and

I had some men out to re-bury them. Every heavy shell hereabouts disturbs some wretched, half-decayed soldier. Then I went off hunting for fuses, and round again into the disused trenches, unutterably filthy, but not as full of rats and mice as our used ones are. The dugouts had all been used by the Germans, smashed in by our artilery fire, ransacked by our men, lived in for a few weeks and then abandoned. On one there was an illegible German inscription ending, 'So cowardly English and French.' At the back of these were piles of smashed German and English rifles, German hand-grenades, torn equipment, English and German cartridges, and, of course, shells exploded or not, and fuses. Farther back on the other side of the German wire - all smashed to bits - there were a dozen dead men, two of them lieutenants. I got a party of men and buried the poor fellows. They were all blackened, and the hands were almost fleshless. Over each man's mound we stuck a rifle and bayonet; heaps were lying about; and his cap on the rifle butt. Everything about them was mouldering. Some have been buried before and torn up by the shell-fire. One officer who was souveniring found a German's prayer-book, and a bandolier of the Prussian Guard. [Lt. Bernard Pitt, Border Regiment]

In parcelling up his souvenirs to send home to his father Captain Crouch of the Bucks. Battalion exhibited a flippant disregard and even affection for the lethality of the weapons concerned:

I've got some more things for you: (1) a ball bomb, (2) a light friction bomb, (3) nose cap of 77-millimetre field-gun shell, aluminium, and (4) a complete 77-millimetre shell.

Nos. 1 and 2 both have the explosive still in them, but are perfectly innocuous, as there is no detonator in them. They can get thrown about. Live bombs without detonators are used for practice throwing. They can't possibly go off.

No. 4 is rather nice. I found it lying in front of my trenches the other morning. The shell had exploded badly and only the fuse had blown out. The empty case is quite complete and intact. It is the ordinary German field-gun shell which is nicknamed 'Little Willy,' 'Pip-squeak,' or 'Whizz-bang.' The two bombs are of an obsolete pattern. The light friction is a very good bomb charged with high explosive which kills within a radius of about six yards only by the force of the explosion. One can throw them and stand and watch them burst with perfect safety. Other types scatter bits about and have been known to kill at 100 yards. The light friction bomb is merely a tin case full of lyddite.

It should not be forgotten though, that the BEF on the Western Front was, for the first time in British history, largely an army of civilians. The following two extracts show how well, despite the nature of army life and of their environment, these men adapted to them:

One lives here in a way which upsets all one's old ideas of life. One does things without a qualm - latrine fatigue, for example - which would have made one physically sick in England. One seems absolutely cut off from all the decent ideas of civilization, and a letter from home is the only connecting thread. Fancy feeling really clean once more, and free from vermin. As soon as we came out last time, I washed all over in cold water, but it had to be done in full view of the public. [H.S.Clapham]

You say you wonder how the life out here affects me. Well, I find it has very little effect upon me either mentally or physically. I always feel very fit, and my nerves are all right. What I felt most at first was the terrible monotony, the sleeping in dirty barns, eating Army food, vermin, sleepless nights in the trenches, etc., but now I am used to it all. You get into the habit of thinking, even when things are at their worst, that 'even this shall pass away.' The first time I was shelled I really thought I should be killed, but if you steady yourself the first time you never have any trouble afterwards, and experience shows you that the very great majority of shell fire misses its mark. Since I have been made a Sergeant I have really enjoyed life very much. When we are out of the trenches we have a Company Sergeants' Mess, of which I am president, where we get a decent meal cooked by our own cook, and generally get a billet with beds in. We have numerous concerts and dinners organised by the Officers in the Regimental Sergeants' Mess, and above all we have an absolute sportsman for a Commanding Officer. [2nd Lt. T.B. Stowell, MC, St. Pancras Rifles]

3
Vermin

Wherever human beings give them the opportunity scavengers of other species will abound. The lack of washing facilities in the front line made it inevitable that every man would - sooner or later - become infested with lice. The refuse and excrement of the living coupled with the all too often unburied corpses of the dead, including at times those exhumed by shellfire, provided an unrivalled source of nourishment for rats and other animals.

Hygiene was extremely rudimentary in the trenches and for the most part men were only able to undress, bathe and obtain fresh clothing during periods out of the line. All water had to be carried up to the trenches by working parties, so precious little could be spared for washing, which came a poor second to the consumption of tea.

Inevitably, then, all front line troops soon fell victim to one parasite or another. Henry Gregory, at the time a private serving with the 119th Machine Gun Company, described how, in reserve one day early in 1916, men of his unit dealt with their unwelcome companions:

> We got a shock after tea; the 'old sweats' in the hut had their shirts off. They were catching lice, and were all as lousy as cuckoos. We had never seen a louse before, but they were here in droves. The men were killing them between their nails. When they saw us looking at this performance with astonishment, one of the men remarked, 'You will soon be as lousy as we are, chum!' They spent the better part of an hour in killing lice and scratching themselves. We soon found out that this took the better part of an hour daily. Each day brought a new batch; as fast as you killed them, others took their place.

A few days later Gregory himself fell prey to the same affliction:

> About this time I felt a tickling feeling round the collar of my tunic. I took off my tunic to investigate, and found many lice there. This was the beginning and from that time we were never free from them. The longer we were there the lousier we got, and it was almost a truism to say that we only had to lie down and the lice would carry us. They became a torment, that it was well-nigh torture...
>
> A lot of us who were billeted up in the loft, were sitting round the brazier one night. It was cold at this time. We were talking and laughing, when all at once one of the fellows jumped up, saying at the

same time that he could not stand it any longer. We had noticed that he had been scratching himself a lot. He took off his tunic and trousers, afterwards his shirt and pants, which he put on the fire, with the remark that the little devils would not bite again. He got some more underclothes next day from the Quarter Master.

Another man in Gregory's company was even worse affected:

My pal, who did night sentry with me, was called Jock, a big, strapping young Scotchman; a fine fellow he was.

One night, as we lay in bed after doing our two hours' sentry - we did two hours on and two hours off - he was scratching in bed as if he would tear himself to bits.

All at once he said 'Damn this, Gregory, I cannot stand it any longer!' He took off his tunic - we slept in these - then he took off his jersey, then his shirt. He put his shirt in the middle of the dug-out floor and put his jersey and tunic on again. As we both sat up in bed watching the shirt he had taken off and put on the floor it actually lifted; it was swarming with lice.

'Did you see it move Gregory?' he asked, I replied that I had. After this he took it in a field and buried it in the ground, then he got rest for a short time, and sleep.

Men adopted a number of methods to try to obtain even temporary relief from their suffering, as Pte. A.S.Dolden of the 1st London Scottish wrote of a time near Vermelles in August 1915:

We had to sleep fully dressed, of course, and with ammunition and equipment on, this was very uncomfortable for the pressure of ammunition on one's chest restricted breathing; furthermore, when a little warmth was obtained the vermin used to get busy, and for some unexplained reason they always seemed to get lively in that portion of one's back, that lay underneath the belt and was the most inaccessible spot. The only way to obtain relief was to get out of the dugout, put a rifle barrel between the belt and the back and rub up and down like a donkey at a gate post. This stopped them for a bit, but as soon as one got back into the dugout, and was getting reasonably warm so would the little brutes get going again.

Neither were the lice any respecters of rank. Gregory's story (below) illustrates how shared experience in the line to some extent broke down barriers between officers and men:

On another afternoon I went up to the gun position on the main Arras-Cambrai road, with a message for our Section Officer. When I arrived at the top of the dugout steps the Officer was busy chatting. He had not heard me coming. The Officers in the line were just as lousy as the men. I coughed, making my presence known to him, and saluted him. He held his trousers with one hand while he saluted with the other. Under other circumstances, this would have been a very embarrassing situation, but war takes the shame out of men, and you get used to situations that under other conditions you would not tolerate for a second.

While men learnt to live with and endure as best they could the companionship of lice, other pests were capable of provoking far greater revulsion. Lt. Vaughan, with the 1/8th Warwicks in April 1917, recorded in his diary a singularly unpleasant encounter:

At the Epéhy crossroads, we found a huge cat squatting on the chest of a dead German, eating his face. It made us sick to see it, and I sent two men to chase it away. As they approached it sprang snarling at them, but they beat it down with their rifles and drove it into the ruined houses. Then we covered the body with a sack, and went on... [later] we saw the sack we had thrown over the dead Jerry heaving up and down, and there was pretty pussy, still rending and tearing the body; so we shot it and continued our march to Longavesnes.

This was admittedly an exceptional experience, but the reality of routine life was only marginally less distasteful:

The outstanding feature of the Armentières sector was the extraordinary number of rats. The area was infested with them. At the rear of the trenches there were huge holes from which earth had been taken to fill the sandbags which formed the parapets. These holes filled up with water, and at night one could see the snouts of rats as they pushed their way across. It was impossible to keep them out of the dugouts even. They grew fat on the food that they pilfered from us, and anything they could pick up in or around the trenches; they were bloated and loathsome to look on. We were filled with an instinctive hatred of them, because however one tried to put the thought out of one's mind, one could not help feeling that they fed on the dead. We waged ceaseless war on them and, indeed, they were very easy prey because owing to their nauseating plumpness they were slow of foot. We would wait and watch for them as they left the water and climb awkwardly on to the boards at the bottom of the trench. Then with a run we would catch them squarely with a mighty kick, and there would be one less to batten on us.

We used to tie our food in sandbags, and these we would hang from a rafter of the dugout. The rats would get the food though, and to do that they must have climbed down the string.

One night a rat ran across my face. Unfortunately my mouth happened to be open and the hind legs of the filthy little beast went right in.

On another occasion a rat fell from a rafter just over the head of Robertson, the fellow who was sleeping next to me. 'Robbie' quickly closed his hand on his overcoat and the rat was caught and speedily finished off. [Dolden]

And further:

In this same barn one evening just after tea, a lot of us were in the barn talking. Rations had been distributed, and each man's rations were put on the top of his bed, which were all fixed in the same way round the barn. As we were talking we heard what appeared to be a fight between rats on the top of the barn where the wheat was kept. They were screaming and carrying on, as if they were pulling one another to pieces. Evidently they were making their way to the edge when all at once a great big rat, almost as big as a cat, fell off the edge of the wheat on to one of the men's beds.

It tried to get away, and we all made a rush for our entrenching tool handles, which had an iron band round one end. We all made a dart for the rat, which by this time was running from one bed to another trying to find a way of escape. We hit it with our weapons as it jumped from one place to another. This could not go on for long, the way it had been pounded, and at last it came to a standstill and laid across a man's rations of bread and cheese, with two legs over one side, and the other two over the other side. One of the fellows gave it another blow, when somebody shouted, 'What about the rations underneath it?' We now threw the enormous rat out of the building.

When the man came back who owned the rations, and was told of what had happened, he was in the frame of mind to throw them away, but on second thoughts he decided to keep them, otherwise he would have had nothing to eat next day. He took out his jack knife, cut about half an inch off the half loaf, a thin piece off all round the cheese and put it away for next day. [Henry Gregory]

At times, considerable ingenuity was brought to bear on the problem:

Sometimes the men amused themselves by baiting the ends of their rifles with pieces of bacon in order to have a shot at them at close quarters. They skipped about like kittens over the feet of anyone who left the dug-out after dark, and even made free with the dug-out itself.

Our Captain, energetic and hopeful as always, determined to make it rat-proof, and spent the whole of one morning having wire netting nailed over every loophole by which they could enter. It was an arduous job, and one corporal nearly lost his stripes over it, but eventually all

was satisfactorily finished, and the Captain sat down to a game of
bridge in the afternoon with an air of 'something accomplished
something done.' The game was under way a short time when Poulter
found a rat sitting beside him on the bench! Captain Thompson, averred
he had brought it in his pocket, an allegation to which Poulter's love for
practical jokes gave some colour, but I think on the whole the rat came
in on his own to show up the preventive measures. [Lt. Frank Laird, 8th
Royal Dublin Fusiliers]

In hot weather particularly, swarms of flies multiplied, feeding on and
laying their eggs in the numerous corpses:

The first experience I had of rotting bodies had been at Serre, where, as
a battalion, we dealt with the best part of a thousand dead who came to
pieces in our hands. As you lifted a body by its arms and legs they
detached themselves from the torso, and this was not the worst thing.
Each body was covered inches deep with a black fur of flies which flew
up into your face, into your mouth, eyes and nostrils, as you
approached. The bodies crawled with maggots. [Stuart Cloete]

Not all vermin excited the same disgust. The war correspondent Philip
Gibbs met an officer during a visit to the front line at Fricourt in the
summer of 1915 whose views he recorded:

'Rats are the worst plague,' said a colonel, coming out of the battalion
headquarters, where he had a hole large enough for a bed and table.
'There are thousands of rats in this part of the line, and they're
audacious devils. In the dugout next door the straw at night writhes
with them... .I don't mind the mice so much. One of them comes to
dinner on my table every evening, a friendly little beggar who is very
pally with me.'

4
Weapons and Technology

Arguably, the Great War was the first total war. Its sheer scale led to unprecedented demands on civilian populations to sustain the troops at the front; the industrialisation of weapons production massively expanded. Attempts to break the deadlock on the Western Front were not only concerned with using existing technology in ever larger quantities (1.6 million shells were fired by the Royal Artillery in the eight days before the battle of the Somme; in 1918, nearly a million were fired in only 24 hours before the storming of the Hindenburg Line) but also in developing new weapons, as well as modernising old (such as mortars, hand grenades and mines).

The principal weapons employed in trench warfare were the rifle and bayonet, bombs (as hand grenades were then known), trench mortars, and machine-guns. New technology was also developed, leading to the use of gas, tanks and aircraft.

The nature of trench warfare dictated that weapons which projected shells or bombs at a high trajectory, giving 'plunging fire,' were essential. The use of howitzers (as opposed to other artillery pieces) was far greater than ever before, and mortars lent themselves all too well to the state of siege pertaining on the Western Front. However, they were popular with none, other than their own crews. Major R.T.Rees described how trench mortars were generally employed:

> There were at this time in our divisional sector three batteries of Trench Mortars, composed of different personnel and using different weapons. Each worked on its own as a self-contained unit, not supplied or controlled by the troops in whose area it happened to be. This want of organisation was bad in every way, and contributed not a little to the universal unpopularity of the T.M. Officer.
>
> What usually happened was this. The T.M. Officer, having heard of some object within the German line which required treatment, would come up with his team and site his gun somewhere near the support line trenches. He would then proceed to open fire with varying success. If his first round missed our front line, that was something to be thankful for, and the infantry would breathe again and hope for the best. But as his range improved, the enemy, roused perhaps from an afternoon nap, would sit up and take notice, and would before long send urgent messages to their own artillery to suppress this nuisance.

Their artillery, thus appealed to, would open fire at once on retaliation-targets, i.e., tender spots in our line, or even some Brigade or Divisional Headquarters.

Then indeed the fat would be in the fire, and the wretched T.M. Officer, hounded out of the trenches by the enraged infantry, would find himself greeted with sour looks by the headquarters which had just had a shell on its roof.

The attentions of trench mortar batteries provoked a swift response; hence Major Rees' complaints. The Germans opposite the 7th Northumberland Fusiliers at Mount Sorrell in January 1916 indicated their displeasure in a novel manner:

During this stay in the trenches the Germans stuck up a notice board with the following legend: *Attention Gentleman*, and below in German, 'If you send over one more trench-mortar bomb you will get strafed in the neck.' [Francis Buckley]

A trench mortar officer, Lt. Bernard Pitt, clearly enjoyed stirring up trouble until brought sharply back to earth by seeing the consequences of his endeavours:

For an hour, for two hours, I fled along winding alleys, looking for a new position to replace the one we had been shelled out of two days before... we found a new position for our homeless gun, and set men a-delving to house it. Every now and then we encountered officers from the front line, from the supports, from the reserves - cavalrymen, engineers, artillerymen. And they gave us information and curses, and told us their opinions of trench mortar merchants, opinions that can not be set down in black and white, but need blood and sulphur and vivid blue... bombs were prepared, and I telephoned through to the front line that we were going to fire, and they had better get under cover. Then, leaving the gunners to get on with their job, I sped towards the observing station with a panting orderly at my heels. As we went forward we spread the ominous news that we were about to interrupt the peaceful toil of the German brethren, who, industrious and worthy men, were constructing machine-gun emplacements, and sniping posts, and other institutions of Kultur. And as we proclaimed these tidings, all turned and cursed us for interfering knaves and murderous varlets... At the appointed time, "Boom," and our bomb sailed overhead, emitting now and then a flash as the fuse burned round. "Crash," as a column of smoke and flame rose just over the edge of the crater. "Aha, that's got 'em, sir," grinned our sniper. "Repeat, four rounds," was my order, and off dashed the runner to the signal station. "Boom," went over our bombs; "Crash." But the Huns were annoyed. A machine-gun chattered and then "Boom," and a nasty black cylinder came tumbling through the air across to our line. "Crash," said the cylinder. Then another toppled along, but it failed to burst; and another, but it burst in the air, to our amusement. "Cease fire," I had said directly our fifth bomb went over, and now I followed my orderly down the trenches again. But "Whurr" came the shells racing through the air; crash, thud, they went, as they burst or buried themselves in the soft earth. We all crouched as these thunderbolts dashed by. Two dozen or more they sent, and then our guns replied, "Whee," and in the distance "Knock," as they reached their target. We hurried home in high glee, but just as we reached our position the German guns returned to the attack. This time they were right on top of us, earth was flying in every direction and I saw my bombardier run away from his gun covered with chalk and dive into my dug-out. I followed him, and found about twenty men in it, all very glad of the protection. Overhead the shells were bursting, their noise dulled by the thick cover. In five minutes all was quiet, except for the scream of our own shells hurrying over in retaliation. Then we could examine the damage. Nothing had been achieved by all this violence, except that the signallers' dug-out near my gun had had its end blown in. Well, I had ordered lunch at one, and so I cleared my guests out of the dug-out and had a meal, spiced by the thought that Fritz and Hans must have been shaken by our generous gifts, and anticipating more fun in the afternoon. A happy idea occurred to me; I would give them five rounds in the quarries; yes, I would...

[later] There are Red Cross men hurrying about, and I see a splash of blood in the grey slime of the trench; and then another; and a yard further on another. I know what that means, and presently a man crouching on a stretcher-chair is carried by me, his head bespattered with blood, and his expression dazed and patient. Snatches of conversation flit up and down the trench, "Eight of 'em"; "Ten casualties"; "Trench mortars?" "No; whizz-bangs." "A captain wounded"; "One poor chap gone." I feel sick, knowing that my five rounds provoked the Germans to this retaliation. [Bernard Pitt]

It was not only the British who initiated these duels; each side retaliated with as much force as they could bring to bear when the other's trench mortars commenced firing:

The situation in the trenches was getting very bad. Shelling by the enemy's artillery was now less frequent, but the annoyance from enemy trench-mortars was something cruel. Not only large oil-cans, full of explosives, came over both by day and by night, but a horrible 9-inch trench-mortar now made its appearance and blew large craters in the C.Ts. and supports. I had two of the oil-cans pretty close to me at different times, and they were not pleasant. Eventually the trench-mortaring got so severe, that the V Corps had a 12-inch howitzer brought up on the railway, and several of these huge shells were fired into Petit Bois when the German trench-mortars started. [Francis Buckley]

Perhaps even more unnerving than receiving projectiles from above was the prospect of being suddenly blown up from below. Mining, a traditional device of siege warfare, was brought to a new pitch. Under the battlefields of France and Flanders there existed miles of tunnels, and chambers as large as decent sized rooms, filled with tons of explosive. The tunneller's job was to blow the enemy out of his trenches, but his prime concern was often his opposite number mining from the opposite direction. Small charges were laid to bring the enemy's tunnel down on his head; sometimes tunnels met and there was hand to hand fighting in the dark and confined space 100 feet below ground. By the height of the mining war there were over 20,000 men actively engaged on each side.

Tunnelling commenced early in 1915 and was well under way by July of that year, by which time both sides were regularly detonating their mines. H.S.Clapham described the effects of a German mine exploding nearby:

> We were feeling a trifle exhausted at night, and about 10.0 o'clock I was lying in my dugout with another man when there was a big explosion, and the whole ground rocked as if with an earthquake. We tumbled out, seized our rifles, and manned the parapet. A huge cloud of smoke was rising to the stars from a small advanced trench on our left front. We realized at once that the Huns had sprung a mine, but star-shells were coming out of the smoke, and the rifles were hard at it, so we knew the trench had not been wiped out. We stood to, waiting for an attack, but our own guns broke out almost at once and no attack was attempted. Apparently the mine exploded just in front of the parapet, and only a few men were hurt.

Lt. A.J.Samson witnessed the firing of a British mine:

> ...word was passed that a mine was to be exploded not very far away on our left, so we waited for the fun. Rifle fire suddenly opened along a good piece of the front - loud cheering and trench mortars and various means of bringing as many Germans as possible to their front line then followed; then up went the mine and every rifle blazed away on both sides, also many guns. Shrapnel burst nearly over our heads and struck the ground a few yards in front and behind, but nothing came into the trench, fortunately, except mud and dirt, so there were no casualties. The worst of it was we couldn't see what luck the mine had, but the reports which have come in this morning say it was very successful.

The mining war reached its climax in June 1917 with the detonation of nineteen mines under the Messines ridge, the noise of which could be heard in London. One of these sophisticated excavations was examined by Lt. Frank Laird of the 8th Royal Dublin Fusiliers:

In the centre of this Strong Point you could climb out of the trench, cross a few yards of the open, and descend by a narrow stair to where an Engineer officer lived in the bowels of the earth. It was one of the openings of a huge mine (reputed to hold a million pounds of ammonal), which ran under the Alleyman's line at Wytschaete. It had been constructed over a year before, and was now biding its time to go up with its eighteen brethren along the front on the great morning of the Messines offensive in June, 1917. At the top of the Strong Point was another larger opening, with a broad stair leading down to the same mine, which proved a pleasant city of refuge one morning when the Alley-man suddenly took a freakish notion to sweep the Strong Point across with a line of shell fire. In spite of the unevenness of the ground I made exceedingly good time to the mouth of the cavern.

Notwithstanding the effectiveness of mines, and fear engendered by them, machine-guns are the weapons most closely associated with the First World War. Two types were usually employed in the BEF; the Lewis gun, a light air-cooled machine-gun which could be fired by a single man from the hip or from a static position, mounted on a bipod, and the heavier, water-cooled Vickers gun, which was less mobile and required two men to operate it (and which supplanted the earlier Maxim in late 1915). Early in the war, the role of the machine-gun was essentially static and defensive, but once its value had been revealed on the Western Front it was exploited more fully and both heavy and light machine-guns were used for offensive purposes. The expanded rôle of the heavy machine-gun was reflected in the formation of the Machine Gun Corps (MGC) in October 1915. Thenceforth, members of the MGC took their place in any operation, small or large. Corporal Gregory of 119th Company found himself using his gun to support an attack during the Battle of Cambrai:

We had now only an hour left in which to dig the gun positions. It was 4 a.m. when we got back to carry on where we left off. We worked feverishly to get them ready, and we were still digging in the little trench, when all at once our Artillery opened out. We got orders to stop digging, all the machine guns in our lot opened out, and what a bedlam! The roar of the Artillery of all sizes, as they belched forth their messages of death and destruction, was well-nigh deafening. The flashes of the guns lit up the sky a vivid crimson, and the noise as the shells burst, added noise to the din.

After the first five minutes the water in the barrel of our machine gun was boiling, and the gun was puffing like a little steam engine. We could hear the shells doing their work of destruction.

I now took a look at Le Vackeray [La Vacquerie] in front of us. I saw a fair-sized town in ruins, all the houses seemed to be burning at once The place was well alight, and the noise as the shells crashed into the houses with their destroying crash, then the collapse of bricks and masonry, with a cloud of dust with each hit, was terrific.

The enemy had been sending shells over our positions, and as they came crashing all round us we had to take what little cover we could in our small shallow trench. I pulled my tin hat well over my head, and as each shell crashed by our gun position, throwing up a shower of earth, this would descend on top of our tin hats like hail as big as marbles. They had discovered our positions, and they meant to blow them to bits.

It was terrible while it lasted. My head seemed to swell as large as my body, with the continual explosions; it ached and throbbed beyond words, and was well-nigh to bursting point.

His Artillery quietened down, not many of his guns now being in action. How the poor devils in the place opposite to us had fared, God only knew, as it was reduced to ruins, and had been a red hot inferno.

Our gun was not ordered to elevate, as the Infantry were to attack with the bayonet and carry the position. The Officer ordered us to stop filling the belts, as we had got a lot ready. Having nothing to do, and the shells having ceased to come over to our positions, I gazed at the scene in front of us.

Just then the first wave of infantry jumped over the top of the parapet of their trench and rushed forward with fixed bayonets to capture their objective. Shortly afterwards two other waves of infantry followed the first lot. The first wave was now nearing the town, and they disappeared up the streets. We could hear rifle bullets cracking out clear and crisp; they had evidently come across some of the enemy. It would now be short and sharp work. If they did not throw up their hands quickly, they would be dead men.

While this bombardment was going on, orders had to be shouted out at the top of the voice. We were only about two feet away from the Officer, but his shouts were just like whispers to us, the noise was tremendous.

Gregory's fire was one element in a machine-gun barrage, raining bullets over the heads of the attacking infantry into the enemy defences. By the middle of 1918, however, the most important role of the heavy machine-gun was to accompany the attacking troops forward and the Lewis gun had become an integral part of small unit tactics, frequently being used to keep enemy strong points covered while other troops worked round their flanks to surround them:

By the end of August, 1918, the German Army was in full retreat everywhere along the whole battle front and we were soon on our way to Cambrai.

Squads of Germans were continually surrendering to our infantry and many were in a panic as they shouted 'No shoot'. Nevertheless, it was often necessary to mount our guns to give covering fire to the advancing infantrymen in our sector.

In the early days of September we reached the outskirts of Cambrai, where we spent a night in a captured German dug-out.

The assault on the Hindenburg Line between Cambrai and St. Quentin (part of the offensive that ended the war) was gathering momentum and directly it was daylight on the morning of September 12th we left the outskirts of Cambrai and marched across open country, bypassing the city.

Pack mules carried our gear - but after a while we struck so many communication trenches it became necessary to get rid of the mules. Headquarters then sent us a tank - complete with driver - to carry our gear. We were almost at the Hindenburg Line when our tank-driver was shot in the face and killed.

We dismantled our gear again and finished up carrying guns, tripods and other equipment into a trench full of Germans who were waiting to surrender.

We saw the machine-gun that we assumed had killed our driver. The gun was ditched against the parapet, but all we could do was to give the prisoners a nasty look as our infantry-men hustled them out of the dug-out.

Infantry bombing squads began to work their way along a maze of enemy dug-outs, which were palaces compared to most of those we had occupied in the British Lines. I remember one German dug-out in particular: it had forty steps leading down to a veritable home from home, with bread and bottles of wine on tables. There was also a piano, the top of which was covered with picture postcards of places in Germany where, apparently the occupants of the dug-out came from.

'They must have had quite an enjoyable time when off duty,' remarked my section officer. We were not able to sample any of the German luxuries for it became necessary to help our infantry comb the many deep shelters, having a gun ready in case of serious resistance.

Some occupants of these shelters seemed most reluctant to come up and surrender when our infantry chaps shouted down to them, but after a

Mills-bomb had been chucked into the shelter they soon changed their minds. Many young boys were among the men.

Reaching a trench which we took to be a dead-end, we discovered our mistake when about twenty Germans suddenly appeared in our rear and one German opened fire on us. We shipped our machine-gun round and covered them. They immediately offered to surrender - shouting almost in unison - 'No shoot, we got childen at home, war fini'.

We withheld our fire and the Germans (most artillerymen), after giving us small souvenirs as a sort of thanks for sparing them, quietly joined their mates in a main trench, waiting to be marched off to a prisoners' reception depot.

In the next bay to us an infantry N.C.O. was shouting orders to his men over something or other. I recognised the voice and slipped round to confirm my belief. We were neighbours from Oldham. For a few moments we talked of home - as refreshing as rain in a desert - but our talk was ended abruptly as a German tailed mortar-bomb came whizzing over from a section of the German line not far distant and my Oldham neighbour received orders to help sort out other problems.

Our machine-gun section got instructions to move into a valley behind us and take shelter in a captured trench.

As we moved it simply rained bullets. I had one through my haversack and water bottle before finally reaching cover. Luckily for us the Germans were firing too much to our right.

In front of us was a German redoubt of machine-guns. It had to be silenced before we made any further advance.

We waited until after dark before doing anything about it, then in conjunction with infantry scouts, took out a gun and got a closer look at the German strongpoint - which turned out to be several tanks protected with concrete shields and well camouflaged. A miniature fortress.

The tanks were British - captured from our lads during the 1916 offensive, we were told later on.

Next day, preparations were made to subdue this little German fortress which we knew was going to be no picnic.

On the last day of September I believe it was, the assault took place. Field guns of the Royal Horse Artillery first bombarded the enemy redoubts and 126 Machine Gun Company put down a heavy machine-gun barrage in support of the infantry who rushed in and captured the whole outfit, with few casualties. It was now quite apparent that the Germans would much rather surrender than fight. [W.Commerford, 126th Company MGC]

A new type of weapon, used for the first time in the Great War, was gas. A number of different chemicals were employed, falling into three main categories, the least effective of which were the tear gases; the more lethal irritants of the eyes and respiratory tract, such as chlorine and phosgene, which could lead a man to drown in the secretions of his lungs; and mustard gas, which was comparatively less lethal but most effective, causing extremely painful blisters to exposed skin and remaining as an oily liquid on the ground for some time afterwards. Gas was delivered either through static projectors (which relied upon the strength and direction of the prevailing wind) or shells, which could be fired directly into enemy positions, and were much more effective.

H.S.Clapham first encountered gas in the form of fallout from a large attack elsewhere, on April 28th 1915, when the Germans opened the Second Battle of Ypres with a chlorine attack in the northern part of the Salient:

> The same afternoon we had rather a curious experience. Without any obvious reason, everyone's eyes began to smart, until the tears ran down one's cheeks. We heard by telephone that the men in the support line were suffering in the same way. There was no smell or any other natural cause for it, and after a quarter of an hour the worst of it passed off. The Captain came round and told us it was said to be the effect of brick dust, driven down-wind, from the burning of Ypres. It was only when we came out that we found that the Huns had been discharging gas north of Ypres. The gas was practically dissipated before it reached us, but there seems to have been serious trouble with it in the north.

Six weeks later, at Hellfire Corner, Clapham's battalion were shelled with gas:

> About 6.0 p.m. the worst moment of the day came. The Huns started to bombard us with a shell which was quite new to us. It sounded like a gigantic fire-cracker, with two distinct explosions. These shells came over just above the parapet, in a flood, much more quickly than we could count them. After a quarter of an hour of this sort of thing, there was a sudden crash in the trench and ten feet of the parapet, just beyond me, was blown away and everyone around blinded by the dust. With my first glance I saw what looked like half a dozen bodies, mingled with sandbags, and then I smelt gas and realized that these were gas shells. I had my respirator on in a hurry and most of our own men were as quick. The others were slower and suffered for it. One man was sick all over the sandbags and another was coughing his heart up. We pulled four men out of the debris unharmed. One man was unconscious, and

died of gas later. Another was hopelessly smashed up and must have got it full in the chest.

We all thought that this was the end and almost hoped for it, but luckily the gas shells stopped, and after a quarter of an hour we could take off our respirators. I started in at once to build up the parapet again, for we had been laid open to the world in front, but the gas lingered about the hole for hours, and I had to give up delving in the bottom for a time. As it was it made me feel very sick.

Clapham seems on this occasion to have encountered chlorine. But mustard gas was far more debilitating:

We came to a shell hole in which there was an unusual kind of yellow powder, and a peculiar smell. I took a good sniff and declared that there had been gas in the shells. This was something new, for gas had not been sent over in HE shells before. Robertson took a sniff and said it was not gas, and a long argument ensued during which we both took a few new sniffs and then went along to the dugout to call the Gas Corporal. When he appeared we set the case before him and he came along to the shell hole. He took a mild sniff and then chased off like mad yelling 'Gas'. The sequel to this came later in Army orders, for that night every unit was warned that the Germans had started to put gas over in high explosive shells.

I was very lucky to get away with that 'packet' as lightly as I did, for I must have taken quite a lot of gas into my lungs with the many sniffs that I took. The ground had become so impregnated with the gas that all the troops were ordered out of the area, and the trench was put out of bounds. I was unwell during the morning, and had a shocking headache, and completely lost my voice, and soon Robertson was affected in the eyes. At 10.30pm the Germans made a raid on our front line, and when our guns answered the SOS signal it was like all hell let loose. The enemy put up a gas barrage over our trench, and we had to lie with our gas masks on. The shelling kept up for about an hour and a half.

The next day Robertson was worse, and had to be led to the Aid Post with a bandage round his eyes, for he could not bear the light on them. There was a continuous stream of water running from my eyes, and they were extremely inflamed and very sore. I was in chronic pain, as my head, throat, eyes and lungs ached unmercifully. In addition, the mustard gas had burnt me severely in a certain delicate part of my anatomy that is not usually displayed in public! [A.S.Dolden]

Another innovation first seen on the Western Front was 'liquid fire,' as the flamethrower was known at the time. Jets of blazing petrol or oil were projected under pressure from a cylinder carried on an infantryman's back or larger, static containers which had a longer range but were too cumbersome to be moved out of a trench. Their short range (20-40 yards) and the danger to the operators inherent in their use meant that they were used rarely. Guy Chapman witnessed a German attack on a pillbox during the Third Battle of Ypres:

> Under cover of the hurly-burly of shelling on our plateau and the thick mist, the enemy had concentrated a number of trench-mortars against our segment of line. They pounded it lavishly for ten minutes. Then the defenders suddenly saw advancing towards them a wave of fire. The enemy were attacking under cover of flammenwerfer, hose pipes leading to petrol-tanks carried on the backs of men. When the nozzles were lighted, they threw out a roaring, hissing flame twenty to thirty feet long, swelling at the end to a whirling oily rose, six feet in diameter. Under the protection of these hideous weapons, the enemy surrounded the advance pill-box, stormed it and killed the garrison. Shorman, its commander, was last seen by Bevan and Digby, who were lying out in front, wounded and being carried away. Bevan himself had been shot in the stomach; but Digby, stayed with him and in the end managed to drag him back to our line. In the meantime, the enemy was consolidating the captured pill-box; but Whitehead and C.S.M. Edmonds, collecting a few men to carry for them, furiously assailed the place and bombed their way into it. Most of the occupants were killed, and six surrendered.

The supreme weapon of the Great War, however, was artillery. The vast bulk of artillery fire was 'indirect' - that is, the gun crew could not see where their shells were landing, owing to geography and distance - and so their fire relied for accuracy on direction from artillery observers. There were usually junior gunner officers known as 'Forward Observation Officers' (FOO's), either sent forward to a front line observation post or, less commonly, skywards in observation balloons (in addition, artillery observation was carried out by the RFC in both aircraft and balloons). Vantage points for FOO's were diverse, ranging from the front line trench itself, via haystacks (early in the war) to convenient church steeples. A novel type of observation post, which became popular, was described by Major R.T.Rees:

> I got my first glimpse of a live German by what seemed to me a most ingenious device. Our Company Head-Quarters was near a row of pollarded willows, now scarred and bare, but with fairly thick trunks. One night some Engineers appeared and cut down one of these trunks, substituting for it another, exactly similar in size and colour and clinging ivy, but made of steel. The motive of this extraordinary procedure became apparent when one found in the steel tree a narrow staircase with small openings for observation. It was through one of these slits

that I caught a brief glimpse of an enemy working-party behind the lines.

Arthur Behrend (90th Brigade, RGA) recounted in his memoirs a vivid account of the crucial and dangerous work of the balloon observer:

When I arrived the following afternoon the balloon was close-hauled and swaying uneasily in the breeze. Its basket, a few feet above my head, was swaying too. The balloon was attached to its winch by a slender cable of steel wire, and the winch was bolted to the floor of a lorry which, though mobile, looked substantial enough to allay my passing fears that it might rise from the earth and follow the balloon into the air. Two men in R.F.C. uniform were standing by at the winch, and one of them showed me how to fit the harness of a folded parachute to my back.

It was a sunny afternoon, a particularly beautiful one on account of the number of small fleecy white clouds between us and the clear blue sky, and Cleaver glanced at them as we were clambering into the basket. "One thousand feet," he ordered the winch corporal. "No smoking, mind," he said to me.

There were no further preliminaries. the winch began to hum, and up we went. Cleaver turned to me. "The visibility's perfect, I know," he said. "But all these low clouds are an invitation to any lurking Hun. Sorry about that because I wanted to take you up to fifteen hundred."

The basket was made of wicker and its sides breast high. Inside there was just room for the two of us to stand upright; the equipment consisted of a telephone, an aneroid barometer, and a compass.

Our rate of ascent if slow seemed steady, and we were soon out of earshot of the winch gear. An upward glance reassured me that the balloon looked more than large enough to take good care of me, and I gazed downward. The cable appeared woefully thin, and it needed a real effort to take my eyes from it. By now the winch was a couple of hundred feet below, and I could see the white blobs of the winchmen's faces each time they looked up to watch our progress. Having reached the conclusion that if the cable parted there was nothing anyone could do about it, I took my Zeiss glasses from their case and slung them round my neck. Here, compared with my only previous experience of the air - in a Nieuport monoplane - there was an unpleasant sense of insecurity. When sitting in an aeroplane the sense of detachment is complete, but standing in an airborne basket seemed neither one thing nor the other. The wretched cable still made us part of the ground, and that was the first of several times that afternoon I felt sorry for balloonatics.

At six hundred feet we were free of most earthly noises, and again I looked down. For the first time I saw the front line as it really was, mile upon mile of it. Now running straight, now turning this way or that in an apparently haphazard and unnecessary curve, now straight again, it stretched roughly north and south till it vanished in both directions in sheer distance. The depth and complexity of the German trench system surprised me, and of the opposing belts of wire, dull brown and rusting, there was considerably more on the German side than on ours. No Man's Land, much wider in places than I had realized from any map, looked like a long-neglected race-course by reason of the distinctive greenness of its bare but relatively undisturbed turf. To me it was like one of those bird's-eye drawings so popular in the illustrated weeklies of that time, except that no artist had   conveniently inserted place-names alongside the more famous strong points and ruined townships of the Somme.

Far behind in enemy territory I saw factories with smoking chimneys and pleasantly normal villages, and the view was so extensive that I counted six streaks or plumes of steam from the engines of equally normal trains. The winch was now so tiny that it was hardly visible, and only the glint of the nearest couple of hundred feet of cable reminded me that we were still connected to the ground. It was such a good day for visibility that every balloonatic, British and German alike, seemed to be taking the air; north and south I counted twenty-three balloons, all lined up at regular intervals of say a mile and a half and all apparently suspended in nothing. There was comfort in numbers, I thought. And no wonder they were called sausage-balloons, I thought too.

Artillery was active on both sides of the line, on the whole a curiously silent activity, though by some acoustic freak occasional booms reached our ears. Yet the landscape was alive with the puffs of bursting shells and the gun flashes of batteries in action, and, like matches being struck in the opposite stand at a football match, the brief glow of some newly-created fire.

All of a sudden the motion, or more correctly the lack of it, changed. In sympathy with the balloon the basket began to tug and sway swinging in what must have been quite a wind. I looked at Hoppy Cleaver but he did not seem concerned; with his glasses to his eyes and his elbows on the edge of the basket to steady himself he was studying something behind the German lines. I understood what had happened.

We had reached our height, the winch was no longer letting out cable, and the balloon was so to speak anchored. This is devilish unpleasant, I thought, and wondered how soon it would be before I was sick. After looking down the cable and finding no palliative there I copied Cleaver by raising my glasses, but through the motion of the basket I found it hard to keep them fixed on any given spot.

Hoppy Cleaver laid the folded part of his parachute over the edge of the basket and indicated to me to do likewise; then, picking up the telephone, he said into it, "Tell the battery we're ready now."

The shoot of 300 rounds we were about to observe was being fired by Toc 1; I had chosen it in preference to the afternoon shoots of our 6-inch batteries because I imagined 9.2 bursts would be that much easier to see. Their target was a 5.9 battery engaged by us several times before and known for its viciousness no less than for its recuperative powers.

"See the target area all right?" Cleaver asked, and I admitted I didn't.
"You will if you look in the right direction. Try ten degrees left of where you're looking now."
I did. "Afraid I still can't get it," I said at last.

"I'll show you on the map first," said Cleaver kindly, one hand holding the receiver to his ear. "Here. Agreed?... Now look where I'm pointing - never mind the basket turning, you'll soon get used to that - and you'll see the grey smoke of a train, it's probably burning wood. Got it?... Two fingers left there's a house with its windows catching the sun... Good. And half a mile in front of that there's a small roundish wood quite by itself. Got that too? ...Running across the front edge of the wood there's a sunken road - you can't see it but it's there all right - and the hostile battery's just beside it. It's in it, in fact 'No. 1 fired!'"

By using the edge of the basket I managed to steady my glasses on the front of the wood, and twenty seconds later Cleaver said, "Did you get it?"
"No."
"Outside the field of your glasses, I expect. It was short." He telephoned a correction... 'No. 2 fired!'"

I saw that one. From the faint blur of smoke it had landed plumb in the wood, but owing to the distance and the jerking basket I could not for the life of me judge whether it was over, right, or both. Hoppy Cleaver knew, and another crisp correction was telephoned down.

Half a dozen more rounds fell one after another, all more or less visible.

"I'm no damned good at this," I said. "I see them all right, but from this low angle of sight I can't say if they're out for line or for elevation."
"They're all O.K. for line. 1 and 3 are still shooting short, all the others are a bit over."

More corrections, and rounds began to fall in and around the target area.

"They've hit something," from me. "That's some of their ammunition going up."

Ranging ended, and Toc 1 proceeded to gunfire of 50 rounds per gun. As a result the target area, half the wood too, became obscured by smoke. There were three more fires, and it seemed clear that Toc 1 was giving that German battery hell.

By now I felt quite at home in the basket, and there was so much of interest in the world above and below that all fears of sickness were forgotten. Through my glasses the fleecy clouds were lovely, and from them I looked north, then south - "My God, what's that?" I asked.

A balloon - the fourth from us - was emitting oily black smoke. Then it sagged, and the whole of it burst into bright red flame. The volume of black smoke soared and became tremendous.

The swaying of our basket ceased because the winchmen had seen it too - we were being hauled down.

"There's the Hun that did it!" I said, still watching through my glasses. "He's tackling the next one now."

Its occupants had not waited. Two tumbling bodies. Then two parachutes opened and floated gently earthwards. An anti-aircraft battery opened up, its white burst dotting the sky at the right height. Otherwise its shells were absurdly wide of the mark. The Taube, unworried by them, came on in a leisurely if determined way and set the next balloon alight in exactly the same way as the first. I was relieved to see he did not dive to shoot up the parachutists. By this time the first balloon, or what was left of it, was dropping like a blazing paper bag.

Still unperturbed, the Hun came on to the second from us. I could see his swift tracer bullets going into it, and then I heard the sharp rat-tat-tat of his machine-gun. It too went up in smoke and flame, and down it came more quickly than the others. The Taube was skilful in avoiding it, but it was touch and go if it would catch up the two parachutists.

The next balloon to us was, like ourselves, perceptibly lower. But nothing like low enough, and as the Hun came on towards it I saw its two balloonatics scramble over the edge of the basket and drop. Both parachutes opened, but one seemed to take a long time about it.

Hoppy Cleaver was now standing on the edge of our own basket, and I saw him tighten his harness and finger the release-box. "Mind the cable when you jump," he said to me.

Finding it hard to choose between watching him and the Hun plane, I settled for the latter and saw it set alight our nearest neighbour as easily and quickly as the previous three. Then, skirting the smoke and flame, it flew on in our direction. I felt a totally different kind of detachment.

This can't mean me, I thought. I looked to see if Cleaver was still there; to my surprise he was getting back into the basket and I remember thinking for a one-legged man he was remarkably nimble. He was looking at me, I remember too. I glanced again at the Hun. Still tailed by the hot but inaccurate fire of two if not three anti-aircraft batteries, he had turned away and was streaking for home.

Cleaver said, "He must have run out of incendiary. All the same 4 balloons in one sortie isn't bad going."

During the rest of the haul-down we did not speak, and when we reached the ground neither of the winchmen who helped us out so much as grinned.

"Come into the mess and have a drink," Cleaver said.
"I don't know about you but I could do with one myself."
"Tell me, why did you get back into the basket?" I asked. "Before the Hun turned off, I mean."
"To throw you out, of course, You were my guest, and I knew you hadn't the sense or guts to get out yourself."
What he said was true.
"But don't you worry about it," he was saying. "And anyway you'll be able to tell your Colonel we balloonatics always do our best."

At the start of the war, aeroplanes were regarded as being useful only for reconnaissance, but once the trench war had become established and the dominance of artillery an accepted fact, their potential for observation was realized. This in itself led to further expansion of their rôle, since to shoot down the enemy's observation planes was to reduce the accuracy of his fire, as was the destruction of his observation balloons. Specialised types of plane were developed to meet these diverse roles; and although 'bombers' as such had not been developed at the start of the war, from an early stage aeroplanes were employed to drop a variety of potentially lethal projectiles on the enemy:

One morning, while we were working in our orchard an "Albatross" appeared and hovered over the town, to the intense indignation of four "Archies", who literally smothered the blue sky with their shrapnel bursts. Being a dead calm, frosty day, the puffs of white smoke hung about for a long time. Before going the Hun plane swooped down to about 6,000 feet and dropped two bombs. I heard them "whiffling" through the air. They landed close enough for us - on each side of the barn our men were billeted in. One was a dud, but the other blew a hole as big as a cart-wheel in the garden, and what was worse blew our signalling sergeant head over heels into the latrine pit! It was all rather a joke, and the men were lucky to see bombs, as the enemy so far has used them but seldom. [Lt. Col. N.Fraser-Tytler]

This incident took place in December 1915; as the war progressed, aerial bombing became considerably more effective:

> The enemy airmen were putting their loads down a few hundred yards away on our horse-lines. I was not particularly frightened. Newcomers to battle rarely are. It is when you have been engaged in active warfare for a few weeks that you begin to get scared and with every bombardment or air raid you become more and more terrified.
>
> When the bombs had ceased falling we went over to see what damage they had done. I saw my first dead man twisted up beneath a wagon where he had evidently tried to take shelter; but we had not sustained many human casualties. The horses were another matter. There were dead ones lying all over the place and scores of others were floundering about screaming with broken legs, terrible neck wounds or their entrails hanging out. We went back for our pistols and spent the next hour putting the poor, seriously injured brutes out of their misery by shooting them through the head. To do it we had to wade ankle deep through blood and guts. That night we lost over 100 horses. [Dennis Wheatley - August 1917]

A further development was the use of aircraft for low-level ground attack - 'strafing.' The 2nd Coldstream were subjected to this in Spring 1918:

> We received a great surprise in our part of the line one day when we were suddenly attacked by aircraft. It was the Richthofen Circus, as it was called. Baron Richthofen was a German air ace who operated with a picked squadron of planes all painted in brilliant colours - scarlet, yellow, blue and orange. Suddenly these monsters swooped down on us as if they were giant birds of prey, banked, and poured machine-gun fire into our trenches. This was, I think, almost the first time the infantry were strafed at close range from the air. It was a very frightening experience and took some standing up to. One had a great desire to run away. They were so big, so near, the roar of their engines so loud, their occupants - in goggles and flying helmets - so inhuman-looking, that for an instant or two one was bewildered. But that did not last long. We poured rifle and Lewis gun fire into them and they veered off. I do not think they were more than forty feet above us as they dived and banked. We did not bring any of them down but I do not think they liked our fire. They certainly did not come back for more. But our Lewis guns did bring down aeroplanes - one or two in the whole war - and the troops, by firing at them from the ground, disturbed them, kept them up, and made their reconnaissance more difficult. [Stuart Cloete]

Notwithstanding the vital role of aircraft, the Great War could only be won by breakthrough on the ground. The most important technical innovation to this end was the tank. Despite initial official scepticism about the concept of the tank itself and continuing doubts in some quarters regarding its usefulness in action, it became increasingly important towards the end of the war. Tanks were first employed on 15th September 1916, on the Somme, when the tactics of their use had not yet been properly developed, but where their performance nevertheless gave an indication of their potential. However, they were vulnerable to shellfire and, the early models especially, to mechanical breakdown. In addition, they were exhausting to operate, being extremely hot, cramped and noisy and filled with exhaust fumes (when in 1918 some roomier models were used to carry troops forward, it was found that the infantrymen became unfit for combat owing to the conditions inside the tanks).

Major W.H.L.Watson of No. 11 Company, Heavy Branch MGC (later to become the Tank Corps) discovered this at Bullecourt in April 1917:

> All the tanks, except Morris's had arrived without incident at the railway embankment. Morris ditched at the bank and was a little late. Haigh and Jumbo had gone on ahead of the tanks. They crawled out beyond the embankment into No Man's Land and marked out the starting-line. It was not too pleasant a job. The enemy machine-guns were active right through the night, and the neighbourhood of the embankment was shelled intermittently. Towards dawn this intermittent shelling became almost a bombardment, and it was feared that the tanks had been heard.

> Skinner's tank failed on the embankment. The remainder crossed it successfully and lined up for the attack just before zero. By this time the shelling had become severe. The crews waited inside their tanks, wondering dully if they would be hit before they started. Already they were dead-tired, for they had had little sleep since their long painful trek of the night before.

> Suddenly our bombardment began - it was more of a bombardment than a barrage - and the tanks crawled away into the darkness, followed closely by little bunches of Australians.

> On the extreme right Morris and Puttock of Wyatt's section were met by tremendous machine-gun fire at the wire of the Hindenburg Line. They swung to the right, as they had been ordered, and glided along in front of the wire, sweeping the parapet with their fire. They received as good as they gave. Serious clutch trouble developed in Puttock's tank. It was impossible to stop since now the German guns were following them. A brave runner carried the news to Wyatt at the embankment. The tanks continued their course, though Puttock's tank was barely moving, and by luck and good driving they returned to the railway, having kept the enemy most fully occupied in a quarter where he might have been uncommonly troublesome.

Morris passed a line to Skinner and towed him over the embankment. They both started for Bullecourt. Puttock pushed on back towards Noreuil. His clutch was slipping so badly that the tank would not move, and the shells were falling ominously near. He withdrew his crew from the tank into a trench, and a moment later the tank was hit again.

Of the remaining two tanks in this section we could hear nothing. Davies and Clarkson had disappeared. Perhaps they had gone through to Heudecourt. Yet the infantry of the right brigade, according to the reports we had received, were fighting most desperately to retain a precarious hold on the trenches they had entered.

In the centre Field's section of three tanks were stopped by the determined and accurate fire of forward field-guns before they entered the German trenches. The tanks were silhouetted against the snow, and the enemy gunners did not miss.

The first tank was hit in the track before it was well under way. The tank was evacuated, and in the dawning light it was hit again before the track could be repaired.

Money's tank reached the German wire. His men must have 'missed their gears.' For less than a minute the tank was motionless, then she burst into flames. A shell had exploded the petrol tanks, which in the old Mark I. were placed forward on either side of the officer's and driver's seats. A sergeant and two men escaped. Money, best of good fellows, must have been killed instantaneously by the shell.

Bernstein's tank was within reach of the German trenches when a shell hit the cab, decapitated the driver, and exploded in the body of the tank. The corporal was wounded in the arm, and Bernstein was stunned and temporarily blinded. The tank was filled with fumes. As the crew were crawling out, a second shell hit the tank on the roof. The men under the wounded corporal began stolidly to salve the tank's equipment, while Bernstein, scarcely knowing where he was, staggered back to the embankment. He was packed off to a dressing station, and an orderly was sent to recall the crew and found them still working stubbornly under direct fire.

Swears' section of four tanks on the left were slightly more fortunate.

Birkett went forward at top speed, and, escaping the shells, entered the German trenches, where his guns did great execution. The tank worked down the trenches towards Bullecourt, followed by the Australians. She was hit twice, and all the crew were wounded, but Birkett went on fighting grimly until his ammunition was exhausted and he himself was badly wounded in the leg. Then at last he turned back, followed industriously by the German gunners. Near the embankment he stopped the tank to take his bearings. As he was climbing out, a shell burst against the side of the tank and wounded him again in the leg. The tank was evacuated. The crew salved what they could, and, helping each other, for they were all wounded, they made their way back painfully to the embankment. Birkett was brought back on a stretcher, and wounded a third time as he lay in the sunken road outside the dressing station. His tank was hit again and again. Finally it took fire, and was burnt out.

Skinner, after his tank had been towed over the railway embankment by Morris, made straight for Bullecourt, thinking that as the battle had now been in progress for more than two hours the Australians must have fought their way down the trenches into the village. Immediately he entered the village machine-guns played upon his tank, and several of his crew were slightly wounded by the little flakes of metal that fly about inside a Mk. I. tank when it is subjected to really concentrated machine-gun fire. No Australians could be seen. Suddenly he came right to the edge of an enormous crater, and as suddenly stopped. He tried to reverse, but he could not change gear. The tank was absolutely motionless. He held out for some time, and then the Germans brought up a gun and began to shell the tank. Against field-guns in houses he was defenceless so long as his tank could not move. His ammunition was nearly exhausted. There were no signs of the Australians or of British troops. He decided quite properly to withdraw. With great skill he evacuated his crew, taking his guns with him and the little ammunition that remained. Slowly and carefully they worked their way back, and reached the railway embankment without further casualty.

The fourth tank of this section was hit on the roof just as it was coming into action. The engine stopped in sympathy, and the tank commander withdrew his crew from the tank.

Swears, the section commander, left the railway embankment, and with the utmost gallantry went forward into Bullecourt to look for Skinner. He never came back.

Such were the cheerful reports that I received in my little brick shelter by the cross-roads.

The need for mutual support between infantry, tanks and aeroplanes, in conjunction with a protective artillery barrage, was recognized well enough by Autumn 1917 for the near-breakthrough at Cambrai to occur. But even then, if this co-operation failed, the consequences could be disastrous:

At 10.30 A.M. the barrage fell and we could see it climb, like a living thing, through the wood and up the hillside, a rough line of smoke and flame. On the hillside to the left of the wood we could mark the course of the battle, - the tanks with tiny flashes darting from their flanks - clumps of infantry following in little rushes - an officer running in front of his men, until suddenly he crumpled up and fell, as though some unseen hammer had struck him on the head - the men wavering in the face of machine-gun fire and then spreading out to surround the gun - the wounded staggering painfully down the hill, and the stretcher-bearers moving backwards and forwards in the wake of the attack - the aeroplanes skimming low along the hillside, and side-slipping to rake the enemy trenches with their guns.

We watched one tank hesitate before it crossed the skyline and our hearts went out to the driver in sympathy. He made his decision, and the tank, brown against the sky, was instantly encircled by little puffs of white smoke, shells from the guns on the reverse slope. The man was brave, for he followed the course of a trench along the crest of the hill. My companion uttered a low exclamation of horror. Flames were coming from the rear of the tank, but its guns continued to fire and the tank continued to move. Suddenly the driver must have realised what was happening. The tank swung towards home. It was too late. Flames burst from the roof and the tank stopped, but the sponson doors never opened and the crew never came out... When I left my post half an hour later the tank was still burning. [Watson]

The battlefield of 1918 fundamentally differed from its predecessor of 1914 in the sheer volume of firepower available. All the weapons discussed in this chapter were designed to increase one's own firepower or to diminish that of the enemy, with the result that the much sought breakthroughs of 1915, 1916 and 1917 finally occurred in 1918.

5
Trench Life - Operations

While fatigues, carrying parties and the like took up the bulk of the front-line soldiers' time, the adversarial side of trench warfare manifested itself in raiding and patrolling. They were offensive measures, actively carrying the war to the enemy. The objects of both were to dominate No-Man's-Land in order to discourage German raids and patrols, while at the same time keeping morale up and maintaining 'offensive spirit' (or so higher command levels intended). In addition, information of military value could be obtained by taking prisoners (in order to assess the quality and freshness of the troops opposite) and also by seeing the state of readiness of the Germans either for repelling or carrying out an attack.

Whereas raids were 'one-off' operations, patrols were a standing feature of day-to-day operations. The former were generally intended to enter the German lines, both to cause alarm and inflict casualties, with the acquisition of prisoners often the ultimate prize. Patrols, on the other hand, did not necessarily set out to make contact with the enemy (although the duties of 'offensive patrols' sometimes included disruption of their working parties) but to investigate features in No-Man's-Land in order to see whether likely outposts were garrisoned and German working parties active. Stealth was the key to patrolling and so the size of patrols was kept to a minimum - as few as two men, though sometimes as many as 30, and occasionally more; the smallest raids consisted of about a dozen men, and on rare occasions whole battalions were involved. While patrols relied on no more than the machine-gunners and rifles of their own battalions for covering fire, raiders could call upon the support of their local artillery to assist them.

In the slang of the front line, any offensive operation was known as a 'stunt;' Capt. Crouch described an offensive patrol:

> We had a great stunt last night, which I hope may earn a D.C.M. or two for B Company. Combie, who is my second in command, as you know, took out a large patrol to round up some Boches who were suspected to be occupying some poplars and a sunken road about 700 yards from our and 100 yards from their trenches. Smaller patrols of my company had found them there two nights in succession. His scheme was to bomb them out of their post at the end of the poplars and drive them up the

road into the arms of another party. Lance-Sergeant Baldwin put four bombs into the Boche post; these were followed by loud shouts and groans. The Boches manned the whole line of poplars and opened fire and threw bombs. About twelve of them charged along the road towards our own trenches. Lance-Corporal Colbrook stood in the middle of the road shouting, "Hands up." The Boche was shouting "Deutscher, Deutscher," evidently taking our people for Boches. Colbrook would have been mopped up, but Corporal Baldwin and Goldswain each put a bomb into the middle of them, knocking out all but three. These swerved round Colbrook and began firing from the hip. One charged on to Goldswain, who fired his rifle from the "on guard" position when the Boche was practically on to his bayonet. A Boche bomb then burst behind Goldswain, throwing him down nearly on top of the dead Boche. Another was also shot and the remaining one fled in another direction. Heavy Boche reinforcements came charging down the road, and nearly bagged Corporal Baldwin and Co., who escaped by the skin of their teeth. The patrol was then reorganised, and Combie made a counter-attack, driving the Boches out of their listening-post again, but the Boche reinforcements occupied the line of poplars and opened fire and threw bombs. We have three men very slightly wounded in the face by bits of bombs, including Alan Crouch and Goldswain. The patrol retired in fine order, halting occasionally and facing about in correct style! Combie reckons he put out from twelve to fifteen Boches in all, killed and wounded. Anyhow, it was a very successful little scrap.

Army tradition and the men's expectation dictated that raids and patrols be led by an officer. Company commanders and above were discouraged (or even forbidden) from taking part owing to the difficulty of replacing seasoned officers. Major R.T.Rees of the Loyal North Lancs. recounted that:

> To go myself was impossible, for there was a very strict order that no officer of the rank of Captain, or over, should take part in patrols in front of the line. Breach of that order meant immediate court-martial. I therefore put a Subaltern and the Sergt.-Major in charge of the party, and explained my plan for surrounding the men, with the caution that there must be no noise or shooting. But I did two very stupid things, first, in allowing a tot of rum to be served out to the party, and second, in allowing the Sergt.-Major to fetch it while I was issuing my instructions.

> What had occurred was this. They had followed my directions and located the men correctly, and had almost surrounded them when, for some incomprehensible reason, the Sergt.-Major shouted, "Fire," and loosed off his revolver. His immediate neighbours followed his example; so that our men on the opposite side of the circle lost their heads and returned the fire, very much as men of Somerset did to the men of Devon over the Doone Valley, while the four Germans, like the Doones,

escaped in the confusion. Luckily there were no casualties, but my reception of the party was, I am afraid, lacking in cordiality.

Following this débâcle, Rees took matters into his own hands:

This failure led me next day to a decision which might have had serious consequences, in view of the order which I have mentioned above.

It seemed to me of great importance that a reliable report should be made as to the condition of the wood, and how far it would be practicable for troops to advance through it in the next attack. This could only be done by day; but we were forbidden to move by day beyond our front line, and I, in addition, was forbidden to patrol. There are times, however, when orders must be liberally interpreted, and I felt that this was one of them.

Accordingly, in the middle of the afternoon, Sergt.-Major Pasquill and I quitted our front line as unostentatiously as possible, and crept along, using all the cover we could, until we had passed our advanced post, to their great astonishment, and then crawled another hundred yards or so towards the German lines. We were now on the crest of the hill, and apparently in full view of the German advanced post. However, as nothing happened, and this spot afforded a good field of observation, we took cover in a convenient shell-hole, and I began to make some notes which I felt pretty sure would be very useful. It was quite clear that the greater part of the wood was fairly open and would not present much obstacle to an advance, and I whispered my opinion to the Sergt.-Major. Receiving no reply, I looked round, and found that I was alone. The Sergt.-Major had disappeared. To look for him then was out of the question; so I went on with my report, and had just finished it when old Pasquill reappeared, his face wreathed in smiles.

"I've been part way down the hill," he whispered, "and seen a dug-out full of them. Shall we go for 'em?"

I hastily disclaimed any desire for glory, and reminding the Sergt.-Major that he was too old and too valuable to be such a fire-eater, I recommended a speedy and careful return to our own lines.

The disadvantage of patrolling in the dark was outweighed by the danger of doing so in the daytime. But one zealous subaltern followed his commanding officer's instructions to the letter:

One of our lads did a gallant thing yesterday afternoon. He was left behind with a patrol to go out after dark to try and find another officer, who got into the German trenches yesterday morning with four men, and after killing four Germans (as a reprisal for raiding his company the night before) was dangerously or mortally wounded outside the enemy wire on his return, and had to be left (by his own order). The C.O. sent orders to the officer who was to search "to go out immediately," meaning to add "after dark," but being in a hurry, he forgot these important words. No one, of course, dreams of going into No Man's Land by day; but this youth never hesitated to ask if there were not some mistake, and leaving his patrol behind in our lines, just went off by himself at 3.30 p.m. He was, of course, seen almost at once and heavy machine-gun fire was opened on him; but this didn't stop him, and he crawled and ran all the 200 yards across the open to the wire and got into some little depression where the M.G. couldn't see him. Had a good look round for the officer he was out to find, failed to see him, so made a good examination of the wire and then came back under fire all the way... I have put him up for a D.S.O., and I trust he will get it. [Frank Maxwell, VC]

By its very nature, a patrol did not know what to expect; however carefully prepared (as in the following anecdote), a foray into Mo-Man's-Land could not always be expected to achieve its objectives:

On February 14 I was told to organise a series of bombing parties, one from each company, to visit the German advanced trench at different times during the night and if possible to bomb German parties working there. I decided to accompany the first party, from A Company, between 8 and 10 P.M. Sergt. Dorgan, an experienced patroller, went with me, also L.-C. [Lance-Corporal] Lowes, Ptes. Austin and Gibson, and two other bombers. As it was very wet, I had a sandbag taken by each man to lie down on. The scheme was to creep right up the new trench near the hedge, and await the arrival of the German working-party. So we crept out along the wet ground and got to the trench, which was about two feet deep. We found no one there, and Pte. Austin went on into the hedge to keep a look-out. In the hedge were found a German sniper's plate, a steel shield with a loop-hole in it, and a German entrenching tool, like a small spade. These were at once annexed. Then we lay down again on the sandbags and waited with eyes and ears straining for about an hour. But no Germans came, though we had one warning from our sentry to get ready to fire. After that, cold and thoroughly soaked, we returned in triumph with the sandbags and our spoils, which we placed in our own trench. [Francis Buckley, 7th Battalion Northumberland Fusiliers]

Siegfried Sassoon wrote in his diary of a patrol where the objective itself was unattainable:

About 8.30 in the evening went out with two bombers, Grainger and Leigh, and O'Brien, to fetch in a supposed German body who was reputed shot the previous night when they came across cutting our wire. It was bright moonshine and very still when we had got out about fifty yards and were up against our wire, we observed four Germans crawling over towards us. Withdrew fifteen yards to a big shell-hole and when they came to our wire we chucked twelve bombs at them and I pursued them, hoping to collar a wounded one. Most unlucky, they all cleared off. Then we got to the boots which had been seen from our trench and found a very old (French) body, at least six months old. Brought in the boots - one of them with half a leg attached (and sent it down to Battalion Headquarters).

Following the German withdrawal to the Hindenburg line in March 1917, it sometimes proved difficult even to find their front line. However, once it was located, daylight patrolling was as dangerous as ever if the party were spotted:

As soon as I arrived at company headquarters I sent for the sergeant-major - a really old hand - a small rugged man with a big moustache and the heart of a lion.

He came in and saluted.

'Sergeant-major,' I said, 'get hold of six good men. We have to take a patrol into the wood, which will take an hour or so. You will send out ahead two scouts, the second man fifty yards behind, you and I fifty yards behind him. The others will be in pairs acting as flank guards about one hundred yards on each side of us.

'Very good, Sir,' he replied.

'We start in half an hour, taking as little as possible; just rifles and a bandolier to each man.'

We started from company headquarters and soon reached the wood, where we found our progress was very slow, owing to the fallen trees.

Quickly losing sight of our line behind us we proceeded slowly and cautiously for about half a mile into the wood, when the advance scout sent back a message reporting that he could see in front of him a system of trenches guarded by barbed wire.

Ordering our men to be ready to support us I went forward with the sergeant-major to investigate.

We found that the trees had been cleared to give a field of fire in front of the wire, and that there was a gap through which we could reach the trench. Without a sound we crawled down the path through the wire, ready for anything. We came to the trench itself.

Looking over the top we found it empty, but a little to our right we saw what was obviously the entrance to a dugout, as it had a blanket covering the door.

'Sir,' whispered the sergeant-major, 'if you will be ready with your revolver I will pull the blanket back with the point of my bayonet; I expect the Bosche are asleep.'

I got ready, thrilled to the marrow.

'Ready, Sir!' he exclaimed, wrenching away the blanket.

There was no one inside.

We found a scrupulously kept small room, six rifles neatly stacked against the wall in a rack, a pile of bombs, tins of water, cases of ammunition, piles of blankets, etc.

We heaved them all out into the bushes. The Germans would be annoyed when they came back that night.

We proceeded to explore the trench system for about two hundred yards on either side. I made a rough sketch giving its position in the wood, and in my report stated that cavalry could not possibly circumvent it.

We then ordered our scouts forward, proceeding onwards in the same formation for about another half mile. Once again the scouts ahead halted and we went forward to see for ourselves what was the matter.

The leading scout crept back on all fours.

'Bosches are just ahead in the village, Sir. Hundreds of them, not more than half a mile in front,' he muttered hoarsely.
'Right,' I whispered. 'You all stay where you are and make sure you are not seen. I am going forward to see for myself.'

I crept forward to the place the man had come from, and a most interesting scene met my eyes.

I could see the village of Havrincourt, quite undamaged by shell fire, about half a mile away, nestling in a hollow below me. On the left was the Canal du Nord, with its bridges destroyed, and on the opposite slope the trenches of the Hindenburg line.

I sat down on a fallen tree to draw a rough map of the ground I could see, putting in the broken bridges, etc. I also wrote a report.

All this time I could see the German soldiers walking about the village on their various jobs or lying on the grass in the sun. The sergeant-major lay besides me smoking his pipe.

Suddenly, to my utter amazement, an observation balloon started to rise under my very nose it seemed; it must have been concealed in a hollow where I could not see it. Slowly it rose to about two hundred feet, becoming stationary almost above us. We could see the two men in it looking down with field glasses.

'Keep quite still, Sir,' whispered the sergeant-major. 'They may not see us.

Just then they did see us. We could see the officer with the glasses pointing down towards us; he reached for his telephone; we could imagine him reporting our presence. What was to be done?

'We must get back at once!' I exclaimed to the sergeant-major. 'Tell the men to go back in the same formation.'

Four guns spoke in the distance. Four shells shrieked over to fall in the wood, a good three hundred yards away.

'They have spotted us,' he shouted.

He shouted to the men to hurry. We ran as best we could, stumbling over the branches. Four more shells burst with a 'crump' over us, but high up; balls of black smoke blew away in the wind. I could imagine the Bosche officer in the balloon shouting guttural directions to the batteries through the telephone.

Four more shells arrived. This time too close for comfort, just over our heads. They had got the range; rapid fire commenced; we had hardly time to drop when we heard the shriek of the shells coming. They were firing with high velocity guns and firing them as quickly as they could load.

A salvo dropped right in the middle of us, bursting right at the height of our heads. Chips whistled through the foliage; clouds of black smoke choked us. I was getting panicky, so were the men; as soon as we moved another salvo arrived. We were all wounded, none of us seriously. My hand was bleeding pretty badly.

Something had to be done, and that quickly, or we should have the Huns from the village after us.

I got up and shouted: 'Every man run fifty yards to the right and then double back towards home, every man for himself.'

The sergeant-major and I ran like hares, dropping behind trees each time we heard the guns fire. They lost the range a bit; we were scattered and not so easy for the people in the balloon to see.

Back through the wood we ran, panting for breath, our clothing torn, faces blackened. We were a dishevelled party when we once again emerged from the wood to find all our troops standing up wondering what all the shooting was about. They thought that a miniature war had started. [Capt. Geoffrey Dugdale]

For reasons of safety, sentries were informed of any party operating in No-Man's-Land in front of them and most importantly the time and place at which it was intended to leave and return to the British trenches.

> We had a curious little bombing-post outside the front line at H.4, which was only held at night. It was inside our wire, but you could only reach it by clambering over the top of the parapet after dark. The post was connected by a string to a sentry-post in the front line. And various signals were arranged to warn the sentry in the front line as to what was going on, for example, two jerks on the string: 'Man returning to trench' three jerks: 'Enemy patrol on right,' and so on. [Francis Buckley]

If these plans were not followed exactly, alarm and confusion could result:

> A man came rushing to me with the news that the enemy were in the line farther along the trench. I had within reach at the time only a subaltern, the Sergt.-Major and two servants. When I informed old Pasquill of the crisis he remarked, 'Well, Sir, we'll — soon 'ave 'em out again.' So I headed a procession along the fire-trench, followed by the subaltern, who, I afterwards discovered, was holding his revolver full cock against the back of my head. He was followed by the Sergt.-Major holding in his hand a Mills bomb with the pin already out, so that the least slip would have sent us to glory. To crown all, we found that the 'enemy' were a patrol or our own, who were seen coming in at the wrong place. [Major R. T. Rees]

Raids, as larger affairs, required more complex planning:

> We have raids almost nightly - 50 men and a couple of officers. Artillery preparation for about an hour on a fairly wide front so as to keep the Germans in the dark as to where the actual entry is going to be made into the trenches, then they ring off for 5 minutes; the raiders rush across, and the Artillery lengthens the range a bit and forms a barrage behind the sector which is being raided. The raiders are generally over for about half an hour, and at a given signal are supposed to leap out of the trench and return with as much plunder, human and otherwise, as they can get. That is the programme, which of course is subject to alterations according to the preparedness of the German. If the latter has been properly ragged by the bombardment they generally get back intact. [Capt. H.Dundas, 1st Scots Guards]

Frank Maxwell, in a letter to his wife, stressed the problems which could be encountered and the possible results:

> To-day I have been hard at it till 4 p.m. without stirring from my dug-out, working out a raid I have to make to-night. Very short notice,

and over absolutely strange ground for my people. Still, I am glad to
have the opportunity, and if it only works out successfully it will do
them a power of good and buck them up. Yet one day scarcely gives me
a chance of working out a good show for them, and I am wondering
whether what I have evolved will be productive of anything. With a
little luck it may. I have gone in for a strong raid, and am sending over
four officers and about 100 men with orders to *mob* the Germans - jump
in on top of them and scupper all they can. The difficulty is the getting
to them, for the distance is, for trench warfare, considerable, and has to
be done by compass bearings, and the way may be easily lost. Then, if
they got there, there may be no G.'s [sic] to kill or bring back. In these
shows one has the run of a large group of guns, and you just tell them
to fire here for so many minutes, 'lift' to there for so many more, etc.,
and it is done, or tried to be done. Much too often, however, something
goes wrong, and guns or infantry get tangled up in their plans, with the
result that our infantry run into the fire of our guns, and have to come
back for fear of being killed. I begged to be allowed to have my little
jaunt without guns, so as to surprise Bosch, unwarned by artillery fire
that something with a bayonet or bomb might follow, but was
disallowed for certain good reasons.

Although battalion HQ usually conceived the plan for a raid, the
participants made their own preparations too. Since fighting was likely
to be at close quarters, and manoeuverability of the essence, rifles were
viewed as being too cumbersome at just under four feet long, and the
raiders equipped themselves with revolvers and bombs and especially
made knuckledusters, knives and a variety of vicious-looking clubs.
Again, Siegfried Sassoon entered in his diary a particularly full
description of an unsuccessful raid on the Somme. Sassoon won the
Military Cross for this night's work:

May 25th 1916

Twenty-seven men with faces blackened and shiny - Christy-minstrels -
with hatchets in their belts, bombs in pockets, knobkerries - waiting in a
dug-out in the reserve line. At 10.30 they trudge up to Battalion H.Q.
splashing through mire and water in the chalk trench, while the rain
comes steadily down. The party is twenty-two men, five N.C.O.s and
one officer (Stansfield). From H.Q. we start off again, led by
Compton-Smith: across the open to the end of 77 street. A red flashlight
winks a few times to guide us thither. Then up to the front line - the
men's feet making a most unholy tramp and din; squeeze along to the
starting-point, where Stansfield and his two confederates (Sergeant Lyle
and Corporal O'Brien) loom over the parapet from above, having
successfully laid the line of lime across the craters to the Bosche wire. In
a few minutes the five parties have gone over - and disappear into the
rain and darkness - the last four men carry ten-foot light ladders. It is 12

midnight. I am sitting on the parapet listening for something to happen - five, ten, nearly fifteen minutes - not a sound - nor a shot fired - and only the usual flare-lights, none very near our party. Then a few whizz-bangs fizz over to our front trench and just behind the raiders. After twenty minutes there is still absolute silence in the Bosche trench; the raid is obviously held up by their wire, which we thought was so easy to get through. One of the bayonet-men comes crawling back; I follow him to our trench and he tells me that they can't get through: O'Brien says it's a failure; they're all going to throw a bomb and retire.

A minute or two later a rifle-shot rings out and almost simultaneously several bombs are thrown by both sides: a bomb explodes right in the water at the bottom of left crater close to our men, and showers a pale spume of water; there are blinding flashes and explosions, rifle-shots, the scurry of feet, curses and groans, and stumbling figures loom up from below and scramble awkwardly over the parapet - some wounded - black faces and whites of eyes and lips show in the dusk; when I've counted sixteen in, I go forward to see how things are going, and find Stansfield wounded, and leave him there with two men who soon get him in: other wounded men crawl in; I find one hit in the leg; he says O'Brien is somewhere down the crater badly wounded. They are still throwing bombs and firing at us: the sinister sound of clicking bolts seems to be very near; perhaps they have crawled out of their trench and are firing from behind their advanced wire. Bullets hit the water in the craters, and little showers of earth patter down on the crater. Five or six of them are firing into the crater at a few yards' range. The bloody sods are firing down at me at point-blank range. (I really wondered whether my number was up). From our trenches and in front of them I can hear the mumble of voices - most of them must be in by now. After minutes like hours, with great difficulty I get round the bottom of the crater and back toward our trench; at last I find O'Brien down a very deep (about twenty-five feet) and precipitous crater on my left (our right as they went out). He is moaning and his right arm is either broken or almost shot off: he's also hit in the right leg (body and head also, but I couldn't see that then). Another man (72 Thomas) is with him; he is hit in the right arm. I leave them there and get back to our trench for help, shortly afterwards Lance-Corporal Stubbs is brought in (he has had his foot blown off). Two or three other wounded men are being helped down the trench; no one seems to know what to do; those that are there are very excited and uncertain: no sign of any officers - then Compton-Smith comes along (a mine went up on the left as we were coming up at about 11.30 and thirty (R.E.s) men were gassed or buried). I get a rope and two more men and we go back to O'Brien, who is unconscious now. With great difficulty we get him half-way up the face of the crater; it is now after one o'clock and the sky beginning to get lighter. I make one more journey to our trench for another strong man and to see to a stretcher being ready. We get him in, and it is found that he has died, as I had feared. Corporal Mick O'Brien (who often went patrolling with me) was a very fine man and had been with the Battalion since November 1914. He was at Neuve Chapelle, Festubert and Loos.

I go back to a support-line dug-out and find the unwounded men of the raiding-party refreshing themselves: everyone is accounted for now; eleven wounded (one died of wounds) and one killed, out of twenty-eight. I see Stansfield, who is going on all right, but has several bomb-wounds. On the way down I see the Colonel, sitting on his bed in a woollen cap with a tuft on top, and very much upset at the non-success of the show, and the mine disaster; but very pleased with the way our men tried to get through the wire.

In addition to the artillery support mentioned by Frank Maxwell (above), other weapons were detailed to support the raiding party. Machine-gunners made their own preparations:

T— and I, as 'gun numbers,' were deputed to stand by to open fire with our machine-gun to cover the raiding party. It was rather 'jumpy' work waiting for the show to start. Surely enough at 3 o'clock, 'bang, bang, bang,' came from the German front trench, showing that our men were in it and bombing along it with their hand grenades. T— and I opened fire at once, and did not cease, except to reload, until we had fired over two thousand rounds. We had, as usual on these occasions, fixed a screen of wet sandbags in front of the gun to conceal the flashes as much as possible, but the Boches were soon searching for us with their shells. A loud whizzing noise, growing into a piercing scream, a deafening crash, and we were thrown together into the bottom of the gun emplacement and smothered in mud. A big shell had landed just behind us, but beyond a shaking we were unhurt, and at once sprang up and resumed our firing. The water in the barrel casing of the machine-gun was now boiling, and was roaring through the rubber escape tube into a bucket of water to be condensed. The sound of bursting grenades and rifle fire came to us in the intervals, so the raid was still in progress. We reloaded, fired another belt through (250 rounds), and then paused. Now all is quiet in front; the raid is evidently over. [H.Raymond Smith]

And so did trench-mortar officers:

I discovered on my return that we were shortly to do our first big show. The Irish Rifles were to raid the German lines, and the Trench Mortars were to cut the wire for them, or rather, to blow it away. This was to be done by firing the big bombs which I have already described, and using percussion fuses, so that the bomb would burst directly on impact and clear several yards of wire.

A great deal of preparation was necessary. Emplacements had to be prepared for twelve guns, with protection against enemy fire, great stacks of ammunition had to be provided and carried up, and of course the greatest care was necessary in timing the whole affair. We had also to register with care, in order to get something like the correct range without giving the whole show away beforehand. Unfortunately the enemy retaliated by shelling the Headquarters of the Infantry Brigadier concerned, and destroyed his favourite sofa. There was trouble about that, but it passed over.

At last everything was ready, the day arrived, and we found ourselves waiting in our appointed places for the bombardment to begin.

For most of us this was the first experience of real battle, though of course we had all been under shell fire many times before; and it is idle to deny that the period of waiting just before a biggish show is due to begin is trying to the nerves. I have done it many times since, but the first time was the worst. You look at your watch and see that there is still a quarter of an hour to go. Has anything been left undone? The O.C. Batteries all have their orders, and it is too late to bother about them now. Runners? Yes. They are with you. Signallers? Yes. Stretcher-bearers? Yes, assisted by the Padre. Still ten minutes. Those stretcher-bearers will have their work cut out if we draw a heavy fire, as we probably shall. Tell the Padre to be sure not to go outside the flimsy shelter looking for trouble. Still five minutes. Telephone rings; the Division want to know if all is ready. Yes. All ready and waiting. I step outside the trench. All peaceful and quiet, and the sun sinking in the West. Back to the shelter. Padre smoking his pipe and reading the 'Daily Mail.' Poop! Surely that is half a minute too soon. No. Poop! Poop! Poop! from all around, and Crash! Crash! Crash! as the bombs burst - in the enemy wire, we hope. Our bombardment has begun.

During that bombardment we fired seven hundred and fifty bombs, and cut most of the wire, we hope. But long before it was over the enemy had realised that there was something important afoot, and had concentrated on us all his available artillery, and even old 'granny', the twelve or fifteen-inch howitzer from near Lille. It is an extraordinary experience to hear one of those enormous shells approaching. The sound resembles nothing so much as the roar of an express train rushing through a station, followed by a crash which makes you think the end of the world has come. Some of our guns were knocked out, and wounded were being brought in. The Padre, entirely disregarding my instructions, was here, there, and everywhere, carrying stretchers, binding up wounds and administering consolation. Through all this hubbub there were incessant messages from the Artillery and Divisional Headquarters to know how things were going.

At last came zero-hour, the time for the infantry to go over, and our part was done, though the enemy, of course, continued shelling as hard as ever. Within twenty minutes the Irishmen were back in our lines with a few prisoners and a good many 'souvenirs.' Then gradually the firing

died away and at length peace reigned again over those torn and
shattered acres. [Major R.T.Rees]

Despite careful organisation things could still go badly wrong:

A night or so later, our raiding party crept out from the right company's
line and lay waiting for the 60lb T.M.'s to finish the breaking of the wire.
A wind had risen during the afternoon and was now blowing across the
front. The twenty-four men lay in the rank grass with Batty, Gwinnell
and Perkins in front, waiting for the toffee-apples to lift and waver into
the wire in front. The trench mortar fired; but the registration had been
carried out when there was no wind. The breeze caught the bomb,
carrying it down the line. It exploded a few yards from the attacking
group.

'I say, guv'nor,' said Private Billett to Gwinnell: 'I'm 'it in the bleedin'
arm.'
'Shut up,' growled Gwinnell. 'So am I.'
'Are yer, guv'nor!' returned Billett. 'I'm sorry to 'ear about that.'

Gwinnell staggered up, with three wounds in the leg, Perkins hit in both
arms; but Batty lay still. A splinter had gone straight through his brain.
Eight other men were hit, and there was no more to be done with the
raid. Gwinnell, bleeding from his wounds, shepherded the men back
and brought in Batty's body. And save for the burial of the quiet clay in
the valley behind Point 147, that was the end. [Guy Chapman]

The vital tasks of raiding and patrolling provided a diversion from the
other routines of trench life, and for many soldiers they were the only
direct contact with an otherwise unseen enemy. But they were
constantly reminded of the latter's presence through shell- and gunfire.

6
Under Fire

Five of us had spent the night patrolling and were returning to Brigade H.Q. when the enemy sighted us and put a barrage along the duckboard track we were following. Early dawn broke in the east, and a grey light filtered eerily through dim cloud-masses to a desolate world of brown, touching the skeleton woods strangely, and blackening the edge of ridge where the German trenches lay. First one shell dropped ten yards behind us, then one came screaming so close that we dropped in our tracks and waited for the end. I got right under the duckboard track, and the hail of shrapnel and mud on it was thunderous enough to frighten the most courageous. Then we stood up, all safe though muddy, and with a "Run like hell, boys", went off in a devil's race, with shells bursting at our heels, for half a mile, dropping at last in complete exhaustion in a trench out of range...

When we left the Menin Road and took to the duckboards at a time when the enemy places a barrage on them, the most careless of us cursed the man in front of him if he happened to pause a minute. It seemed the best solace for excited nerves to keep going, no matter whether into or out of danger. Yet, luck stood by us; in spite of our over-zealous artillery, not a shell dropped near us until we reached our trenches, and then we had it stiff. A sergeant and two privates were blown to pieces twenty yards from me: all that night and early morning we lay in the shallow trench, trying vainly to keep knees from shaking and teeth from chattering, with a deadly sick feeling in the stomach as bits of shrapnel hit the side of the trench with a dull thud and earth was shaken over our face... All we could do was to lie motionless on our back and pray that the enemy had not seen us. I tried to sleep, but nervous excitement kept me awake all day until night, when we dug out a new trench... Yet my first experience of death was worse than this. Our battalion had entrained almost as far as Ypres, and we rested beside the railway for some time, with the engine standing stationary, sending a high pillar of smoke into the air. I expect the German observation balloons had seen it, for the enemy began to place shells on each side of the railway at regular intervals for about two hundred yards. Of course, we side-slipped until it stopped. Then we began to cross the railway: our two companies had just got over when I heard a scream of a shell. Instantly we got on our noses: I looked up cautiously, just in time to see it explode in a thick mass of the other companies on the railway. The scream of despair and agony was dreadful to hear, men shell-shocked out of reason and others dying of frightful wounds. That shell caused sixty casualties and shook the whole battalion for several days. Even when going through the market square of Ypres, beneath the yellow flash of great howitzers and the roar of naval guns, we thought shells were bursting among us and looked fearfully at every corner, nerve-shaken and absolutely afraid. The sudden roar of a gun made us start guiltily, half-ashamed, and yet unable to control our agitation. That cry of dying men will ring in my ears a long time after everything else will be forgotten.' [Lt. Hugh Quigley, 12th Royal Scots, Passchendaele, 1917]

Shellfire seems to have been far more feared than either rifle or machine-gun fire. Bullet wounds were viewed as being 'cleaner' and more survivable, whereas the wounds inflicted by shell splinters and shrapnel were far more mutilating.

The fear of imminent death or wounding was exacerbated by the knowledge that the shells were aimed in one's general direction, their approach could be heard and that there was nothing one could do to control one's destiny. By contrast, by the time a bullet was heard, it had already gone past, and in general, there was a perception that one could, by one's posture, have some control over the effects. For instance, troops moving in No-Man's-Land knew not to lie down if a machine-gun opened fire, since they were trained at 'grass-cutting' level and so to lie down risked a head or body wound, whereas a standing man presented a smaller target and if hit, a greater likelihood of receiving a non-fatal wound.

The notorious Ypres Salient, heavy with British batteries and surrounded by German artillery, was a particularly 'hot' sector to be in:

Our second two days were much more lively. A lot of shelling went on, and it came from such unexpected quarters that one never felt certain whether the shells were from our own or Hun guns. British shells were crossing our lines diagonally and falling on the Hun trenches in front. One or two Hun batteries in front were shelling our rear. Some 17-inch things were passing over bound for Ypres itself. Another battery was putting big crumps right across us to a small hill, three hundred yards on our left. Another on our right was pelting us with whizz-bangs, and another still farther to the right was sending small crumps right down the length of our trench, knocking branches off the trees above us and falling at first fifty yards beyond the right-angle, but later much nearer. These last came with a peculiar scream of their own, and always in salvoes of three. Every time we heard the scream we had to make a rush for the end of the traverse, which was the only shelter available.

As time went on the Huns improved their range, and the big stuff fell all around us, covering us with litter. Coming as they did, right down the trench, from one side, they were rather nerve-racking things. I don't know whether it was a result of the general state of my nerves, but I had the wind-up more properly that I ever remember before. [H.S. Clapham]

The evident fear engendered by shelling is quite understandable given its devastating effect:

It was here that a subaltern was annihilated by direct hit from a whizz-bang. A booted foot and some bloody earth were all that were recovered to be placed in a sandbag and decently interred. The adjutant inherited the ambiguous task of explaining to his relatives exactly why it was not possible to send home his personal effects. [Guy Chapman]

The following passage shows a marked lack of appreciation of the thoughts uppermost in the mind of the average mortal when under shellfire:

A few Sundays ago I was taking a Service in an 'Upper Room' at Philosophe when the Boches began to drop heavy stuff round about us. The whole of my sermon was punctuated by the well-known Whirrrr-r-r-R-R CER-R-RUMPH, and the only annoyance of which I was conscious was that some of the soldiers - there were about 160 - kept glancing uneasily out of the windows while the shell was still "whirring" until the ultimate "CRUMPH" announced that it had found some other billet - much the same annoyance as when someone faints in Church, and half the congregation turn their heads to watch them being carried out, and you feel inclined to make petulant remarks.

After the sermon we were singing "The King of Love my Shepherd is," and no doubt some of us were thinking of the appropriateness of the fourth verse, when a young Gunner Officer hurried in with profuse apologies and a polite but firm message from his Superior that this service must stop at once," and "the men disperse!"

As the service was to have been a celebration of the Holy Eucharist - in fact, as I said, we had already got as far as the sermon - I obtained his consent to invite any small body of men to stay who wished to do so dismissing the remainder with The Blessing.

Not a man of the 160 stayed, so I reluctantly gathered up the sacred
vessels (I had another celebration that morning elsewhere), and followed
them. [Anonymous padre, 'E.A.F.', *Vermelles*, late 1915]

Charles Edmonds was far less sanguine when being shelled:

I never could stand shell-fire. I got into a thoroughly neurotic state
during the day. Enduring a bombardment is the opportunity for that
kind of nervous disease which made Dr. Johnson touch every post as he
walked along Fleet Street. You think of absurd omens and fetishes to
ward off the shell you hear coming. A strong inward feeling compels
you to sit in a certain position, to touch a particular object, to whistle so
many bars of a tune silently between your teeth. If you complete the
charm in time you are safe - until the next one. This absurdity becomes a
dark, overpowering fatalism. You contemplate with horror that you
have made a slip in the self-imposed ritual, or that the augury sign of
your own invention shows against you. You imagine that the shells are
more deliberate and accurate than could be possible. They seem to have
a volition of their own and to wander malevolently until they see a
target on which to pounce; the fierce roar of their near approach; they
defy your mute relief when they fall far away, by sending slivers of
jagged steel sighing and murmuring hundreds of yards towards you,
long after the shock of the explosion is spent and gone.

Every gun and every kind of projectile had its own personality. Old
soldiers always claimed that they knew the calibre of a shell by its
sound and could always foretell which shells were going to fall
dangerously close. Yet far more than they calculated depended on the
range and the nature of the intervening ground. Sometimes a field gun
shell would leap jubilantly with the pop of a champagne cork from its
muzzle, fly over with a steady buzzing crescendo, and burst with a fully
expected bang; sometimes a shell would be released from a distant
battery of heavies to roll across a huge arc of sky, gathering speed and
noise like an approaching express train, ponderous and certain. Shells
flying over valleys and woods echoed strangely and defied anticipation;
shells falling in enclosed spaces simply arrived with a double bang and
no warning at all. Some shells whistled, others shrieked, others wobbled
through space gurgling like water poured from a decanter.

So all the day you listened, calculated, hoped or despaired, making
imaginary bargains with fate, laying odds with yourself on the chances
of these various horrors. One particular gun would seem to be firing
more directly on you than the others. You would wait for its turn so
intently as to forget other perhaps more real dangers. At last it comes.
You hold frenziedly on to the conversation; you talk a little too fast;
your nerves grow tense, and while you continue to look and talk like a
man, your involuntary muscles get a little out of hand. Are your knees
quivering a little? Are you blinking? Is your face contorted with fear?

You wonder and cannot know. Force yourself to do something, say something, think something, or you will lose control. Get yourself in hand with some voluntary action. Drum out a tune with your finger-tips upon your knee. Don't hurry - keep time - get it finished, and you will be safe this once. Here superstition and neurasthenia step in. Like the child who will not walk on the lines in the pavement and finds real safety in putting each foot on a square stone you feel that your ritual protects you. As the roar of an approaching shell rises nearer and louder you listen in inward frenzy to the shell, in outward calm to the conversation. Steady with those nervous drum-taps on your knee; don't break time or the charm is broken and the augury vain. The shell roars near. What is Thorburn saying?

"Oh yes!" the rations came up at nine o'clock, enough for twice our numbers." (Explosion!)

After a while, experienced soldiers learned intuitively to determine whether shells were falling near enough to harm them:

It was about this time that I suddenly realised that I had become acclimatised to shell fire; not that I liked or had ceased to fear it, but that I was able to discriminate between a shell that was coming near and one that was far enough away not to worry about. Some officers recently arrived from England were responsible. They were in charge of one of the working parties, and while we were standing in a group, not far from Plug Street, we heard the whine of a German shell. I looked instinctively in the direction of the church to see the usual cloud of dust and stones, and at the same time I realised that the officers with me had ducked. I was certainly no braver than they were - quite the contrary; but my ear had somehow become attuned, so that as soon as the first sound was heard I knew approximately where the shell would burst. The possession of this 'shell sense' must have been a great relief to one's nervous system and it is possible that some of the worst cases of nervous breakdown occurred in men who never acquired this valuable instinct. [Stephen Foot, RE]

Foot developed an apparent sang froid through familiarity; the author Dennis Wheatley did so as a result of affecting a monocle, bought just before he went to France:

When I eventually arrived on the Western Front I found that this useless triviality, adopted only out of vanity, had there a really valuable function. If a shell explodes near one or there is a sudden burst of machine-gun fire, the natural instinct is to fall flat, or at least jerk one's head down. But if you do so when wearing a monocle it falls out; and having to pick it up makes you look an awful fool. Therefore, rather than lose face in front of my men, when coming unexpectedly under fire

82

I always remained erect, thereby earning a reputation for bravery which I certainly did not deserve.

Some unfortunates, however, simply lacked the mental wherewithal to realise what was going on, as was the case with one of Lt. Arthur Behrend's (90th Bde. RGA) gunners:

> Gunner Freshwater, the hardest of hard workers and a first-rate handyman, had one peculiarity. Unless desire for some essential such as leave or food or a new pair of boots compelled him to open his mouth and speak, he had not been known to say a single word to anyone during the year he had been with us. The Colonel, who was bad at remembering names, had once hailed him with, "Come here, carpenter!" Gunner Freshwater had taken no notice. The Colonel went close to him and said, "Didn't you hear me calling you?" Freshwater looked at him in his queer way and then said slowly, adding "sir" as an afterthought, "Yes, I heard you. But I'm not a carpenter. My name is Gunner Freshwater." He had one further eccentricity. When given a job to do, he would work like a horse till it was time for breakfast or dinner or tea or bed. But once one of those times arrived he would stop work suddenly, even if half way up a ladder with a sandbag on his back. Consequently Gunner Freshwater carried on when the shell fell.
>
> "Get under cover!" roared the Sergeant-major, the only person from whom Freshwater was prepared to take orders.
>
> Freshwater paused with his barrow in the middle of the road, and looked to see who was shouting. As he looked a second shell tore over our heads and burst with a rattling report at Freshwater's very feet. When the smoke and the dust had cleared away, we could see him lying dead on the road with his overturned barrow beside him.

Given the sheer volume of shelling on the Western Front, to survive in the front line for any length of time required more than just experience:

> Our luck held good all the time we were in the orchard. Once, just after a gun had been pulled forward to permit improvements to its platform, a 5.9 landed plumb on the empty platform. Another time three gunners had a fairy-tale escape. Our dug-outs are merely little scratchings in a bank under a hedge, and on this afternoon I heard a dud land in the bank. On investigation I found it had gone through ten feet of earth (in the bank) into a dug-out where three men were lying; it passed over one man's back, slightly bruising his ribs, and came to rest with the fuse touching the clay of the far wall. Three scared men crawled out of their hole very speedily, and I looked and saw lying there a silvery 5.9-inch shell, polished by its passage through the earth. [Lt. Col. N.Fraser-Tytler]

Stephen Foot recalled two inordinately lucky escapes:

On one occasion the Colonel and I were walking together when a shell came so close to us that he actually felt the heat of it as it passed. We fell to the ground and the shell burst so near that we were on the edge of its crater, but though covered with mud we were unhurt. In those days, provided the ground was soft, shells penetrated deeply before they burst, with the result that they were comparatively innocuous. Later on, both sides invented a special quick-acting fuse designed so that the shell burst the moment it touched the ground. The resulting crater was insignificant and all the pieces of shell spread out above ground with much more deadly effect.

"Duds" were quite common. On one occasion I was sitting in the downstairs room of a small house that was being used as the Headquarters of a Field Battery. My job was to discuss with the O.C. of the Battery the construction of an Observation Post. I was seated at a table near the window, he was standing alongside; at the back of the room were two or three junior officers; a gramophone was playing. Suddenly with a resounding crash a German shell came through the wall behind me, struck the table on which my arm was resting and passed through the plan of the Observation Post which we were examining. I wonder if anyone who has never had a similar experience could guess what was the immediate result of this happening. Certainly it was a complete surprise to me. The moment before the shell arrived we were in broad daylight; a moment afterwards we were in pitch darkness. We groped our way from the room and to our amazement found that I was the only person hurt; and my injuries were merely a few scratches on the face and hands caused by bits of brick. The reason for our escape was clear. Lying just outside the house, with its nose sticking into the ground, was the German shell - a dud; it had passed right through the house without exploding. The darkness was caused by the fact that the room was filled with brick-dust.

It is not for nothing that the Great War has been referred to as 'the war of the guns.'

7
Fear & Shellshock

In the Great War for the first time, men were subjected to lengthy periods of continual danger. For it was essentially a four year siege, other than in its opening and closing phases. Combined with the debilitating effects of trench life, this constant danger induced high levels of stress in the frontline troops. In its most extreme form, this stress led to 'shellshock.'

This phenomenon was hitherto unidentified; as such, it was not readily accepted as a medical condition by much of the army hierarchy and medical establishment. Psychiatry was in its infancy and there was then a tendency to view mental disorder as a reflection of moral weakness. In army circles this reinforced the view that shellshock was bad for morale and its spread should be discouraged. This hesitancy to accept shellshock meant that whenever possible it was played down. Nevertheless, it was gradually recognized and debate about its nature and treatment arose. It came to be viewed as an anxiety neurosis, rather than an extreme manifestation of simple fear, which is after all an obvious concomitant of battle. Shellshock was unpredictable in onset - shells were by no means the only trigger - and the symptoms were various. Fortunately, while fear was almost universal, the incidence of shellshock was relatively low. Fear of danger was compounded by 'fear of fear.' Ordinary soldiers were often terrified of breaking down in front of their comrades, and officers in front of their men. In his memoirs, Stephen Foot, an engineer officer, analysed his feelings:

> Looking back now, I find it difficult to recapture the motive which made me desirous of getting a wound stripe. Later on, towards the end of the Passchendaele Battle, I definitely wanted to be wounded in order to get out of it all; but that was the result of a protracted stay in the Ypres Salient. In 1915, although I was often intensely frightened, yet I think I should have refused to clear out to a place of complete safety even if I had been given the chance.

> I had an uncomfortable feeling that in order to do one's duty it was necessary to get killed, or to risk getting killed all the time; and to be wounded showed that one had at any rate taken a step in the right direction. There was certainly nothing heroic about this feeling; on the contrary, the truth was that whenever I was in serious danger I was

almost completely paralysed by fear. Only too well I remember sitting with Coffin on the fire-step of a trench during an intense bombardment, when it seemed certain that we must be killed. Shells fell all round us; in the bays of the trench on each side; in the parapet above our heads, spattering us with mud; each moment threatened to be our last, and my fright was such that I was conscious of biting on the stem of my pipe to prevent my teeth from chattering. If I had been alone on that occasion I believe that I should have been cowering at the bottom of the trench in hopeless terror; it was the presence of others that saved me. Just as in boyhood I had acted a part, trying to appear natural when walking across a room, so now I was acting again, counterfeiting bravery. In the presence of danger my cue was "nonchalance," but such an attitude was the exact opposite to my real feelings.

On another occasion I was making a report on the state of the wire entanglements in front of our trenches. Snipers were active in that part of the German line, and as it would have been almost certain death to put one's head above the parapet, I was using a periscope. Unfortunately, at one point there was a single sandbag lying on top of the parapet, and, when I leant the periscope against it, confidently thinking that my head was protected by at least three feet thickness of earth, a sniper's bullet came through the single sandbag and missed my head by about two inches. If nobody else had been there I feel sure that I should have collapsed at the bottom of the trench, overcome with fear; but another officer was with me. Instinctively I acted my part: "That is what one might almost call an 'inner,'" I remarked, as I wiped the mud from my face.

Charles Edmonds found that keeping himself occupied helped him cope with fear. He described a German counter-attack on the Somme and his attempts to keep cool:

"Stand to," there was a shout; "they're coming!"

My servant and another man who had been hanging about beyond the sentry-post came flying round the traverse.

"Allemans," they said; "they're coming!"

This was a very different matter from running about in noise and darkness. I suddenly thought of Prussian Guardsmen, burly and brutal, and bursting bombs, and hand-to-hand struggles with cold steel. My first impulse was to tell Bickersteth. It was his responsibility now.

'Thud!' went a loud noise along the trench, and the air shook and whined with flying fragments.

I felt myself turning pale.

I found I was walking slowly away from the danger-point. "I must go and tell Bickersteth," I excused myself. I passed the word down the dugout. Then I pulled myself together and got up to the front somehow. The men too were very panicky. Poor devils, they hadn't had a good sleep or a square meal for three days.

'Thud' went a bomb three bays up the trench. I licked my lips and felt for my revolver.

'Thud' went a bomb two bays away.

I was standing at our extreme right flank where we had posted a sentry two bays beyond the half-finished bomb-stop.

"Come along, let's get back to the bomb-stop," said I not very bravely. Just then round the traverse from the dugout came Serjeant Adams, an old volunteer of many years' service in England. He was smoking a pipe and had a thin smile on his face.

"What's that, sir," he said pleasantly, "go back? No, sir, let's go forward," and he tucked his rifle under his arm and strolled along the trench alone - still smiling. A bomb burst in the bay beyond him. He climbed the traverse and took a snapshot with his rifle at some person beyond. A group of men stood wavering, and then I went and took my place beside him on the traverse.

Thirty or forty yards away I saw a hand and a grey sleeve come up out of the trench and throw a cylinder on the end of a wooden rod. It turned over and over in the air and seemed to take hours to approach. It fell just at the foot of the traverse where we stood, and burst with a shattering shock.

"The next one will get us," I thought.

Serjeant Adams pulled a bomb out of his pocket and threw it. I did the same, and immediately felt better. A young Lance-Corporal, Houghton, did the same. The next German bomb fell short. Then someone threw without remembering to pull the pin, and in a moment the bomb was caught up and thrown back at us by the enemy.

I snapped off my revolver once or twice at glimpses of the enemy. A little of last night's feeling was returning. Adams and Houghton were moving forward now, and I was watching them over the traverse, when I had the impression that someone was throwing stones. Suddenly I saw lying in the middle of the trench a small black object, about the shape and size of a large duck's egg. There was a red band round it and a tube fixed in one end of it. What could this be?

I guessed it must be some new sort of bomb.

It was lying less than a yard from my foot; I was right in a corner of the trench. What was I to do? In an instant of time I thought: Had I the nerve to pick it up and throw it away? Should I step over it and run? or stay where I was? There was no room to lie down. But too late. The bomb burst with a roar at my feet. My eyes and nose were full of dust and pungent fumes. Not knowing if I was wounded or not, I found myself stumbling down the trench with a group of groaning men. One of them was swearing and shouting in a high-pitched voice and bleeding in the leg. All the nerve was blasted out of us.

I fetched up almost in tears, shaken out of my senses, at Bickersteth's feet. My clothes were a little torn and my hand was bleeding, but that was all.

Bickersteth was very cool. He was watching the fight through a periscope and organising relays of bomb carriers.

"You must get these men together, Edmonds," he was saying, "and make a counter-attack."

"I'm damned if I will," said I; "I'm done for," and I lay and panted.

He looked at me and saw I was useless. I hadn't an ounce of grit left in me.

It was Wells who rallied the survivors and went up again to find my revolver, "shamefully cast away in the presence of the enemy," and Serjeant Adams still holding his own.

"Come along, Edmonds," said Bickersteth, and in a minute or two I felt better and went up. We got the Lewis-gun out and the whole party moved forward. Houghton was throwing well. We rushed a bay, and Houghton, who was leading, found himself face to face with a German unter-offizier, the length of the next bay between them. He threw a lucky bomb which burst right in the German's face. Their leader fallen, the heart went out of the enemy's attack. At the same moment there were two diversions. An 8-inch shell, one of those which had been falling occasionally on our right, suddenly landed right in the bay behind the German bomber, and his supporters fled. So ended their attack. But as we moved forward a sniper fired almost from behind us. I felt the bullet crack in my ear, and Corporal Matthews, who was walking beside me, preoccupied and intent, fell dead in the twinkling of an eye. I was looking straight at him as the bullet struck him and was profoundly affected by the remembrance of his face, though at the time I hardly thought of it. He was alive, and then he was dead, and there was nothing human left in him. He fell with a neat round hole in his forehead and the back of his head blown out.

Private A.S. Dolden took a dim view of one frightened officer he encountered:

> At dark we went out again to the advance post in 'No Man's Land'. There was a pioneer battalion (The Cheshires) digging in the trench, so we had to go nearer to the German lines to act as a covering party while the digging was in progress. The next night we had just been relieved from the bombing post about midnight, when a Captain of the REs. wanted us to guide him to the advance post. We did this, and it then transpired that he wanted us to act as a covering party to his men while they were working out there. There was no need for a covering party, but the real trouble was that the Officer had 'the wind up' badly. He fairly gave us the 'pip', for as we walked on in front he and his party would crouch down every time a German star shell went up. In an endeavour, therefore, to create confidence in his party, we strutted about 'No Man's Land' as if we did not know what fear was.

One soldier recorded his feelings before and after going into action:

> Yesterday we were told we were 'for it' on the 16th, and ever since then great preparations have been taking place. We have arranged to leave all our spare food and effects with a pal in the transport. Our section commander has been attached to the Salvage Corps, so he does not got up with us. He had appointed a substitute, and made a list of men who are to take charge of the section in turn, if things go wrong with those above them. I come some way down, so I am not likely to have much responsibility.
>
> Everyone is suffering more or less from "wind up". It will be our first real show, and I suppose a certain amount of "wind" is natural. I certainly feel it myself, although I try not to show it. Anyway, we shall see what we shall see...
>
> [later] We have lost half the battalion and nearly all our officers, including the Colonel and the Second-in-Command. Those of us who are left look worn and old, and our nerves are in tatters. We wake up with a start, and if a shell bursts a mile away we jump out of our skins. I am inclined to curse anything and anybody. I suppose that is nerves, too. [H.S. Clapham, HAC]

An outward appearance of calm and authority could sometimes be used to help a man to contain his fears, as the following two extracts show. In the first, Charles Edmonds simply refused to countenance the 'nerves' of one of his men:

> An N.C.O. came up and said that Private Eliot wished to speak to me. The man was a mere boy, whom I had known in England, and I felt flattered that he should apply to me rather than Bickersteth for whatever

help I could give. I found him crouched against a chalk-heap almost in tears. He looked younger than ever.

"I don't want to go over the plonk," he flung at me in the shamelessness of terror, "I'm only seventeen, I want to go home."

The other men standing round avoided my eye and looked rather sympathetic than disgusted.

"Can't help that now, my lad," said I in my martinet voice, "you should have thought of that when you enlisted. Didn't you give your age as nineteen then?"

"Yes, sir. But I'm not, I'm only - well, I'm not quite seventeen really, sir."

"Well, it's too late now," I said, "you'll have to see it through and I'll do what I can for you when we come out." I slapped him on the shoulder. "You go with the others. You'll be all right when you get started. This is the worst part of it - this waiting, and we're none of us enjoying it. Come along, now, jump to it."

And he seemed to take heart again.

[later] ...I wandered up the trench and noticed Eliot, the boy who had wanted to stay behind. He was sitting on the fire-step joking with his neighbour, with his fears forgotten. He agreed with me that things weren't so bad, after all.

During the battle of the Somme, Anthony Eden witnessed an officer being 'brought to his senses,' with gratifying results:

A while later I was surprised to see a subaltern from one of the battalions holding the line in advance of us walking briskly back from the front only a few yards away on our left. Signing to me to stay where I was with our runners and small headquarters staff, Foljambe walked across, stopped the young officer and was soon talking quietly but insistently to him. The boy who looked rather dazed but otherwise well enough, listened and replied and then after a pause looked again at Foljambe, turned and walked back the way he had come.

Foljambe later told me what had happened. He had asked the boy what he was doing; the reply came that he was suffering from shell-shock and was on his way down the line. Foljambe asked him if he had his company commander's sanction. The subaltern replied that he had not, that he had been knocked over by a shell blast and badly shaken. His company commander had not been in reach, so that he had handed over to the nearest N.C.O. Foljambe had told him that he should not have done that and persuaded the boy to rejoin his company and try to carry on...

[several days later] As we were preparing to leave, without regret, our headquarters at Factory Corner, the commanding officer of the Fusilier battalion with whom we had been sharing the space spoke to Foljambe of the exemplary conduct of one of his subalterns, how he had rallied his men in conditions of the utmost danger, adding that this subaltern was due to report at battalion headquarters at any time now and that he would like Foljambe to meet him.

A few moments later there was a clatter on the cellar steps and there emerged from the semi-darkness the young officer of Foljambe's encounter a few mornings before. Foljambe congratulated him warmly and the subaltern and I exchanged cheerful grins. Had I been a little older I might have reflected on the many facets of courage. Foljambe was genuinely delighted.

Shellshock proper could not, however, be dealt with by reassurance or example. Where it was correctly diagnosed, cases were hospitalized:

It was while I was in this Field Hospital that I saw the first case of shell shock. The man was on a stretcher in a tent directly opposite to ours. There was a railhead behind Fins, and the enemy used to shell this with large shells several times a day.

The shell shock case had been brought down during one morning. The enemy opened out about dinner time, as usual, with his big guns. As soon as the first shell came over, the shell shock case nearly went mad. He screamed and raved, and it took eight men to hold him down on the stretcher.

He kept up a listening attitude for other shells coming over, and with each shell he would go into a fit of screaming and fight to get away. The sweat stood on his forehead in large beads. At last they had to strap him down. He was there until nearly tea time, before they removed him further back. He was a very bad case.

It is heartbreaking to watch a shell shock case. Their terror is indescribable. The flesh on their faces shakes in fear, and their teeth continually chatter. I am sure that if he had been kept there much longer, he would have gone out of his mind; he was not so far off as it was.

On another occasion when in this sector, it was night, and the enemy were putting over to our trenches their usual nightly strafe. He was pouring his shells all over our trenches, when all at once an infantry man jumped up on top of the parapet and made for the enemy trenches. He had suddenly gone shell shock with the continual strain of being under fire. That was the danger with shell shock cases, they did not know what they were doing, or where they were going, but just wandered anywhere, and more often than not a shell or bullet was the end.

When shell shocked they would shriek, kick, struggle and foam at the mouth. It was a fearful job to keep them in hand and prevent them from doing harm to themselves. When they went over the top in this manner they were described as missing; what their end was in many cases nobody knew.

Shell shock was brought about in many ways: loss of sleep, continually being under heavy shell fire, the torment of the lice, irregular meals, nerves always on end, and the thought always in a man's mind that the next minute was going to be his last. It was enough to wear down iron, leave alone flesh and blood. The strain got too great, then shell shock followed.

We had a case which happened in our section of the front line one night on the Cambrai Front, of a man who was near to shell shock; he was just on the border line. He had been out this night with a raiding party, but getting the "wind up," had turned back.

The first that we knew of him, was when we saw in front of our gun positions. About twenty-five yards ahead, something white was moving. We challenged in the usual way, and the Corporal was ready to open fire upon the moving target. He answered the challenge and put up his hands. He was near enough then for us to make out that he was one of the Infantry men from our part of the line. He had lost his tunic and his shirt was all torn. He was as white as a ghost, and had got the "wind up" badly. He told us that he had been fast on the barbed wire in front, and that the enemy were coming over in droves.

All the machine gun teams were ordered to stand to in readiness for any emergency. He told his tale all down the trench to such an extent that he put the "wind up" the whole company of Infantry, and we found out that they left the trench.

The cases described by Corporal Gregory (above) may be said to conform to the stereotype of shellshock. In the next extract, Major R.T.Rees leaves it unclear whether the officer in question was technically shellshocked or not; it is apparent that the disorder affected different people in different ways:

On our second night, about an hour after the relief had taken place, the servant of the Platoon Commander in the advanced post appeared at my dug-out with a request that I would come up at once, as his officer had gone mad and was shooting right and left. I had heard several shots, without thinking anything of it; but I recollected that this officer, who had only just joined us, had been invalided before with a bad attack of

malaria, and it was only at his own urgent request that I had consented
to take him up to this sector.

I hastily accompanied the servant into the wood, and had almost
reached the post when I was suddenly ordered to halt. There, just in
front, was the poor fellow covering me with a rifle. I stood motionless,
while the servant, with great presence of mind, crept round a bush into
the trench, gripped the rifle and disarmed him after a brief struggle. His
nerve had gone completely. He had been imagining an enemy behind
every bush, and wild shots had resulted in the death of his Platoon
Sergeant, one of my best men, whom I had been rapidly promoting. Nor
was this all. The men had naturally become jumpy, and therefore, after
sending the officer down to Battalion H.Q., I remained with the platoon
for the rest of the night.

The journalist Philip Gibbs gave an outsider's view of shellshock. While
displaying some of the class prejudices of his time, he was a trained
observer, willing to and capable of understanding the condition:

Shell-shock was the worst thing to see. There were generals who said:
"There is no such thing as shell-shock. It is cowardice. I would
court-martial in every case." Doctors said: "It is difficult to draw the line
between shell-shock and blue funk. Both are physical as well as mental.
Often it is the destruction of the nerve tissues by concussion, or actual
physical damage to the brain; sometimes it is a shock of horror
unbalancing the mind, but that is more rare. It is not generally the slight,
nervous men who suffer worst from shell-shock. It is often the stolid
fellow, one of those we describe as being utterly without nerves, who
goes down badly. Something snaps in him. He has no resilience in his
nervous system. He has never trained himself in nerve-control, being so
stolid and self-reliant. Now, the nervous man, the cockney, for example,
is always training himself in the control of his nerves, on 'buses which
lurch round corners, in the traffic that bears down on him, in a thousand
and one situations which demand self-control in a 'nervy' man. That
helps him in war; whereas the yokel, or the sergeant-major type, is
splendid until the shock comes. Then he may crack. But there is no law.
Imagination - apprehension - are the devil, too, and they go with
'nerves.'"

It was a sergeant-major whom I saw stricken badly with shell-shock in
Aveluy Wood near Thiepval. He was convulsed with a dreadful rigor
like a man in epilepsy, and clawed at his mouth, moaning horribly, with
livid terror in his eyes. He had to be strapped to a stretcher before he
could be carried away. He had been a tall and splendid man, this poor,
terror-stricken lunatic.

Nearer to Thiepval, during the fighting there, other men were brought
down with shell-shock. I remember one of them now, though I saw
many others. He was a Wiltshire lad, very young, with an

apple-cheeked face and blue-gray eyes. He stood outside a dugout, shaking in every limb, in a palsied way. His steel hat was at the back of his head and his mouth slobbered, and two comrades could not hold him still.

These badly shell-shocked boys clawed their mouths ceaselessly. It was a common, dreadful action. Others sat in the field hospitals in a state of coma, dazed, as though deaf, and actually dumb. I hated to see them, turned my eyes away from them, and yet wished that they might be seen by bloody-minded men and women who, far behind the lines, still spoke of war lightly, as a kind of sport, or heroic game, which brave boys liked or ought to like, and said: "We'll fight on to the last man rather than accept anything less than absolute victory," and when victory came said: "We stopped too soon. We ought to have gone on for another three months." It was for fighting-men to say those things, because they knew the things they suffered and risked. That word "we" was not to be used by gentlemen in government offices scared of air raids, nor by women dancing in scanty frocks at war-bazaars for the "poor dear wounded," nor even by generals at G.H.Q., enjoying the thrill of war without its dirt and danger.

One may contrast the view of a professional soldier to that of Gibbs. While accepting that a problem existed, a RAMC doctor, Colonel F.A.Symons, showed limited understanding of it. In 1914, shellshock was already being observed but not yet classified as a disease in its own right:

Cases of shock began to present themselves. An officer, quivering, lay on his face and groaned at the memory of the awful shelling he had gone through. It was not fear which obsessed him. His nerves simply refused to serve him further. He was but the forerunner of many others.

As late as June 1916, some regular officers seemed unwilling to comprehend and were even disdainful of the condition:

One of my subalterns is said to be suffering from 'shell shock,' a new disease since I was young, and has gone away for two months' rest at the base or at home, I don't know which. Not that there have been enough shells lately to shock his maiden aunt; I must see if I cannot find a small shell with a low standard of propriety to shock me. [Major Francis Graham RFA]

Another regular officer seems to have been prepared to admit the existence of a problem, but his ideas regarding its treatment were decidedly brisk:

Yesterday, when I halted in my walk round the men's quarters here, there was one wretched looking scarecrow standing shaking and perfectly senseless amongst the others of his section. The kind fellows were going to send him to hospital, and all that, but I told them not to, pointing out that he had been through the mill and only wanted rest and food and quiet to be perfectly all right; whereas, if they sent him to hospital, wouldn't all the doctors say that he was a funk, which would be bad luck on him, and bad for the regiment. New idea! which was immediately seized, and one man said he would get to work and shave him and clean him up, and all the others were going to help.

As a matter of fact, it is a terrible ordeal for men who have only become soldiers in the last few months - even weeks. But in the majority of cases, nerve breakdowns are curable by brutal, rather than by sympathetic treatment. Thank goodness, some army commanders are beginning to realise this... [Frank Maxwell, VC]

Shellshock could be just as long-lasting and maiming as the loss of a limb. Whether the result of physical damage to the brain or mental disorder triggered by battlefield stress, it has been a subject for debate ever since. In more recent years it has been accepted and put into modern jargon as 'PTSD' or 'Post-traumatic stress disorder'.

8
Wounds, Death and Burial

Men faced the near-certainty of being wounded when serving in the front line in different ways; not only the prospect of being wounded, but the type of wound that might be suffered was the subject of frequent discussion. On the Somme in 1916, Anthony Eden was adjutant to his battalion. Towards the end of a day of heavy fighting, he was directed by his CO to go up to the front line in order to see how one company had fared:

> At the outset I walked into a stretcher party bearing one of the most intelligent of our young officers. He had only joined us a short while before. I asked him where he had been hit and he looked up at me, smiled and said a little ruefully, 'In the stomach.' We both remembered how a few nights before some of us had been discussing, as was common enough in a Somme interlude, where we would prefer to be hit. Each had his preference, an arm, a shoulder, a leg; we had all agreed that the stomach was the one to be feared. Next day I learnt that Anderson had died before reaching the casualty clearing station.

While stomach and abdominal wounds were almost invariably fatal (especially given the absence of antibiotics, which had not then been discovered), many men harboured the hope that if they were hit, the wound would be light enough to get them out of the line for a time or even back to hospital in England - universally known as 'Blighty,' A colleague safely on his way down the line with a 'blighty' wound and so out of danger was envied by his fellows. A 'blighty' meant an honourable passage away from the trenches and their attendant horrors to warmth, clean sheets and ultimately, the comforts of home, whereas to leave one's comrades without good reason was viewed as unacceptable. This wish for a light wound distracted men from the reality - the risk of permanent disablement by the loss of a limb or blinding; gross disfigurement; lying untended, alone and in agony in a shell-hole in No-Man's-Land, not knowing when or whether help might come. In truth, as Charles Edmonds discovered, even a 'blighty' was still a painful wound and no soft option:

> Towards midday, the enemy shelling really began. Black shrapnels crashed overhead and huge crumps burst round us among the ruins. We all crouched down in our one huge shell-hole, which I began to regret, as a single shell in it would kill us all. One or two men were hit;

especially, I remember, one who was standing up with sleeves rolled up, when a shrapnel burst right above us. A sliver of steel came down and hit him lengthwise on the bare forearm, making a clean cut three inches long between the two bones, as if his arm had been slit with a knife. To my horror the wound gaped open like a freshly cut shoulder of mutton. Though this was as "Cushy" a wound as man could desire, the sight of it cured me of hoping for a "blighty one." The victim agreed with me, for he danced and cried out with the pain.

Stuart Cloete, on the other hand, regarded his 'blighty' as a piece of good fortune:

The German's cheek lay along the butt of his rifle. I could see the black hole of the muzzle. I could see the point of the bayonet. That was the focus of everything. The man, the rifle ending in a steel point, the whole weight of it ending in something little bigger or sharper than my mother's embroidery scissors that were shaped like two gilded cranes. A point was a point.

I moved towards him with my pistol in my hand. My feet dragged. As I advanced the rifle barrel continued to move, following me. Why didn't he shoot? Why didn't he? Why did he hold fire? Suddenly I ran to close in. As I ran, he fired. I spun round and sat down. I felt no pain. I felt as if someone had hit me in the shoulder with a great wooden mallet with such force as to knock me over. Now he was coming for me. The bayonet was lowered. I got the full perspective - the point, the blade, the rifle and the big man leaning forward as he ran. He became enormous, a giant. The rifle was a battering ram, the bayonet a lance. When he was almost on me I fired. As he fell, I fired again and he fell on me. Now I began to think about myself. The war had got away from me. I could see the men very small against the horizon as I sat on the ground. I had not tried to get up yet.

We had been in the second wave, mopping up, throwing bombs into dugouts and taking prisoners. Soon the Huns would drop a barrage behind our advance. Meanwhile there was a very pleasant sound of our shells going like the rush of birds' wings over my head. I stood up. I did not feel too bad. Now I had to make the big decision. I could go on fighting and be a hero... On the other hand I had ample excuse to walk off and leave the war... I felt this 'blighty' was the last present I should get from Mr Luck. We had been over the top six times in four weeks and had never lost less than fifty per cent in casualties. I was the last officer but one who had come through. I had always felt luck to be expendable and I had had about my share. Now I had my blighty and was off. I bent down and took the dead German's belt. I wiped the blood off it on his trousers, removed the bayonet scabbard and fastened the belt with its *Gott mit Uns* buckle round my own waist. Souvenir, I thought, and a good one. I felt somewhat elated.

If a man were wounded in No-Man's-Land, his comrades' immediate concern was - if possible - to help him, and if he could be moved, to get him back to medical treatment in the British lines. The state of the terrain and the attentions of the Germans meant that this was not always easy:

> ...at that moment my servant was hit, and badly too, in the right breast. I wondered if they would come for us, and I got his rifle ready; but I don't think the Bosche has much initiative. The crater was partly full of water, and still worse, it was a crater near or in a ditch. These craters are so many bogs, and you can imagine what happened. "Sir, give me a drink. Oh, Sir, do get my legs out!" He was slowly sliding down the crater, with his legs buried and doubling underneath him; but I got him out and pushed him further up, but seemed stuck for ever myself. At last I got one leg out, and by scooping with my hands and lying on one side (and it seemed after ages of pulling without a sign of movement), at last I was out. It was useless to creep back for help, for how could stretcher-bearers come out there and call for help? The Bosche could be there first, and why should he know he had got one of us? Yet how to get him back? I shouldered his rifle - I didn't think a revolver alone good enough - and hauled the poor chap to the edge of the crater. He stuck it well, but it must have been horrible. Then a friendly gunner from somewhere put a few rounds of shrapnel bang on the very spot from which we had been sniped. I found I could not manage the rifle, but I got poor old Barnbrooke up and carried him a few yards; more was impossible, the mud is so horrible. We had started off that afternoon at 3, and now it was past midnight, so you may imagine how hopeless one's strength seemed to be, just when it was wanted. Those few rounds of shrapnel gave us just the little chance; but the snipers started again, and the edge of the wood was still 80 yards off. I thought the poor chap wanted me to leave him; he was as plucky as could be all the time. I told him we would be alright in the wood; couldn't he manage to walk a wee bit? So I got him up, and with his arm round my shoulder, we pushed ahead a few more yards, then another rest, and I carried him again, and though you could scarcely believe it, he was game enough to walk another bit, when suddenly we heard a whispered call: "This way, Sir. Here you are, Sir" and at last we were in one of our own shell-holes. It was some time before we could get the stretcher-bearers down, and a hard time it is for those poor fellows, but thank God, we got him up to our own pill-box. [Major S.H. Baker, Gloucestershire Regiment]

During an attack on a German strongpoint on the Somme, Capt. Gilbert Nobbs (London Rifle Brigade) was shot and blinded. Having been hit near the enemy lines, his chances of help from his own side were non-existent:

I was quite conscious and thinking clearly: I knew what had happened and what would happen; I remembered every detail.

My head at the moment was inclined to the right, for I was shouting to the men. Like a flash I remembered that about fifty yards to the left of me there was a "German strong point" still occupied by the Germans. A bullet had entered my left temple; it must have come from a sniper in that strong point, for I found some days later that it had emerged through the centre of my right eye.

I remember distinctly clutching my head and sinking to the ground, and all the time I was thinking, "So this is the end - the finish of it all; shot through the head, mine is a fatal wound."

Arnold jumped up, and catching me in his arms, helped me back into the shell-hole... [he] was busy tearing open the field-dressing which I carried in a pocket in my tunic.

"Use the iodine first, Arnold; it's in the pocket in a glass phial."
"The glass is broken, sir."
"In a piece of paper there are two morphia tablets - quick, better give them to me."
"They are not here, sir." And he bound the dressing round my eyes as the blood trickled down my face... I remembered no more.

I do not know how long I remained in this condition. I remember gaining consciousness and finding Arnold by my side.

Something terrible was happening. I gradually began to realize that another attack was taking place over my head. This time the fire was coming from both sides. A stream of bullets seemed to be pouring over the shell-hole. The meaning was obvious: a German machine-gun had been placed in the trench ten yards away, and its deadly fire was pouring over the shell-hole in which we lay. Loud explosions were taking place all round us, and with each explosion the earth seemed to upheave, and I felt the thug, thug of pieces of metal striking the earth close by; whilst showers of earth kept falling on my body. I couldn't last long.

How long this lasted I cannot say. I was weak; my shattered nerves could not stand such a terrible ordeal. I lay huddled and shivering at the bottom of the shell-hole, waiting for the jagged metal to strike my body, or to be hurled, mutilated, into the air.

Again I became unconscious. When I next recovered my senses, Arnold was trying to lift me, to carry me away, but his strength was not equal to it. He laid me down again.

The firing had ceased. He seemed to be peering out of the shell-hole and talking to me. I think he was planning escape. It must have been dark, for he seemed uncertain about the direction.

Then I began to vomit; I seemed to be vomiting my heart out, while Arnold seemed to be trying to comfort me.

I again became unconscious. When I regained consciousness for the third time it seemed to me that I had been insensible for a great length of time. But I seemed to be much refreshed, although very weak.

Everything was silent, uncanny; I could see nothing, hear nothing. Yes, I remembered; I was shot blind, and I was still in the shell-hole. I felt my head; there was a rough bandage round it, covering my eyes. The bandage over my right eye was hardened with blood, and dried blood covered my left cheek. My hair was matted with clay and blood; and my clothes seemed to be covered with loose earth.

But what did this uncanny silence mean? - Arnold, where was he? I called him by name, but there was no response. I remembered the firing I had heard: yes, he must be dead...

I did not know at the time, of course, what had become of Arnold; but I found out later.

Fearing I was dying when I lapsed into unconsciousness again, after my fit of vomiting, he decided under cover of darkness to try and find his way back to the British lines to bring me aid.

After stumbling about in and out of shell-holes, he suddenly saw the barrel of a rifle pointing at him from a trench close by, and following him as he moved; and a moment later he was a prisoner.

Understanding German, he told his captors that I was lying out in No Man's Land, and begged them to send me medical aid; and they answered that stretcher-bearers would be sent to make a search... Presently I heard some one crawling towards me. A few pebbles rolled down the slope, and there was silence again. I felt that he was looking down at me. Again a shuffle, and a quantity of loose earth rolled down the slope, and he was sliding down towards me... I lay perfectly still. He seemed to be bending over me undecidedly. I thought he might believe me dead and go away without finishing me off, to seek the cause of the shout elsewhere.

I raised myself on my elbow and turned my face towards him. Then, to my astonishment, he put his arms around my body and raised me up. What strange wonder was this? He put my arm around his neck, and with his own arm around my body, he raised me to my feet. But I could not stand. Then, placing both arms firmly around me, he dragged me out of the shell-hole. I felt myself being dragged several yards, and then he stopped.

I heard many voices talking below me. What would happen next? Then several hands caught hold of me, and I was lifted into a trench.

Some one gave an order, and I was dragged along the trench and round a corner. More voices seemed to come from still farther below. Some one picked hold of my feet, and I was in a dugout... A voice asked me a question in English, but by this time I had collapsed completely. I tried to speak, but no sound would come from my throat. My head seemed to be an enormous size; my jaw would not move. I felt some one examine my tunic and examine my pockets. No, there were no papers there. I heard some one say, "Hauptmann." Then more talking.

A cigarette was put in my mouth. I held it between my swollen lips, but could not inhale. A sharp command was given, and once more I was lifted up on to some one's back, and was being dragged down a long communication trench.

I was able presently to realize that I was in a dressing station, for I was laid on a stretcher. Some one bent over me, evidently a medical officer.

In contrast to the above, when Lt. Leslie Yorath Sanders suffered a superficial wound at Hill 60, near Ypres, in April 1915, his trauma (both mental and physical) was far less:

I was wounded slightly in the right shoulder by a shell which burst a couple of yards away half-right. I went into the crater... to investigate the wound; another shell came over my head as I did so and burst a yard or two in front of me, without, however, damaging me. The marksmanship displayed by the German artillery was not brilliant. Finding the damage slight, I made my way without much difficulty to the dressing station in the cutting; Trench 38 had been so smashed up by artillery that I followed instead a path along the edge of the cutting... An iodine dressing having been applied, I walked back to Ypres; luckily no shells fell near me during the walk. A straggling procession of walking cases were following the same path. In Ypres I was astonished to find the shops only just opening. I and three others went into one place and had a cup of coffee, then made our way to the main hospital. Here the wound was re-dressed, and I was inoculated with anti-tetanus serum. I was then, after some waiting, put on board a motor ambulance and taken to the clearing hospital at Poperinghe. I had a meal here, and about 3 p.m. the motor ambulance came again and conveyed us to the railway station, where we went aboard the ambulance train. After many waits and very slow progress between whiles, we reached Boulogne about 10.30 p.m. Once more the motor ambulances were waiting, and I was carried to the Casino at Wimereux.

Another young officer wrote home - very much in the language of his class and public school background - of his wounding and his passage through the machinery of the Royal Army Medical Corps from the front line to No. 14 General Hospital, Wimereux (formerly and subsequently the Hotel Splendide) in February 1916:

L.B.W., B.Fritz. Put my leg in front of a straight one. I hope you got a note from Pat and I suppose by now you have got some sort of intimation from the War Office. Apparently I have been pretty lucky. The bullet went in behind the knee, and came out just below the knee-cap. The x-rays show that it has gone through without touching anything of importance, which the doctor tells me is pretty fortunate, as there are some unpleasant parts in your knee to get damaged. Anyhow, it is not painful - only a bit stiff and throbs occasionally.

We had had a very heavy 3 days in the front line - perfectly horrid time. We were looking forward to buses, which were waiting to take us right away. Just getting out of the danger-zone, we got picked up by a stray machine-gun, just chance shots of course. I heard phizz, phizz, phizz, phizz, and about the fifth one I didn't hear copped me behind the knee, and sent me head over heels. I sent the platoon on, and the sergeant sent a corporal to get a stretcher-bearer, while my servant, who was with me, bound me up. I was wearing thigh gum-boots, which he had to cut off, and - rather a bore - he had to cut my breeches up. Anyhow, he made quite a good job of it, and carried me under cover as there were some more pellets dotting about.

The corporal went back to Battalion H.Q., and in about ½ an hour there was a tremendous hue and cry. Puffing and blowing, Major Benson, the Adjutant, and the M.O. came hurrying up as if the world had come to an end. Very good of them, as they were all dead beat, and it was a long way to come. The M.O. put a proper dressing on it, and then between them, with the help of a stretcher-bearer, they carried me down to the dressing station, where I was left in charge of some R.A.M.C. orderlies who made me tea, and fed me with cigarettes. About an hour afterwards a motor ambulance turned up, and took me along to the first town, to the forward hospital. The doctor here happened to be L.G.Brown, the Rugger International, a very pleasant person. He inoculated me against tetanus, and dressed me, and I got a wash and rid of some of my muddy clothes.

They only kept me there an hour, and another motor took me to the first clearing hospital, where they again examined me in bed and gave me lunch.

Just getting to sleep after lunch, they had me out of bed, and put me in an enormous and beautiful hospital train - destination, Boulogne. This was 2, and we arrived at Boulogne, after a very hot but comfortable journey, at about 10.

These trains are wonderful things. They gave us an excellent tea and dinner on board. They came round before dinner, and asked what we should like to drink; provided whisky, beer, etc., ad lib., comfortable beds, and nurses and doctors trotting about all the time. We found more motors at Boulogne, which brought us out here, "The Hotel Splendid," [sic] Wimereux. A really beautiful place - "every convene," as Phil Ray used to say. It's beautifully got up, and most awfully comfortable. I share a room with a man in the Shropshires. We seem to have about a dozen sisters, who are all most attentive and pleasant. One night nurse's name is Heaton Ellis, a cousin of the Heddon Court one. We are deluged with food, fruit, flowers and papers, etc. In the morning a sergeant comes round to know what paper you require, and the barber comes along to see if he is wanted, so altogether we are being looked after in some style. It is certainly a great thing to be in sheets once more.

When this writer, 2nd Lt. J.S.Tatham (9th King's Royal Rifle Corps) was wounded, he was not fighting in a major action and so his treatment and evacuation were swift. Philip Gibbs described a different scene in the aftermath of the battle of Loos, when sheer numbers put the medical services under strain:

To onlookers there were some of the signs of victory on that day of September 25th - of victory and its price. I met great numbers of the lightly wounded men, mostly "jocks," and they were in exalted spirits because they had done well in this ordeal and had come through it, and out of it - alive. They came straggling back through the villages behind the lines to the casualty clearing-stations and ambulance-trains. Some of them had the sleeves of their tunics cut away and showed brown brawny arms tightly bandaged and smeared with blood. Some of them were wounded in the legs and hobbled with arms about their comrades' necks. Their kilts were torn and plastered with chalky mud. Nearly all of them had some "souvenir" of the fighting - German watches, caps, cartridges. They carried themselves with a warrior look, so hard, so lean, so clear-eyed, these young Scots of the Black Watch and Camerons and Gordons. They told tales of their own adventure in broad Scots, hard to understand, and laughed grimly at the killing they had done, though here and there a lad among them had a look of bad remembrance in his eyes, and older men spoke gravely of the scenes on the battlefield and called it "hellish." But their pride was high. They had done what they had been asked to do. The 15th Division had proved its quality. Their old battalions, famous in history, had gained new honour.

Thousands of those lightly wounded men swarmed about a long ambulance-train standing in a field near the village of Choques. They crowded the carriages, leaned out of the windows with their bandaged heads and arms, shouting at friends they saw in the other crowds. The spirit of victory, and of lucky escape, uplifted those lads, drugged them. And now they were going home to bonny Scotland, with a wound that would take some time to heal.

There were other wounded men from whom no laughter came, nor any sound. They were carried to the train on stretchers, laid down awhile on the wooden platforms, covered with blankets up to their chins, - unless they uncovered themselves with convulsive movements. I saw one young Londoner so smashed about the face that only his eyes were uncovered between layers of bandages, and they were glazed with the first film of death. Another had his jaw blown clean away, so the doctor told me, and the upper half of his face was livid and discolored by explosive gases. A splendid boy of the Black Watch was but a living trunk. Both his arms and both his legs were shattered. If he lived after butcher's work of surgery he would be one of those who go about in boxes on wheels, from whom men turn their eyes away, sick with a sense of horror. There were blind boys led to the train by wounded comrades, groping, very quiet, thinking of a life of darkness ahead of them - forever in the darkness which shut in their souls. For days and weeks that followed there was always a procession of ambulances on the way to the dirty little town of Lillers, and going along the roads I used to look back at them and see the soles of muddy boots upturned below brown blankets. It was more human wreckage coming down from the salient of Loos, from the chalk-pits of Hulluch and the tumbled earth of the Hohenzollern redoubt, which had been partly gained by the battle which did not succeed. Outside a square brick building, which was the Town Hall of Lillers, and for a time a casualty clearing-station, the "bad" cases were unloaded; men with chunks of steel in their lungs and bowels were vomiting great gobs of blood, men with arms and legs torn from their trunks, men without noses, and their brains throbbing through opened scalps, men without faces...

As the men in the front line grew accustomed to living with wounds and death on such a regular basis it is not surprising that their attitude became somewhat matter-of-fact. In a deserted inn which Major R.T.Rees had chosen as battalion HQ, believing it to be safely out of range of German observation:

There was an almighty crash, and a turmoil of smoke, dust and flying fragments. We were nearer the enemy, I suppose, than we had thought, and the smoke of the fire had given us away. Anyhow, he put a shell very accurately through the roof, and it was that which caused the disturbance.

When the smoke cleared I found myself "unmannerly breech'd with gore," with my wristwatch no longer on, but in the wrist. The staircase, however, was still intact, so I went down and found one of my

Subalterns, startled out of his sleep. We picked out as much of the watch as we could (a good deal of it still remains inside), and he tied up the broken joint for me, with the encouraging remark, "I'm afraid you will lose the hand, Sir."

The tension of battle could push soldiers to an extreme, of almost ignoring the wounded:

The strange thing was that during the whole of the attack I felt absolutely callous and indifferent to everything except pushing on. For example, I came across two men of another battalion, one with his leg shattered and the other with arm smashed to pulp. They had both been bandaged up, but one was in such agony that he clutched at my foot and implored me to give him his rifle so that he could shoot himself. I gave them my water and cut their equipment away to ease them, but the predominant feeling in my mind was one of impatience. [2nd Lt. T. B. Stowell, St. Pancras Rifles]

In hospital however, it was impossible to ignore the sufferings of the wounded, even for so seasoned a soldier as Siegfried Sassoon:

I listen to the chatter of the other wounded officers in my room, talking about people being blown to bits. I remember the chap at the C.C.S. with his jaw blown off by a bomb ('a fine looking chap, he was,' they said). He lay there on the bed with one hand groping about on the bandages that covered his whole head and face, gurgling every time he breathed. His tongue was tied forward to stop him swallowing it. The war had gagged him - smashed him. (Me it had spared.) People looked at him and tried to forget what they'd seen. 'Not expected to live...' Surely he would be better dead. All this I remembered, while the desirable things of life, like living phantoms, stole quietly into my brain; looked at me wistfully, and crept away again... beckoning... pointing... 'To England in a few days...' and I know it's wrong... I know that I shall go there, because it is made so easy...

On occasion, a man could be written off by his comrades as dead or about to die; but this was not always the case, as the following two extracts show:

During the night a 'Scottish' patrol brought in a private of the Fusiliers who had been lying out in an unoccupied trench in 'No Man's Land' since 1 July [1916] - in all thirteen days. He had been unconscious for most of the time, and only remembered two dawns. Despite the long exposure great hopes were entertained for his recovery. He did, in fact, fully recover and on one noted occasion he was able to attend as a visitor a 1st Battalion reunion at the headquarters of the London Scottish Regiment in Buckingham Gate. He was, in fact, a guest of one of the members of the patrol that found him. [Private A.S.Dolden, London Scottish]

Poor Bill H— was shot through the head by a sniper. The bullet went in at the top of his forehead and came out a little further back. He received first aid and was taken on a stretcher down to the dressing station. We naturally made certain [sic] his wound was fatal, but some weeks afterwards were delighted to hear that he was in a base hospital and making progress towards recovery. [Cpl. H. Raymond Smith, 1/8th Worcesters]

As men became inured to wounds, so they also did to the sight of corpses. Each side found it difficult to bury its dead owing to the proximity of the other, and the recovery of bodies from No-Man's-Land was almost invariably too risky an undertaking. Near to the front line, the remains of those killed in action were almost ubiquitous; where burial had been attempted, it was frequently a hurried affair of interment in a shallow grave. And these graves were all too easily disturbed by shellfire.

Not yet having become accustomed to the more unpleasant sights of the battlefield, Charles Edmonds was somewhat taken aback by the easy going familiarity of his sergeant towards the dead:

Presently Sergeant Coke, a fair-haired, pleasant-mannered young man, drifted into conversation with me.

"There's a lot of dead Boches along here, sir," he said cheerfully.

This roused my interest, for curiously enough, though I had six months' service in France and had often seen men hit, it had always been in well-ordered trenches, where casualties were soon disposed of; and I had never seen a corpse.

"Come along, sir," said Sergeant Coke, leading the way over the holes and hummocks of chalk. "When we were up at Messines they lay about thick. I pulled the teeth out of one of them and made a necklace of them. All the chaps used to rummage round them for souvenirs. Careful, sir, look out for this wire! They used to smell in the summer when the flies were bad. Do you know what we are up here for, sir?"

"No," said I, a little disgusted.

He chattered on in a silky civilised voice. "The chaps are pretty tired, sir. Some of them didn't get any sleep at all last night with the shelling, and they'd been up since two o'clock yesterday. Captain Mayhew didn't like it a bit. He said C company had touched lucky as usual. They had a man hit in C company."

"Yes," said I, "he was a policeman."

"Look at this, sir!" gloated Sergeant Coke. 'This' was a rusty tangled framework made of iron stakes and barbed wire of the kind which soldiers call a 'knife-rest.' It had been struck by a sixty-pound trench mortar bomb of which the stem lay close by. In the middle of the tangle, as if the wires had been carefully twisted round it, was a bundle of rags. They were grey and of fine texture, like my own khaki, obviously the ruins of an officer's uniform. It was only when I noticed two smartly booted and gaitered legs in tan leather protruding from one end of the bundle, that I realised it was anything more than rags. No other sign of humanity was visible.

A.O.Pollard of the HAC, however, was not revolted but intrigued by what he found on an excursion into No-Man's-Land:

I spent as much time as possible roaming round No Man's Land. The Huns were now eight hundred yards away and there was plenty to see in the intervening space. On one of these excursions I came across an excellent Burberry with only five small shrapnel holes in it and which I promptly annexed. By it, in the bottom of the shell-hole where I found it, was a solitary head. It stood upright in the centre of the crater and there was no trace of the body to which it belonged anywhere near it. For some reason it fascinated me. It looked so droll and yet so pathetic. To whom had it belonged? Was he friend or foe? Had death overtaken him whilst he was dashing forward in a charge full of the lust of battle or had he been cowering down in sickening fear, his nerve shattered by the thunder of bursting shells? I hoped he was a fighter who had gone down with his face to the enemy, his courage high and his mouth set in grim determination. That was how I hoped to die if I had to; though I should have liked one second's warning so that I could breathe Her name. Afterwards, if my head remained to mark the spot, I should like it to be pointing to the trenches I had never reached.

Whereas it was considered legitimate to take souvenirs from German dead, British corpses were generally left alone unless it was for the purpose of salvaging rations or equipment:

During this period of hibernation war became more and more a matter of housewifery. Salvage was the fashionable winter amusement. The order had gone forth that no man was to return from the front line without some derelict article, a hat, a bomb or two, a barbed-wire picket, a Lewis-gun drum. Some units affected to despise this domesticity, boldly returning nil reports. Not so ourselves, Smith saw in this last brain-wave an idea which might be turned to our own profit. This area was strewn with dead. The dead had haversacks. The haversacks had socks. A unit was still judged by the number of men who developed trench feet during the winter. Defeating this disease was a matter of dry socks. The allowance was two pairs per man, both of which were usually wet through in the course of a couple of days. Now thanks to salvage, we acquired some thousands of pairs of unauthorized socks. The colonel himself took the lead. Pipe in mouth he might be seen hopping, carrion-crow-wise, from body to body in the appropriately named Opaque Wood, returning home towards lunch time with his runner, their arms full of necessaries for the battalion. Occasionally I accompanied him on these jaunts: but my stomach was too queasy. Smith's mind was actively interested in all phenomena. He was as interested in a dead as in a living man, wanted to know just why the corpse lay in that position, speculate on the caprice which had left a head and a leg with no body to join them. Though I could look on bodies unmoved, I could not abide bare fresh bones: and after a morning in which the colonel tried vainly to interest me in a complete jaw without skull or cervicle, and with the teeth still flecked with blood, I excused myself from further operations. [Guy Chapman]

Despite the difficulties inherent in conducting burials in the fighting zone, it was deemed necessary to do so, both on grounds of hygiene and respect for one's comrades and foes. Capt. H.Raymond Smith wrote of his work commanding a divisional burial party:

I was appointed to the command of a burial party in place of O—, who had gone to the R.F.C. Here we operated from the old dugout in Pope Avenue in front of Gouzeacourt [sic], which I have already described. I shared the mess with two padres - one Church of England and the other Wesleyan. In the morning we went out and collected the dead, British and German dead were placed side by side in one big grave, and the padre conducted the burial service over friend and foe alike. During the progress of this work, which took a long time, as the battlefield was very extensive, my sergeant and I came upon a terrible sight. We approached a tank which had been struck by a direct hit from a shell in the fore part; the shell had gone clean through the thick armour plating and burst inside. We entered through the tiny door in the side of the tank, and a ghastly sight met our eyes. Three charred bodies lay inside the tank; all the clothing had been burnt off them, and they were unrecognisable. We got them out and buried them in a shell hole. No doubt they were killed instantly by the explosion of the shell inside the tank, and their bodies burnt afterwards.

Corps, as well as divisions, appointed officers to locate bodies and undertake their interment. While the nature of their duties was important, it also brought out a macabre streak of humour in those engaged in less morbid tasks:

We have had no more Infantry guests - even the "Body Snatcher" or "Cold Meat Specialist" (Corps Burial Officer) has left us to rejoin his battalion. The latter was a very cheery Irish boy who had messed with

us for ten days; we never learnt his real name, since he always answered
to the above sobriquets. He was in charge of our area and was most
useful in removing our pet aversions, which otherwise might have
remained unburied for months. [Lt.Col. N. Fraser-Tytler]

When the 20th Division was hard pressed by German counter-attacks at
Cambrai, all available troops were needed in the front line. Capt. H.
Raymond Smith (still in command of his divisional burial party) was
summoned to his Battalion HQ:

> Descending the steps, I am ordered by the Commanding Officer to take
> my party into the frontline. I return to them, a hasty word of command,
> and off we go. The journey up Pope Avenue seems longer than usual,
> and the terrible shelling still continues. Suddenly I feel a catch in the
> throat, and we halt, and put on our gas masks. The gas shells are
> dropping behind us, and the fumes are drifting back on us. After a time
> I am forced to remove my gas mask, as when it is on I am unable to give
> an order. We reach the headquarters of another unit, who prove to be a
> battalion of the Berkshires. I enter their dug-out, but am at first unable
> to speak on account of the gas I have inhaled. At length I am able to tell
> them that I have come to reinforce them. "What is your party?" asks
> their Commanding Officer. "Divisional Burial Party" I reply, which
> seems to have a depressing effect upon them!

It was an important part of the duties of any individual who conducted
a burial to mark its site and to report who was interred there (whenever
this had been or could be ascertained) and the precise location of the
grave. Early in the war, this tended to be haphazard, but the
importance of care of the dead to both civilian and military morale was
recognised in the establishing of the Graves Registration Commission
(the forerunner of the Imperial and later Commonwealth War Graves
Commission) in March 1915, to whom all details of burial were passed
whenever possible.

Individual graves were initially marked using whatever means were
available; at best, this took the form of a rough wooden cross, but other
expedients sometimes were employed. Lt. Col. Fraser-Tytler
encountered an unusual example:

> On our way home Macdonald and I visited the cemetery. Rows of
> corked whisky bottles, with names, etc., inside mark the graves, until
> they can be replaced by the wooden crosses. We stayed while a padre
> read the service over a man buried that morning, a short service
> somewhat interrupted by the German reply to our shoot.

1. An officer of the Great War: Capt. H. Dundas, Scots Guards; see text.

2. A 'ranker' of the Great War: Rifleman G. Brown, Rifle Brigade.

3. Open Warfare: Battle of the Marne, 1914. 1st Middlesex First-Line transport struck by shrapnel at Signy Signets, 8th September. Nine horses were killed; the man with the goggles belongs to the Intelligence Corps and is bady wounded in the head and his face covered with blood.

4. Trench Warfare: A 'high command' trench, probably in the Ypres Salient early in 1915. The men are not yet equipped with steel helmets.

5. Trench Warfare: 'High command' trench running through the ruins of St Eloi, early 1915...

6. ...and the view of the crossroads in the middle of the village at about the same time. Not long after, even these ruins were completely pulverised.

7. Oblique view of St. Eloi from an observation balloon. The legend in the top right-hand corner of the photograph gives the balloon and map references and date. The black smudge above the crossroads refferred to in the previous caption is a shellburst. Note the four large mine craters, the scene of heavy fighting in 1916.

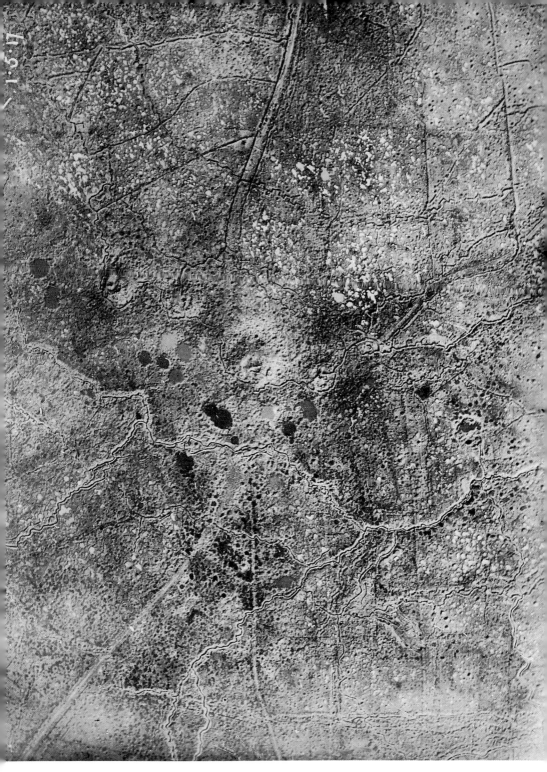

8. Vertical shot of St. Eloi, which the legend shows was taken by B Flight, No. 6 Sqdrn. RFC on 1st May 1917. The close proximity of the opposing lines can be discerned in the vicinity of the craters.

9. Trench Warfare: Battle of Messines. View of Oosttaverne Wood, showing captured German trenches, 11th June 1917. Heavy bombardment has reduced the trees to matchwood.

10. Mud: Tank wrecked in Inverness Copse, 25 September 1917. During the Third Battle of Ypres this position changed hands nineteen times.

11. Trench Warfare: Working party of the York and Lancs. Regiment repairing the parapet. Arras front, 12th January 1918.

12. Mud: Officers of the 12th Royal Irish Rifles wading through the mud of a fallen-in communication trench, the result of a thaw after weeks of snow and frost. Essigny, 7th February 1918. Fifth Army troops, they had recently taken over from the French 6th Division.

13. Technology: An Australian Lewis gun team in a front line trench, Garter Point, near Ypres, 27th September 1917. This picture also shows a trench mortar and a quantity of entrenching tools, and is clearly posed.

14. Technology: Machine Gun Corps troops manning heavy machine-guns just behind the front line. The gun on the right is a German one; that on the left a Vickers.

15. Technology: Mk. I tank at Flers (D17), 17th September 1916. Flers was taken on 15th September with the aid of tanks, the first time they were used.

16. Technology: Battle of Cambrai. Tanks passing captured guns at Graincourt on their way to the attack on Bourlon Wood, 23rd Novmber 1917. Note the 'unditching beam' on the back of this Mk. IV tank.

17. Technology: A bombing 'squad', c.1915. Each man wears a grenade waistcoat, a short-lived item of equipment (see Chapter 1). The front two men each hold a No. 1 grenade and the sack held by the man on the left presumably holds more bombs.

18. Technology: Guardsmen manning a bombing post. Ypres Salient, April 1916.

19. Technology: Canadian Scottish moving up to the attack on Cambrai. Note the wirecutter attachments on the rifles of the first and third men and the rifle grenades carried by most of them. The breeches of the rifles are protected from mud by cloth covers.

20. Sniping: A section of the Queen's Regt. display their standard Lee Enfield rifles equipped with telescopic sights.

21. Technology: A light trench mortar battery displays two of its 3" Stokes mortars (and mascots) outside its billet in France. The chalk billetting mark on the door behind them indicates that this is the 23rd Light Trench Mortar Battery, 23rd Brigade, 8th Division.

22. Technology: Heavy trench mortars. British 9.45" mortar crew in an old German trench in Pigeon Wood, Gommecourt, March 1917. The projectile being loaded was known as a 'flying pig.'

23. Open Warfare: The German March Offensive. Field-gun batteries in action in the open. 28th March 1918. Albert Area.

24. Open Warfare: Battle of the Canal du Nord - infantry supports going forward. 4th Canadian Division, 27th September 1918. Note marks left by caterpillar tracks.

25. Open Warfare: Battle of the Canal du Nord. A Field Dressing Station; note prisoners bringing wounded in on the 4th Canadian Division front, near Moeuvres, 27th September 1918. In the background artillery is going forward; owing to the depth of the initial objective, batteries were compelled to move forward into captured ground to continue firing the barrage.

26. Technology: 12-inch howitzer in action; near Aveluy Wood, September 1916. Note hoist to lift shell into position; also overhead camouflage to impede aerial observation.

27. Technology: RFA Forward Observation Officer observing from the firestep of a trench. His linesman stands by his side communicating by telephone with the Battery. Note notice-board marking a bomb store. Near Croiselles, 4th January 1918.

28. The Somme: A group of war graves. Note German shells in wicker cariers, wrecked railway line in the foreground and transport wagon going towards the line in the background. Northern corner of Bernafay Wood, September 1916.

If it could be arranged, it was deemed proper for a padre to perform a brief funeral service and one of his more important duties was to minister to the dead:

> The chief occasion on which a Chaplain would go out in the ordinary course would be to bury the dead on the battlefield after an engagement. The risk of this varies, of course, with the distance from the enemy's firing line. In some cases it is absolutely impossible, in others there is no risk at all: sometimes it is just a case of "chancing it."

> The first experience I had of this sort of thing was a short time after the battle of Loos. We were occupying some trenches which had been taken from the enemy at that battle, and sleeping in dug-outs which had recently been German. Just behind us, on what had been the battlefield, lay the bodies of many brave men who had fallen, and during the night a party of ours went out and buried as many as they could find. We buried 25 men, all of them belonging, I think, to the gallant Devons, in five graves, and five times I repeated a very abbreviated form of the burial service. Digging the graves, although we made what use we could of shell holes, and collecting the bodies, many of which were entangled in the German barbed wire, took us exactly 2 and a ½ hours. Not one of us was hit that night; as a matter of fact, there was a certain amount of haze and I think we were invisible to the Germans, but they had a machine gun playing slowly and systematically across the ground from a slag heap called the dump, and we had ample opportunity of hearing all the bullets had to say for themselves. ['E.A.F,' *Vermelles*]

Although it was not always feasible to give soldiers burial as individuals, the role of the padre did not diminish in importance:

> As I was approaching the quarry I saw a procession of soldiers headed by a parson in his surplice. He had a book in his hand, and the soldier who was behind him was carrying a half-filled sandbag. There was a newly opened mound of earth, and they all ranged themselves round this. The parson was reading the burial service. This being over, the sandbag was put into the grave, which was then filled in.

> When I got to the place where this had been taking place, I enquired what had been the matter, and was told that the half sandbag of remains that they had just buried comprised all that was left of eleven men. These men were new out from England, and had only arrived the night before. They were billeted in the sunken road by the quarry, and a German shell had come over and landed right on top of their billet, scattering them in all directions. [Cpl. H. Gregory]

Capt. Crouch of the Bucks. Battalion recorded the views of a fellow officer on such an abrupt and mutilating end:

> Birchall says that he doesn't want to get killed a bit. He wants to die at the age of ninety-five and be buried by the vicar and the curate, and his funeral attended by all the old ladies of the parish! He strongly objects to large objects of an explosive nature being thrown at him, and then his remains being collected in a sandbag and buried by ribald soldiery and dug up again two days later by a 5.9!

A footnote to this light-hearted piece records sadly that Captain Birchall died of wounds, in July 1916.

While exhumation by shellfire was not uncommon, it was not its sole cause. Crouch wrote to his father:

> Thanks for your letter. I was awfully glad that the Bosche helmet is such a success. Would you like a skull to go with it? The rain is disclosing all sorts of interesting souvenirs behind my trenches. There is a little osier-bed in front of a hedge, and evidently two shallow pits were dug and dead Boches were bundled in anyhow. The pits are now sinking a little, and boots, bones, clothes, and all sorts of debris are sticking out. There are two fine skulls there. I carried one on the end of my stick and planted him at the head of a communication trench, but it has been removed.

To underline the magnitude of the task of honouring the dead of the Great War, by the provision of a named grave, it should be pointed out that the memorial to missing of the Battle of the Somme, at Thiepval, bears the names of some 74,000 men; that at Ypres (the Menin Gate), some 55,000 and these are only two of 16 such memorials. The work of burying and recording the dead occupied the then Imperial War Graves Commission throughout the 1920s and 1930s and its work continues to this day.

9
Religion & Superstition

Under wartime conditions, the pursuit of religious faith necessarily took second place to a host of other activities. The spiritual needs of all religions were nevertheless ministered to by the Army Chaplains Department, but individual chaplains faced numerous obstacles in fulfilling their rôle.

The traditional peacetime duties of the padre, which chiefly consisted of officiating at the weekly Church Parade were eroded by the constraints under which chaplains on the Western Front worked. Church Parades were impossible in the front line and so the padre's most useful contributions were at a more practical level, such as conducting burials, reassuring the wounded at dressing stations, and distributing such luxuries as cigarettes and chocolate. In addition, some felt obliged to distribute advice of what one author described as a 'virilist' nature, such as exhortations to 'scrag the Boche.'

One Church of England chaplain described his difficulties in following his ministry. Normally suitable premises tended, given the view from their spires, to be misappropriated by others. Having found his way to the village church at Vermelles, he was confronted by discouraging signs:

> "Troops are warned not to loiter at these cross-roads as they are frequently shelled. *N.B.-This includes officers.*" The italics are my own. Then we enter the Church and the most extraordinary scene of wreckage presents itself.

> The floor is thickly strewn not only with the ruin of the fallen roof but with innumerable broken cane-seated chairs, fragments of the pulpit and stalls and debris of everything imaginable. The great beam of the roof cants downwards from the eastern gable at a dangerous angle, and the stairs leading to the organ-loft are torn and twisted. The Chancel, over which rises the battered tower, is completely bare, but an altar still stands at the east end of the North Aisle, just by the tiny doorway leading to the tower staircase. As we approach this altar, with probably a deep sense of reverence - and a sort of "here is something left which suggests worship - and I want to say my prayers" feeling, our eye catches a notice nailed to the door of the staircase opening just beside the altar - "This is an Artillery Observation Post. Please keep away." ['E.A.F.']

If premises proved to be a difficulty, the army authorities were another matter:

> After consultation with the R.C. and Presbyterian Padres, I wrote a humble request to our Brigadier that we might have Church Parade at 9 a.m., and march off at 9.30: or if that was impossible, as it well might be, since the whole Division (12 Battalions, besides Artillery, R.E.'s, R.A.M.C., &c., &c.) was on the move, and times and routes had to be minutely adjusted to avoid congestion, I suggested that when we had got off the track of the rest of the troops, the Brigade might be allowed to fall out for half an hour, and have a Voluntary Church Parade in a field under their respective chaplains. I also quoted what the Corps General had recently told us at Béthune about the paramount importance of Honour, Duty and Discipline being inculcated by the chaplains, and pointed out that the period of Corps Rest was the one great opportunity we had of getting the men together, since at ordinary times they were frequently debarred from attending Service. I also suggested that if everything else failed, Monday or Tuesday of that week might be kept as "Sunday." The Brigadier was entirely sympathetic and forwarded my request to the Divisional General. The reply was a telegram despatched at 9 p.m. on Saturday Evening: -

> "Reference your letter of 5th inst. aaa. Brigade may return to Raimbert by 2 p.m. on Sunday and therefore it would be possible to hold a Voluntary Evening Service. aaa. Owing to training it will be impracticable to hold a Service on Monday."

> On receipt of this wire, I managed to get a 7.30 a.m. Celebration of The Holy Communion for which the Brigadier kindly lent me his dining-room, at Enquin, and a 6 p.m. Voluntary Service at Raimbert put into Saturday Night's Orders, with the result that the Brigadier and I were the only communicants, and as far as I remember nobody at all turned up in the evening.

Another source of frustration was that the troops, while happy to oblige him, frequently failed quite to understand what his wishes actually were:

> It was Holy Week and finding that a Motor Transport Column was billeted in the town, I visited their C.O. to ask if he could find any convenient time for his men to attend Church on Good Friday and Easter Day.

> The C.O. was very pleasant and affable. He was not an "Old Army" officer, but thoroughly competent to deal with his present command, consisting, as it did, of draft horses, motors, and a handful of men, and he had a certain cosmopolitan manner which suggested a voyage or two to Rio or The Cape. He appeared gratified by my offer, and tacitly assuming that I could not have suggested that anyone in their senses

could want to go to Church twice in one week, replied, "Oh, certainly! *Either* day would be perfectly convenient. Which would you prefer?"

It seemed a perfectly simple question, yet it rather non-plussed me. I decided on Good Friday and I thought when I had the men together it would give me the chance of arranging a Voluntary Service for Easter Day. Next day, however, he sent me a message to say that he had forgotten that they had a Gymkhana arranged for the Friday so they would "try to come on the Sunday".

Administering the sacraments proved no easier at less holy times of year:

I had several times taken a Service for [a] Battery at the request of the Artillery Chaplain, who had far too much to do, and one Sunday he asked me to give them a Celebration of Holy Communion.

I went prepared to do so, and found that the place fixed for the Service was a draughty gap between two houses, with a messy sort of yard and all sorts of unmentionabilities in the immediate background. Outdoor services are preferable to indoor in fine weather, but if there is any wind it is almost impossible to have a Communion Service.

Moreover, what was even more to the point, the Sergt.-Major told me that only an ordinary Service had been announced, and that he thought only one man in the Battery was a Communicant and he was on leave, and that they had not had a Celebration since they had been in France.

He also added that he had meant to be Confirmed himself when he was in England and had attended one class, but as he had been obliged to "miss the other two" he had not "been done"! I forget from what part of England he said he had come.

There might, he said, be some Communicants, but he "would soon find out," and before I had realized what he was doing, he turned round to the men, who were drawn up in two double ranks facing one another, down the afore-mentioned gap, (in stentorian tones): "Parade, t'shun. Those who wish to receive Communion one pace forward - March." Naturally no one moved, so he turned to me - "No, Sir, I thought there was none." "Very well," I said, "I will take the ordinary Service," and I gave them a simple instruction on the meaning and use of Holy Communion, and said I would have a Celebration the following Sunday. ['E.A.F.']

Before and during a battle, the padre's role expanded; demand for reassurance was likely to be at a peak and in that context he could both feel and be actively useful:

On the morning before the battle, Friday, Sept. 24, we four Church of England chaplains of the Division met in a bell-tent for a celebration of Holy Communion, six or seven miles back, at a place called Vaudricourt. We knew, of course, that big things were going to happen the following day. Then we went down to visit our respective Brigades.

I will only mention one incident, which I think was probably typical of what many chaplains were doing that day. I came across a young officer in Mazingarbe who was the very finest type of what an officer and a gentleman should be. We talked *choux et raves* for a few minutes, and I saw clearly that he had something on his mind; so when our conversation harked back, as it inevitably did, to the coming fight, I said to him very pointedly, "I know what it is that is troubling you; it is the thought of your people." I knew that he was recently married. "Yes," he replied, "that is just exactly it. One does not mind for oneself." Then I said, "I wonder whether it would help you if I told you something that was said to me the other day - that when Our Lord Himself was giving up His life for what He knew was The Right, even on the Cross He made arrangements for the welfare of His own mother. Don't you think He will feel equally responsible now for anyone you love if it is His will that you should leave them?" I saw a look of relief and joy in the boy's face as he thought it out, and then we shook hands cordially and parted. I never saw him again. He was shot dead the next morning a few yards from our parapet. But I do not think it was "chance" that made me meet him for the first time the day before, or that put it into my head to suggest that thought to him.

I slept that night at Noeux-les-Mines.

Next morning, Saturday, the 25th, the day of the battle, I was up early and went first to the Noeux-les-Mines hospital, where I found 16 fellows who had been wounded on their way up to the trenches the night before by some idiot who had dropped a box of bombs he was carrying. Strange to say, the culprit was about the one man of the party who was uninjured. I stayed and talked to them for a few minutes, and then as nothing else seemed likely to happen there for some time, I got on my bicycle and rode on about three miles to the advanced Dressing Station of an Ambulance at the Villa Arnould at Mazingarbe. It was then about 8 or 9 a.m., and a long stream of "walkers," i.e., slightly wounded but able to walk, were pouring in. I stayed for some hours helping to tie on labels to each patient, before he was sent off in an ambulance car or cart, specifying his name, number, rank and regiment, whether he had been inoculated for tetanus, and whether he was suffering from compound fracture of the arm or Gun-shot wound in the calf. ['E.A.F.']

Despite the Church's view that God was on our side, the foul weather which almost always accompanied British attacks led others to question this:

One must give up the idea of the Deity having or rather exercising any direct control on events - for reasons of course which we can't explain; otherwise, of course, it is patent that any divine intervention which does occur is on the side of the Boches - *i.e.*, the weather. Every time we biff - rain, rain, rain. Of course, that we can ascribe to the Artillery, I'm absolutely certain. It must have the effect of bringing down the clouds - any shattering bombardment. After two fine days it looks as if it was going to rain this evening - for I am going to play fitba' for the Battalion against some one. [Henry Dundas]

Notwithstanding the established consolations of religion, many felt the need to supplement them in other ways:

On Good Friday we had an Easter service, as we were to be in the trenches again on Easter Day. Our padre was Capt. Rev. J.O.Aglionby, C.F., whom we came to know and like very well. The bombers had a day's training at Bruloose, and we were asked to bring our steel helmets, which had just been issued. So I wore mine for the first time. After the practice was over, I was asked to come and see the Brigade Bombing Officer fire off some Mills rifle-grenades, which were a novelty then. Whilst this was going on a grenade burst prematurely soon after leaving the rifle, and a piece came back and struck my helmet, cutting the lining and scratching the metal. After that I would never part with that helmet, though newer ones were issued later on. [Major F. Buckley, 7th Northumberland Fusiliers]

More traditional ways of ensuring good luck were also used:

The church was battered and broken, and there were enormous shell-pits in the churchyard and open vaults where old dead had been tumbled out of their tombs. We walked along a sunken road and then to a barn in open fields. The roof was pierced by shrapnel bullets, which let in the rain on wet days and nights, but it was cosy otherwise in the room above the ladder where the officers had their mess. There were some home-made chairs up there, and Kirchner prints of naked little ladies were tacked up to the beams, among the trench maps, and round the fireplace where logs were burning was a canvas screen to let down at night. A gramophone played merry music and gave a homelike touch to this parlour in war.

"A good spot!" I said. "Is it well hidden?"

"As safe as houses," said the captain of the battery. "Touching wood, I mean."

There were six of us sitting at a wooden plank on trestles, and at those words five young men rose with a look of fright on their faces and embraced the beam supporting the roof of the barn.

"What's happened?" I asked, not having heard the howl of a shell.

"Nothing," said the boy, "except touching wood. The captain spoke too loudly." [Philip Gibbs]

Some men felt that luck was not required; their survival was inevitable:

It was a colonel of the North Staffordshires who revealed to me the astounding belief that he was "immune" from shell-fire, and I met other men afterward with the same conviction. He had just come out of desperate fighting in the neighbourhood of Thiepval, where his battalion had suffered heavily, and at first he was rude and sullen in the hut. I gauged him as a hard Northerner, without a shred of sentiment or the flicker of any imaginative light; a stern, ruthless man. He was bitter in his speech to me because the North Staffords were never mentioned in my despatches. He believed that this was due to some personal spite - not knowing the injustice of our military censorship under the orders of the G.H.Q.

"Why the hell don't we get a word?" he asked. "Haven't we done as well as anybody, died as much?"

I promised to do what I could - which was nothing - to put the matter right, and presently he softened, and later was amazingly candid in self-revelation.

"I have mystical power," he said. "Nothing will ever hit me as long as I keep that power which comes from faith. It is a question of absolute belief in the domination of mind over matter. I go through any barrage unscathed because my will is strong enough to turn aside explosive shells and machine-gun bullets. As matter they must obey my intelligence. They are powerless to resist the mind of a man in touch with the Universal Spirit, as I am."

He spoke quietly and soberly, in a matter-of-fact way. I decided that he was mad. That was not surprising. We were all mad, in one way or another or at one time or another. It was the unusual form of madness that astonished me. I envied him his particular "kink." I wished I could cultivate it, as an aid to courage. He claimed another peculiar form of knowledge. He knew before each action, he told me, what officers and men of his would be killed in battle. He looked at a man's eyes and knew, and he claimed that he never made a mistake... He was sorry to possess that second sight, and it worried him. [Philip Gibbs]

Other men did not feel invulnerable, and indeed their 'second sight' extended to premonitions of their own wounding. One of the many who experienced this was Hugh Quigley of the 12th Royal Scots, during the Third Battle of Ypres.

Last night I had a strangely poignant dream: I was lying in hospital, trying madly to move my legs, both tied down in splints, and biting my lips to overcome pain coming from the right groin. A comfortable wound might be the outcome of the premonition. Let us hope so: then I can see again the Old Country...

[six days later] I got that comfortable wound I mentioned in my last letter: some intuition must have told me what was going to happen. The pain is not too great, although the right leg is useless just now; the doctor says it will come in time. I am expecting to be home in two days.

More unusual was the dream of Desmond Young's father, even before the war had started and his son had donned an officer's uniform:

The latest German surprise involved a curious case of precognition. A couple of years before the war, my father had been engaged in salving a dredger in the Mersey. When my mother came to lunch on board the *Ranger* with some friends, he told them that he had had so disturbing a dream that he had got out of bed and written it down. He was, he said, with others in a ditch at night when he had seen figures advancing upon them. They wore what appeared to be inverted coal scuttles on their heads and had cylinders strapped in front of them. From these protruded pipes, the nozzles of which they held in their hands. Suddenly flames burst from the ends of the pipes and a rolling cloud of fire and smoke swept over the ditch. As he flung himself down to avoid it, other men came rushing up with rifles and fixed bayonets and jumped down upon them. At that moment, when he knew that he was about to be killed, he awoke. The paper has not been preserved but, at the age of 93, my mother, with her remarkably retentive memory, still remembers exactly my father's dream and the names of the guests who were present when he told it...

As it happened I saw the fulfilment of my father's dream. The battalion was in reserve, in shallow dugouts near the Ecole, outside Ypres. It must have been almost exactly 3.20 A.M. when I turned out of my sleeping bag and went out of the dugout to have a look at the night. Far away to the eastward I saw the flames roll over the front line and knew that this was no ordinary bombardment.

Young witnessed the first use of liquid fire by the Germans against British troops, at Hooge on 30th July 1915. He took part in the unsuccessful counter-attack later in the day, when his company suffered severe casualties and he himself was wounded.

Both religious faith and superstition clearly played their part in reassuring many men, under circumstances where any prop was a boon.

10
Officers, Men and the Regiment

The relationship between the officers and men in the Great War was closer than ever before. Before 1914, there had traditionally been a gulf between the commissioned and other ranks, and it has often been remarked that the British Army was run by its NCOs. The army reflected the comparatively rigid class structure of Victorian and Edwardian society. For the families of the men, their going into the army was often viewed with dismay, whereas those of the officers frequently encouraged the taking of a commission to further a tradition of the honourable pursuit of arms. The men might have joined as a last resort, by way of escape from the slums (although there was always a minority who joined willingly, to make a career in the army); the officers were drawn from the gentry and aristocracy, usually requiring a private income to keep them in the fashion demanded by the army. And so it is quite understandable that there was at times a lack of mutual comprehension.

Under active service conditions, with officers and men mixing far more closely than in peacetime, this gulf was gradually reduced. The virtual annihilation of the old army by the end of 1914 hastened this process, for officers in the New Armies, even though they might succeed in maintaining some distance between the men and themselves, were just as much civilians in uniform as the former. But it is important to stress that the gulf never went away; the army itself had mechanisms to prevent it doing so, such as providing each officer with his own soldier-servant, allowing him other privileges such as censoring his own letters and his own supply of alcohol and other luxuries, and trying to ensure that the social background of applicants for a commission conformed to at least some of the pre-war norms.

However, the supply of public schoolboys and university graduates was not unlimited; rapid expansion and disproportionately high officer casualties led to an increasing number of men being commissioned from the ranks. This had been very rare in the pre-war army (although the CIGS from 1915 to 1918, Sir William Robertson, had joined the army in 1877 as a ranker), but it has been estimated that by 1918 about 50% of subalterns had previously served in the ranks. Nevertheless, as far as was possible, the army tried to retain the old relationship between officers and men. Part of a newly gazetted 2nd lieutenant's training was concerned with his acquiring the social graces and bearing expected of one holding the King's Commission. Another general rule was that a newly commissioned officer should not be sent to his old unit, where it might be harder for him to exercise the authority invested in him.

On a more practical level, while all ranks were under military discipline, officers were also permitted the latitude of a considerable degree of self-discipline. This comes out strongly in the manner in which access to spirits for the troops came in the form of the carefully monitored rum ration, whereas the officers' mess, even in the front line, was liberally supplied with liquor. When Capt. Dugdale's men came across a well-stocked German canteen during the battle of Cambrai, he naturally appropriated the best of the booty for the headquarters mess, while leaving the men what he deemed their just reward:

> Down one dugout we found a German battalion canteen, but a lot of our troops had got there first. It was obvious that our presence was very badly needed. The canteen was full of every kind of drink, from beer to brandy. Luckily the men who had discovered this canteen were men of my old battalion, so I asked two of them to collect all the brandy in sandbags, which we took to headquarters. We also took with us a large quantity of butter and cheese. We left the beer for the men to drink. They had earned it.

While Dugdale displayed a 'correct' distance between himself and the men, Lt. J.S.Tatham found himself in a position which would have been inconceivable in the peacetime army:

> In my bit of the trench I was with a corporal and 5 men, and the corporal said "Would you care for a turn of whist, Sir?" So we solemnly sat down and played whist, the corporal, two signallers, and myself, with a pack of very weird and dirty French playing cards, on a mackintosh sheet. Afterwards we devoured a cold pheasant which I had brought up in my haversack, and the corporal man said, "The fust time I've ever tasted this 'ere sort of bird." He was in the retreat from Mons, and is most interesting. By profession he is a postman, and knows my old Joyce Green Hospital well. He is an old 60th [i.e. King's Royal Rifle Corps] man, though, and was in service with one of the regular battalions. They are most amusing, some of these men, and keep me in roars of laughter. The lies they tell are simply colossal, but I think they really begin to believe their own stories. Anyhow they are a tremendous assistance, and are always cheerful and willing even under the worst conditions.

The proximity of his men led Lt. D.O.Barnett, serving with the Leinster Regiment, to observe them far more closely than would have been possible before the war:

> We had a route march yesterday for our health. Rather a good remark I heard when a shell knocked a dug-out flat, with a man called Kerrigan inside. From the heap of débris came a complaining voice: 'My back is broke and they have the rum spilt on us.' (As a matter of fact he was not hurt at all.)
>
> An outpost man reported the other day that he had seen some Germans go into a farm. 'Into the farm they went and the hens I could hear *roarin'.*' That made me laugh solidly for about three hours.
>
> 'There was I feelin' meself all over and askin' the Howly Mother wis I dead or alive.' This after a shell burst.
>
> The following words aroused a sub[altern] from slumber in his dug-out: 'Git up, sor.' 'Wha - what's the matter?' 'There's an officer afther seein' ye.' 'What officer?' 'Sure I don't know his name, but it's a big fat officer that he is.' This with Bullen-Smith a few feet behind!

Barnett's men were not unique in providing their officer with some amusement:

> We are sending a small proportion of N.C.O.'s and men on leave for urgent reasons. The number of moribund relations the army produced at a moment's notice was surprising. My section, foremost in this as in every other department of military science, produced the best liar, and he went on leave to-day. It was apparent from his story that the entire fate of the British Army depended on his going home to see his father, who is, I believe, confined to bed with a slight chill. He (the son) came to me for an advance of pay, but I explained to him that it would cost him little or nothing to sit by his father's bed and hold his hand. However, he thought he might want to buy some medicine or what-not. I recommended the 'Goat and Compasses' as a surgery and capitulated. [Major Francis Graham, RFA]

Frank Maxwell, like Graham a regular officer, displayed the same paternalistic care for his men's welfare:

> ...When we next get out of the line, don't be surprised if I send you home our nice little Canadian doctor to put up for ten days. He has had no leave, and can take none, as he knows nobody at home, his people being in Canada. But leave prospects are poor. One officer, N.C.O., or man every five days! I don't think it is because they mean to be stingy with leave, but because ships go home full up with wounded, or, at any rate, come out full up with drafts, so that accommodation is very limited. That, anyway, is said to be the reason. It is a sad pity that they

can't let every man go home who has not yet been on leave since he came out. There are not, alas! a great many left who came out with the battalion; but those that there are, possibly fifty to a hundred, must want to see their homes badly, poor fellows. I have sent one officer away, Warr, of whom I told you, for he left to join his Territorial battalion going to Gibraltar while on his honeymoon two years ago. The next turn comes round to-morrow, and I am sending an N.C.O. or man; but, as usual, I have managed to pinch a bit, and yesterday squeezed a pass out of the General for Perkes, also a Territorial, who has not been home for two years. He told me in conversation two days ago his mother had been ill, so next day when I went over to the brigade, she, poor lady, "was dying" (I didn't say "to see her son"), and I packed him off this morning, one immense grin, which will, if he doesn't control it, be sure to stick out of the train and get caught in a tunnel, or something dreadful.

The generally amicable relationship between officers and men of the old army also arose in the new:

> It was rather late before I was able to go and visit the company. I found my way up to the first sentry post, where a Private, with an amazed expression, leaped forward and grasped my hand, saying, "I am so glad to see you, Sir." So spontaneous a tribute, though gratifying, was a little surprising, until the lad explained that I had been reported to be dead. The fact was that the Platoon Commander, coming back to report, had found the body of a Captain lying near Company Headquarters and somewhat hastily concluding that the dead man was myself, had reported my decease to Battalion H.Q. and announced that he was carrying on. I replied in the words of Mark Twain that the report of my death was considerably exaggerated, and continued my inspection. [Major R. T. Rees]

The automatic respect for rank of old soldiers led to the occasional surprising exchange, as demonstrated by this scene in a captured German trench on the Somme, as the 5th Royal Warwicks consolidated:

> "Stand to! Stand to! They're coming again!"

> "What is it? What is it?" asks the Colonel. "Damn them! They're all alike. Half-gotten weaklings. What's this panic about?" He gives orders. "This nonsense must stop. We must have some sleep down here. Edmonds, don't let them disturb me and Captain Bickersteth. Oh Lord, what's this?" Unknowingly in the dark he has stepped on Mills, who gives a loud groan.

> "Wounded man, sir," say I, "name's Mills."

> "Well, get him out of the way, Edmonds. Are you badly hurt, Mills? I'm sorry, but they shouldn't have put you here."

> "Oh, it's awright, sir. I'm done for. Fourteen years' soldierin' and they got me this time. Wasn't you as hurt me, sir. Back seems all numb, sir. Can't get warm." He maunders on as the Colonel moves away. [Charles Edmonds]

Respect, however, had to be earned:

> I led the company on to the duckboards at 8 p.m. No sooner had I done so than the enemy opened up with a battery of field guns, the shells falling in salvos on either side of us; it was alarming. I did not know whether to stop or go on. I then remembered my brother's excellent advice: "Always keep on the move," he told me, "if you stop you will lose half the company from men falling out." I hesitated for a second or so, till I heard a voice from the darkness say: "- officer's got the wind up." This decided me.
>
> I went on, the company trailing behind me. I was walking faster to get out of the shell fire; if I had been alone I should have run. [Capt. G. Dugdale]

Capt. Dugdale related the sort of dilemma faced by any inexperienced officer. For them, an important prop could be the steadying effect and example of a reliable NCO:

> At this point we ran into machine-gun fire, the most deadly barrage of all. There was nothing for it but to take cover in the surrounding shell-holes, of which there was a plentiful supply. In my shell-hole the bullets were striking the rear slope; so I crouched against the forward slope as low as possible, being a great coward where machine-gun bullets are concerned. After burrowing in the mud for some time I lifted my head a little and shouted to the Sergt.-Major to ask how he was getting on.
>
> "All right, Sir," came in gruff tones from immediately above my head! With a start I looked up, and there was old Pasquill standing in the open, and contemplatively smoking his pipe. "I think it'll be over in a minute, Sir," he added, as though we were discussing a shower of rain. [Major R.T.Rees]

Most men were happy to be led by and place their faith in an officer (their training having discouraged them from using their own initiative). Lt. H.M.Butterworth's sergeant, a regular whom he regarded highly, gave him a valuable lesson in this:

> No digging or wiring party ever goes without an officer, that is the way to get the men along. If one takes out a party of men somewhere they don't know - in the open probably - to dig, they'll go like lambs as long as they've got an officer with them. The curious thing is that in civilian

life they've probably cursed us as plutocrats, out here they fairly look to us. The other night some time ago, I had some men and had to get somewhere I'd never been to before in —; as a matter of fact it wasn't difficult and we had ample directions, so before we started I was told to send the men with a sergeant. Said the sergeant to me, 'I wish you were coming sir, I don't know the way.' I said, 'My dear man, nor do I.' To which he made this astounding reply, 'Very likely not, sir, but the men will think you do and they know I don't!'

An integral part of an officer's duties was the maintenance of discipline:

At 11 I turned out and inspected the guards. One of the sergeants in charge was dhrunk! Took the necessary steps, put him under arrest, went and got another sergeant to take charge, &c. It was a long but most amusing business, though it was dark as a coalhole and raining cats and dogs. This morning (Easter Sunday) I inspected the guards again, also the canteen and cookhouse. Visited the soldiers-under-arrest, as they are called in Army Orders, and asked for complaints. Private Sherry wanted clean under-clothes! Of course I knew he'd sold them for drink, so I told him to try the pawnbrokers. Loud cheers from the guard and the other prisoners. Collapse of Private Sherry...

[later] This morning I've been giving evidence in the case of Sergt.— charged with being drunk in charge of the quarter guard.

'Lance-Corporal Reilly.'
'Sirr! At elivin fhurty-foive on the nhoight of te t'ird of April I was passin' by the gyardroom an' te orderly officer called me up to look at the sergint. He was dhrunk.
'Corporal Keenan.'
'Sirr! At twilve o'clock on te noight of te t'ird of April, as I was afther postin' te sintries, Oi saw te orderly officer had the gyard turned out. Oi siz, 'Gyard all pres'nt 'n c'rect, sirr.' Siz 'e, 'An fwere's t' sergint?' 'Inside he is, 'siz I, and wid that in Oi wint and there he was lyin' on the bed of him. 'Git up,' siz I, 'sergint; te orderly officer is afther turnin' out the gyard on yez.' Thin te officer came in. 'Oi have the gyard turned out,' siz he, and wid that he shook the sergint and rolled him off the bed. He got up and wint to the door.'
'Was he drunk?'
'He was dazed, sirr, like as afther been woke up out of the sleep.'

And so on. [D.O. Barnett]

Lt. Barnett could afford to be relatively flippant over what was a comparatively unimportant breach of discipline. But for the serious offence of desertion, the death penalty could be imposed. Philip Gibbs encountered an officer upon whose lack of sympathy he remarked:

Going up to Kemmel one day I had to wait in battalion headquarters for
the officer I had gone to see. He was attending a court martial. Presently
he came into the wooden hut, with a flushed face.

"Sorry I had to keep you," he said. "To-morrow there will be one swine
less in the world."
"A death sentence?"

He nodded.

"A damned coward. Said he didn't mind rifle-fire, but couldn't stand
shells. Admitted he left his post. He doesn't mind rifle-fire!... Well,
to-morrow morning -"

The officer laughed grimly, and then listened for a second.

There were some heavy crumps falling over Kemmel Hill, rather close, it
seemed, to our wooden hut.

"Damn those German gunners!" said the officer.
"Why can't they give us a little peace?"

He turned to his papers, but several times while I talked with him he
jerked his head up and listened to a heavy crash.

On the way back I saw a man on foot, walking in front of a mounted
man, past the old hill of the Scherpenberg, toward the village of Locre.
There was something in the way he walked, in his attitude - the head
hunched forward a little, and his arms behind his back - which made me
turn to look at him. He was manacled, and tied by a rope to the
mounted man. I caught one glimpse of his face, and then turned away,
cold and sick. There was doom written on his face, and in his eyes a
captured look. He was walking to his wall.

This attitude was not shared by all officers; Frank Maxwell took a far
less vengeful view:

Had two men up just now for absence without leave, which I am afraid
means desertion and a miserable shooting thereafter. They failed to
march with us as we left our training ground to come up to the battle
area, and a week later "found" themselves at Boulogne. Fairly busy
marching for men who had lost their way, and fairly straight going for
home. Poor devils, I suppose it was cold feet, and they are going to lose
their lives dishonourably now, instead of taking the chance of doing so
honourably a week ago. Another man I had put under arrest for
challenging about the one German who was on the front I have been
jawing about. The man belonged to what is called a "blocking" party, *i.e.*
was blocking passage down the same jolly trench which the General
wanted me to reconnoitre up. Down came a German unarmed and

alone, possibly to see some pal of his among the gruesome slain still lying about in the vicinity (killed by our artillery fire on the 1st). "Halt, who goes there?" shouts our silly idiot; on which Fritz, of course, turns and hooks it round a corner of the very tortuous trench. No one thought this in the least odd behaviour, only, in fact, wondered why I had him arrested when I heard of his performance; nor a long battalion order, informing the regiment that the King pays us to kill Germans, not to warn them to clear out or they will get hurt. A new aspect, which I trust the regiment will appreciate. Anyway, the next man gets court-martialled, so the sooner he does appreciate it the better...

Disciplinary action could be brought about by less serious circumstances and take an unusual form:

I should mention that as a result of his only fault - his sleeping-in habits - Gardiner got into trouble too. Admittedly there were times when he had to do a fair amount of out-of-door night-work, but, as I told him more than once, he was only annoying the Colonel by trying to take advantage of it. I also pointed out that the Colonel, though a bachelor, was well aware no doctor gets called to a confinement every night.

In the end the Colonel got more than annoyed. One morning a quarter of an hour after the breakfast table should have been cleared and Gardiner had not appeared, I saw him writing away in that special book, and when he had finished he tore off the top sheet and handed it to me. "Get this delivered at once," he ordered.

This is what he had written, and I am not relying on memory because I liked his letter so much that I made, kept, and still have, a copy of it:

CONFIDENTIAL

90 BRIGADE
R.G.A.

Lieut. A.N. Gardiner

22/634

You are to get up at such an hour in the morning as to ensure finishing your breakfast not later than 8.50 AM. You are to start your day's work not later than 9.0 AM.

Should you at any time fail to obey this order you are to report in writing to the Adjutant 90 Brigade R.G.A. giving the reasons for doing so.

A.H. THORP Lt. Col. R.G.A.
O.C. 90 Brigade R.G.A.

30.5.18.

No report was received by the Adjutant because Gardiner did not fail again, and it could well be that the Colonel was a better psychologist than any of us knew. [Lt. A.F.Behrend, adjutant, 90th Bde. RGA].

Lt. Gardiner, it seems, heeded the strictures of his CO when they were finally put into writing. But until this happened, he had taken advantage of the leeway in terms of discipline permitted between officers. Lt. Graham and his fellows clearly enjoyed - in both senses of the word - a degree of latitude in their relationship with their CO:

> The Colonel recently, by way of giving observing officers something to do, called for tactical reports at 11.30 a.m. and 4.30 p.m. Finding that observers resisted the temptation to use their brains by simply 'phoning in 'nothing to report', he added a rider to the effect that no detail was too trivial to be noted. This spurred us to action and emulation. One of us reported that 'the Germans were wearing grey uniforms with soft hats, and were digging in their trenches'. Another, of an inventive turn of mind, reported that 'the Germans were wearing grey-green uniforms, that they had a nice bailing tin with a long handle, and that they had red blankets in dug-outs'. I was not going to be out-done by that, so when it came to my turn I reported that 'the Germans had a clean change of under-linen in the dug-outs, and that they wear pink pyjamas at night'. This report was not forwarded to the Colonel.

It was not only his colonel who came between Graham and what he saw as the best way of carrying out his duties. Up to about May 1915, shortage of troops led to the cavalry being employed in a dismounted role:

> I am glad to say we have come to an end of the cavalry in front of us. This is no place for amateurs, and life was too exciting altogether with them about. I think I told you about their attempt to shoot our observer. They were highly suspicious, too, of telephone wires, and it was no rare thing to find our wires cut in about a dozen places. If they found we were observing from the top story of a house, they would come up to have a look; poke their fingers through the roof, put their heads out of the observing hole, and generally behave in a manner calculated to endear them to the heart of the poor devil of an observer, whose only chance lay in not being spotted by the Germans. At last, in desperation, we made out a large placard, and pinned it up in a prominent place downstairs. The proclamation was to this effect - 'The artillery observers do not want *you* upstairs.'

The artillery themselves, however, were not exempt from the wrath of others. In August 1916, on the Somme, Lt. Col. Maxwell found it difficult to raise the artillery support he required:

> My scheme also drew in the gunners, whom I "had" all right. What, quite naturally, they like is to go to bed snug and quietly, and only be ready to run out if we, miles away, send up S.O.S. messages, to say we are being heavily attacked, on which they get to work as quick as maybe. The latter expression of time can be wonderfully quick, if they

have had any indication or warning beforehand; otherwise, I think, you might be dead and gone for all the assistance they could give you. They don't, again quite naturally, see why *I* should call on them to strafe the gentleman over the way, just because *I* think it a good thing. And I haven't the right to order or ask them to do so. If, however, I am being shelled heavily by the enemy, then I may call for retaliation, which is supposed to be given. The gunners, however, had heard of my troublesome ideas on the subject, and didn't mean to play up to it if they could, or dared. When, therefore, my first little missiles hustled through the air, and shortly after what I thought was a German reply (it wasn't in actual fact till later) came back, I called up the liaison officer hard by and told him the enemy were shying things at me, and I wanted retaliation badly. The sleepy fellow played up all right, or tried to - I stood by, so he hadn't much choice - and put the message back by telephone as best he could to his major. Then apparently began a long argument, the latter evidently asking if I hadn't begun first, and so on. Just about then a real fizzer came along, burst in the alley-way outside, and I have no doubt shook the signal officer far worse than it did anything outside (140 lbs. weight of high explosive does make things fairly hum inside these so-called dug-outs, with no windows in them), and conversation became more animated.

"Why, they've just landed a d—d great sausage on to Battalion H.Q., Major." More chat, so I went away to watch things for a bit, then returned. "Well, when are the batteries going to fire?" I asked. "Doesn't your jolly old Major realise that we are being frightfully punished while he is jawing to you? I think it's twenty-five minutes since I suggested that an emergency had arisen." "My Major's a bit sticky, I'm afraid," was the reply. "Why?" "Don't like turning the battery out of bed, I expect, sir." "Oh, that is the game, is it," said O.C. 12th Middlesex [i.e. Maxwell]. "I'll take my battalion out of these sweet trenches, then, and take it back to bed in billets somewhere nice and cosy." On which I left him, to digest the horrid sarcasm as best he might.

It worked out all right, and the "Major" evidently began to think he might get into trouble if he didn't comply (as a matter of fact, I am much more likely to), and I got the guns, also a battery of bigger stuff. That was all I wanted; but they did better, and taking heart of grace, let off another lot, one and a half hours later, when my next packet flew over to the Germans and drew his angry reply.

Relations between arms of the army and units within them were generally more cordial than the above might suggest, even among élite regiments. Animosity generally did not go further than healthy rivalry.

In the village we met a company of Infantry going towards the trenches. "Who are you?" shouts the officer in command. "Rifle Brigade; who are you?" I shout in reply. "Oh, -er, Coldstream Guards," comes the answer in an altered tone. As the two bodies of troops pass each other one of my riflemen remarks chattily to the man next to him "What funny breeches those Guards officers wear, don't they?" at which there is a subdued laugh. This meeting recalled another incident connected with this famous regiment. One morning back in the summer, while at "rest," I was marching my company along a by-road when we met a company of the Coldstream Guards. I saw the Guardsmen come smartly to the "slope" in response to a command, and at once brought my men to the "trail," as an exchange of compliments was indicated. I exchanged a salute with their company commander, and at the same time we both gave "eyes left" as the two companies passed each other. It was then that our quick hundred-and-forty paces to the minute quite threw the tall Guardsmen out of their dignified stride, and I heard several muttered uncomplimentary remarks concerning our quick step and comparative lack of inches! [Capt. H. Raymond Smith, 11th Rifle Brigade]

Regulars traditionally did not rate the Territorial Force very highly, but under the circumstances of the Great War, when other regulars very soon came to be in short supply, and when they had perforce to learn to work alongside Territorials, the traditional dismissiveness evaporated:

Just behind us were two battalions of Regulars. They were very friendly, and I had two cups of tea with a party of them in a sort of "Maiden's Bower" of leafy branches in the heart of the wood. We found we had been sent up for a special purpose. Another battalion, pals of ours, was to try and capture a small piece of trench, which had been won and lost again on the 16th. We were to support, and if the trench were taken, to relieve them and hold on...

My hosts at tea told me that the attacking battalion had particularly requested that we might support them. It was a compliment which we might willingly have dispensed with, but we seem to have gained a reputation as "stickers", and this is one of its penalties. As a matter of fact, we get on very well with the Regulars. They are jolly good chaps. When we take over from another battalion of the division, we often find a message for us nailed up in the dugouts, with drawings of the badges of the two regiments above it.

It is interesting to note the condescension of Clapham, a Territorial, to the men of the New Army, once he regarded himself as an 'old soldier'. In August 1915:

We were relieved by a North Country battalion of Kitchener's New Army - the first I have seen. They were rather quaint birds. They talked as if the War would be over in no time, now that they were out, but as soon as they got into the trench, a lot of them jumped on the fire-step and started firing at our own line, just in front. We had to pull some of them down.

During the course of the war, the fighting qualities of a unit were more important in determining its status than the origin as a regular, Territorial or New Army formation. The Scots enjoyed a high reputation in the eyes of Guy Chapman's RSM:

> He had a number of personal gods, in particular the 2nd Argyles, though he was from the Scottish Rifles himself. His account of that battalion at Loos was epic. 'Sirr,' he would say, 'you never saw men fight like it before, and you never will again. They went over like madmen, and after they were broken, men would come back to us - we had taken over their line - and say, "Ha'e ye a bomb, Jock?" and go in again. One private ran across No-Man's-Land with an apron full of bombs, drew the pin of one, slung the whole lot into the trench and jumped in on top of them. Another stopped to pick up a wounded officer. As he did so, he shook his fist at the enemy and a bullet came through his elbow. He brought his officer in, mortally wounded. He stood, with his own wound undressed, so that the dying man could grip his ankles as long as he was conscious. Then he went back to the German trenches with a pocket full of bombs, drawing the safety pins with his teeth and throwing with his unwounded arm, until he was killed.'

Morale both sustained and was sustained by the achievements of a unit in battle. Another bulwark of morale was loyalty first to the battalion, then to the regiment and in conjunction with these, to the division in which the battalion was included:

> I shall never forget that afternoon in Ypres, when every officer and man we met asked us how our division did in the attack. I was proud of it, too, in some kind of perverse delight, not keen on fighting, yet glad to be in it. Even then, among all that sordid mass of ruins we call Ypres, memory and recollection have given a romantic aspect, as some monument worthy of valour and enshrined in our deeds, where our bravest fought to the last and never yielded. [Hugh Quigley, 12th Royal Scots, 9th (Scottish) Division]

All armies, to be effective, rely on discipline and loyalty. It is testimony to the achievement of those who created and the men who composed the largest army Britain has ever had, that those qualities were maintained as strongly as they were on the Western Front.

11

The Front Line Soldier and the Staff

It is an integral part of Great War mythology that 'The Staff' (including all command functions above battalion level) had no conception of the reality of the front line. This is epitomised by a commonly repeated, perhaps apocryphal tale. Legend has it that Haig's chief of staff in 1917, Sir Launcelot Kiggell, paid his first visit to the battlefield of Third Ypres towards the end of the offensive. As he was driven through the desolate swamp he became noticeably and increasingly emotional, and finally uttered through his tears 'Good God - did we really send men to fight in that?'

It should not be inferred from this that officers of the staff were not fully committed to their very demanding job.

Created almost from scratch, the administration and organisation of some two million men, with additional pressure during active operations inevitably took their toll. Two tragic stories highlight the immense strain that could be involved. It appears that fatigue fatally weakened the constitution of Brigadier-General E.W.Cox, Haig's chief of intelligence from January 1918. Howard Spring, later a noted novelist, served as a clerk at GHQ and remembered how Cox worked like a man possessed during the German offensive in the Spring of 1918: 'Chain smoking cigarettes during day and night, allowing himself little time to eat and no time to rest, he wore his body to a shadow. The time came when the clouds lifted, the tension relaxed, the miracle of salvation intervened. General Cox said he would go for a bathe. His chauffeur drove him to Berck Plage, and the general went down to the sea alone. No one saw the manner of his end. The body was recovered from the sea some time later.' Another tragic senior staff officer at GHQ took his own life when some important documents went missing from his care in the aftermath of the March 1918 offensive.

But notwithstanding this, the experiences of the staff - at divisional level and above, comfortably billeted miles behind the line - were vastly different to those of the front line soldier, and the latter was always suspicious of those perceived not to be taking their share of the burden of fighting and whose presence in the fighting area was mostly conspicuous for its rarity.

This perception was reinforced by the way in which the awards system appeared to operate to the greater benefit of 'desk-bound warriors,' as Desmond Young forcibly described:

> ...when a final D.S.O. came up 'with the rations' just after the Armistice and he [Young's CO] asked me (quite improperly) whether I wanted it, I at least had the grace to say that it ought to go to one of the company commanders, three of whom had been with the battalion from the beginning and had borne the burden and heat of the day. Colonel Feilding was pleased with me. But neither he nor I was much amused when, in face of an order that the last awards should be conferred only for action in face of the enemy, a D.S.O. was given to a member of the Divisional 'Q' staff. Kid Kennedy cynically remarked that the citation must be for 'riding through Contay by day when the enemy were bombing it at night'.

> Can men worry about such trivialities in the setting of a bloody war? The answer, again in Colonel Feilding's words, is that 'a ribbon is the only prize in war for the ordinary soldier. It is the outward visible sign, the ocular proof, to bring home to his people, that he has done well: and, say what you may, a man's prowess, when the war is over, will be assessed by the number of his ribbons... Personally, I often wish that this form of reward did not exist, seeing that ribbons must be distributed by men, not gods. If they were given by God, how many an iridescent breast would cease to sparkle - and the contrary!' Because decorations - and particularly foreign decorations - were quite shamelessly intercepted by the staff; because they were not allowed to be allotted by battalion and brigade commanders, who alone knew the facts, but had to be extracted like back teeth from Higher Authority; because everything depended on the recommendations being written up in a flamboyant and often fanciful style which does not come naturally to the good frontline commander, the vexed question of 'honours and awards' so soured relations between the fighting troops and the staff that it cannot be omitted from any honest recollections of World War I.

Anthony Eden, who had seen heavy fighting all through the Battle of the Somme, recorded in his memoirs his concern regarding the distance of the staff:

> An additional complication in the October fighting was the delay in communication with brigade headquarters which, as Foljambe commented, was too far behind the line. Wires having been repeatedly cut by shell-fire, despite all that our signallers could do, the only sure means of contact was by runner, but our strength in runners was limited and reduced by casualties. Yet it was imperative to keep in touch also with companies and neighbouring battalions. One can only suppose that this distant stationing of headquarters was due to an error of judgment compounded by the worsening weather, which further stretched the

journey for our runners. In any event, during the ten days of our approach march and the battle, I never saw an officer from brigade headquarters except the junior who had strayed into our lines.

Nor did we see anyone from divisional headquarters, which was less surprising. This did not go unnoticed by the riflemen. Some weeks later two of them were on local leave walking across a square in a town behind the Ypres Salient, when the divisional commander and his staff rode glittering by. The general stopped to speak to our men and asked them which battalion of the regiment they were serving with. When they told him he added, 'Good, and were you with me on the Somme?' to which one of them replied, 'We did not see you there, sir.' A good rifleman's story maybe, but it expressed the inner thoughts of many.

Desmond Young, who had seen service in the infantry in the Ypres Salient in 1915, returned to the front in a staff capacity in 1917, after recovering from wounds. Attached to IV Corps HQ, he was surprised to discover that no one from the Corps staff had entertained the notion of visiting the field of the battle they were directing:

We arrived in France just as the first major tank attack was launched, with electrifying success, at Cambrai. Intercepted at IVth Corps Headquarters, which was in nominal control of the battle, I was set to filing signals on spikes in the 'G' Office. Because there was little to do and this seemed a new-model battle that no student of war ought to miss, I asked the G I [i.e. GSO1] whether I might borrow a staff car and go up the line.

Everyone in 'G' Office was much too busy to have any such urge. In those days it was no part of the duty of a corps staff to see what was happening on the spot. The professional staff officer of such a formation was fully occupied with orders and messages. For him nothing was actual until it was on paper, until the flags had been correctly placed (according to the latest information) on the wall map. Though it would have been perfectly easy for the Corps Commander himself or his B.G.G.S. to have flown over the whole battlefield and returned to Villers-au-Flos within an hour, no member of this particular staff had, so far as I know, been forward since the attack started. It had simply not occurred to them.

The G I was, however, a kindly man and indulged my eccentricity. In a Crossley car borrowed from the corps pool I set out - to see a battle as it ought to be seen, spread out before one's eyes, with every landmark easily identifiable, in fine, sunny weather and in almost complete safety. For there was now a lull. The Germans, their supposedly impregnable Hindenberg [sic] Line broken by the tanks within a few hours, were getting their guns back and, as we were to discover, quickly regrouping. On our side, no one had taken the decision to put in the Cavalry Corps, which had been waiting for two years for just such an opportunity as this. There were no other reserves to take advantage of it...

By now I had gone far beyond the point where the driver felt justified in taking a corps car and was rambling about on foot. Presently it occurred to me that I was not in fact a sight-seer and ought to do something to justify my journey. In front, on rising ground, rose the dark mass of Bourlon Wood. It was apparently unoccupied by either side, though the Germans, with their quick eye for country, had realized that it was the key to the situation, and were beginning to infiltrate back into it. Should I not find out what was happening? It would mean a long walk across open country.

At Guards Brigade Headquarters in Havrincourt village, the Brigade Major (Oliver Lyttleton, I fancy, now Lord Chandos), with typical Guards politeness, obligingly lent me a large white horse. On this conspicuous animal I made my way forward to the Brigade Headquarters of Brigadier-General 'Boy' Bradford, who was holding the line. This prodigy, aged twenty-four and already wearing the ribbons of the Victoria Cross, the D.S.O. and the M.C., was not polite when he caught sight of my corps armband, but mellowed when I explained that I was only an attached officer. 'About time we saw someone from corps,' he remarked. 'Now get back as quickly as you can and tell them that with one fresh battalion I can occupy and hold Bourlon Wood. If I don't get it soon the Germans will be back there.'

Feeling that I was carrying the good news to Ghent, I set off at a canter on my white horse for Guards Brigade H.Q. Having handed him in, I ran as fast as I could in field boots to the place where I had left the car. By the time we had fought our way back through the stream of transport to Villers-au-Flos it was already late evening. With suppressed excitement I hurried into the 'G' Office to give Bradford's message to the G I. 'I'm afraid the B.G.G.S. has just gone in to dinner,' he said. 'But I'll see if you can see him immediately afterwards.'

This I did and tried to impress him with the urgency of the case. He was polite and friendly and said that he would take action at once. The orders were in fact issued from the 'G' Office quite early the following morning. By the time they had percolated down through Division, Bourlon Wood - and the battle - were lost.

Clearly, then the lack of proximity of the Staff to the front line left much to be desired. But it also meant that there were occasions when the troops in the front line made convenient arrangements with the Germans to their mutual advantage. Generally these occurred when conditions were such that the trenches on both sides were uninhabitable, or when conditions dictated a mutual suspension of hostilities. Examples would be after a battle when both sides needed to collect their wounded, or (as in the following quotation) to avoid needless bloodshed. The official attitude to such unofficial truces was actively to discourage them, since it was considered vital to dominate No-Man's-Land in order to discourage German raids and lower their morale, while keeping that of the British troops high. The dismay produced by such intervention comes out strongly in this letter written by Capt. H. Dundas of the 1st Battalion Scots Guards on 24 January 1917. The wintry conditions, a sharp frost and the subsequent thaw having made the trenches fall in, it was only possible to move about above ground:

> Up till two days ago a reign of absolute quiet had prevailed. Perfect peace. Every one walked about on both sides. There are no trenches: merely a series of 'islands,' and no communication trenches. The other side are in a similar position, except that their islands are on the top of a ridge and we can't see anything behind. They, of course, can sweep all our islands and the approaches to them, so quiet was essential if any work was to be done, or indeed if any existence was to be continued. So peace reigned. People waved bottles at each other across No Man's Land - wha' a bond is Johnny Dewar even between enemies - and life was very pleasant. We used to walk round inspecting the islands on the top all the time with the German thirty yards away.
>
> But gradually the Divisional Staff decided that this state of affairs must cease. This being so, the Brigadier decided that the Germans must be warned. Accordingly Brodie and I, about seven in the morning, sallied out of our posts across the Boches' lines. Brodie is an excellent German scholar, so we were well equipped - he with speech and I with papers inscribed with a message to the effect that 'after dawn on the 19th all Germans exposing themselves would be shot' (printed in English usefully enough). We stayed on their wire shouting for an 'Offizier.' At last, after much excitement, a small man looking like Charlie Chaplin appeared, with whom Brodie chatted for about twenty minutes, saying how sorry we were that this state of affairs must cease - telling them that all would be well if there were only head-keeping-down by both sides. And so away - not unamusing.

However, staff intervention often comprised frustratingly irrelevant communications arriving at times when the recipients had far more important matters to attend to. Guy Chapman recalled one such episode:

> In the early afternoon the shelling grew lighter. About three o'clock a runner from brigade came staggering in. I tore open the brown envelope, which a glance assured me did not contain relief orders. 'On visiting your horselines today, I found that the grease-traps were not in good condition. For information and necessary action, please. A.B. Area

Sanitary Officer.' It was too grim and too old-fashioned a jest. The brigade runner was thirstily swallowing a mug of tea. 'What time did you start?' I asked him. 'Ten o'clock, sir. I've had to lie up several times on the way.' He had spent five hours crossing two miles of country to carry this triviality.

And again, Captain Philip Berliner of the 2/7th Battalion London Regiment, received the following message at Poelcapelle while being bombarded:

> Please send artificial teeth of 351688 Pte BLOUNT C.L. to this station. D Coy. Passed to you for necessary action please! Captain & Adj., 2/7 LONDON R.

Vaguely worded orders could also be a source of irritation:

> On 6 October we had to 'stand to' at midnight, while our artillery sent over gas from cylinders. These were fired from trench mortars from the front line, and a thousand in all were shot over to the Germans. We had to be prepared in case there was any retaliation, but after some time, as nothing happened, we received orders to 'stand down'.
>
> There was a brilliant exhibition of red tape that night. At 1am we had to put our watches back to twelve midnight to conform with the provision of the Daylight Saving Act. Divisional orders also directed that we should 'stand to' for a gas stunt from 12pm to 1am. We 'stood to' for the required hour, and then thought that we had finished, but no, back went our watches to 12pm and so we had to obey Divisional orders again and do another hour's 'stand to'. [A.S.Dolden]

This apparent unwillingness or inability of staff officers to alter their ideas to changing conditions is futher emphasized - and with more far-reaching effects - by Major R.T.Rees' account of his attempt to change the plan for a raid:

> When the appointed day at last arrived, I noticed in the morning, with great misgiving, that some of our guns were registering on their targets for the evening, and, with still more misgiving, that the enemy replied by registering apparently *on his own front line*. When the Chief Staff Officer of the Division appeared before lunch to ask how things were going, I earnestly called his attention to the significance of these facts. It seemed to me to be obvious, firstly, that the German front line was unoccupied, and, secondly, that when our barrage began, they would put a barrage on their own front line, and we should have to walk right through it. Therefore, since we knew there was very little wire, I requested to be allowed to make the attack without any artillery support at all.

If my request had been made a year later, when even the High Command had realised the futility of advertising an attack and the enormous advantage of surprise, it would certainly have been granted, and the raid would have been a success. At that time, however, such views seemed unorthodox. At any rate very unlikely that enough of us would reach the tunnel to be able to bring back prisoners. However, there was nothing to be done about it except to impress on my officers that the men must not guess our opinion.

Even during the heavy fighting and confusion of the great German Spring Offensive of 1918, Arthur Behrend (Adjutant of a heavy artillery brigade) found that the attitude at Corps HQ markedly lacked the urgency of his own:

I went up the hill to see the Staff Captain about rations and ammunition supply.

As I climbed up the broad duckboard path which was neatly covered with strips of rabbit-wire to prevent you from slipping, I felt even more like a tramp than usual. The lawn was as trim as ever; the garden, fringed with its decorous row of huts, had never looked in better shape. In the middle of the lawn stood the trophy, a German pip-squeak resplendent in its new coat of paint. Above it on a line dangled a row of Magpies shot by the Reconnaissance Officer with the Brigade Major's gun. Sleek and gentlemanly clerks, carrying papers and what not, hurried in and out of the offices. Even the huts with their tarred and sanded roofs, daintily camouflaged ends, and sedate notice boards eyed me askance. I entered a hut labelled AMMUNITION OFFICER where friend Smithers told me - um, yes - that 6-inch ammunition was very scarce owing to the large amounts which had been dumped on the reserve positions and - er - handed over to the enemy. However there were a few thousand rounds lying at Puisieux; we could draw from these if we liked - um, yes - but they weren't likely to be in very good condition because they had been salved nearly a year ago from the Somme. Failing that we would have to send our lorries fifteen miles back to the railhead at Acheux, where ammunition was being sent up as fast as possible; it wasn't considered safe to bring trains any closer to the line - um, yes - under present conditions.

I visited the Staff Captain next. Rations were to be drawn from the railhead at Achiet-le-Grand, which was being evacuated. Everyone could take as much as was wanted, he said, and indents were no longer required.

Then I went into the Counter-battery office, where you could always rely on hearing the very latest news. A clerk was packing a typewriter in the outer room and looked at me in surprise when I asked if anyone else was in. 'Oh no, sir, it's dinner time,' he said. 'They're all in the mess having dinner.'

For the most part, the troops' contact with the staff and senior officers was rare. The feeling of alienation from them left a deep impression on one Machine Gun Corps NCO, who wrote:

> In later years I have often been asked what the trenches were like and how the High Command obtained the vital information from the front on which to base their fateful decisions.
>
> I have always wondered this myself. I do remember my company Commander and his Warrant Officer coming round, also a frightened cinema operator, who put his camera over the top of a communication trench, took a brief exposure and then scuttled away for dear life, but I cannot recall ever seeing a senior officer, much less a general, in any part of the line which I was occupying. Communications were appalling and chiefly made by the two-footed runners - heroes every one. [Anonymous NCO, 168 MG Company]

To some soldiers, the Commander-in-Chief was so remote a figure that they failed to recognise him even when they encountered him in person, but were forthright in their views when told who he was:

> I saw him later, during the battle of Loos, after its ghastly failure. He was riding a white horse in the villages of Heuchin and Houdain, through which lightly wounded Scots of the 1st and 15th Divisions were making their way back. He leaned over his saddle, questioning the men and thanking them for their gallantry. I thought he looked grayer and older than when he had addressed us.
>
> "Who mun that old geezer be, Jock?" asked a Highlander when he had passed.
>
> "I dinna Ken," said the other Scot. "An' I dinna care."
> "It's the Commander-in-Chief," I said. "Sir John French."'
>
> "Eh?" said the younger man, of the 8th Gordons. He did not seem thrilled by the knowledge I had given him, but turned his head and stared after the figure on the white horse. Then he said: "Well, he's made a mess o' the battle. We could 've held Hill 70 against all the di'els o' hell if there had bin supports behind us."
>
> "Ay," said his comrade, "an there's few o' the laddies 'll come back fra Cité St.-Auguste." [Philip Gibbs]

It should not be inferred that no staff officer ever visited the front line, or that all senior officers were wholly out of touch. After some heavy fighting in the Ypres Salient, the 2nd Leinsters were visited in their front line:

> The Brig. General came round to inspect the line with the C.O. The Brigadier said the Battalion had done splendidly, and that the place was thoroughly consolidated: he, however, objected to a German's leg which was protruding out of parapet, and I was told to have it buried forthwith by the C.O. I called Finnegan, and told him to remove the offending limb. As it would have meant pulling down the whole parapet to bury it, he took up a shovel and slashed at it with the sharp edge of the tool. After some hard bangs, he managed to sever the limb. I had turned away and was standing in the next fire bay, when I overheard Finnegan remarking to another man: "And what the bloody hell will I hang me equipment on now?" [Capt. F.C.Hitchcock, 2nd Leinsters]

These visits could introduce a degree of confusion among those not accustomed to dealing with such dignitaries:

> It was of Gen. Hunter Weston that the story was told about the drunken soldier put onto a stretcher and covered with a blanket, to get him out of the way when the army commander[1] made a visit to the lines.
>
> "What's this?" said the general.
> "Casualty, sir," said the quaking platoon commander.
> "Not bad, I hope?"
> "Dead, sir," said the subaltern. He meant dead drunk.
> The general drew himself up, and said, in his dramatic way, "The army commander salutes the honoured dead!"
>
> And the drunken private put his head from under the blanket and asked, "What's the old geezer a-sayin' of?"
>
> That story may have been invented in a battalion mess, but it went through the army affixed to the name of Hunter Weston, and seemed to fit him. [Philip Gibbs]

A revealing example of the gulf between the viewpoints of senior regular officers and junior temporary officers was related by then Lt. H.Raymond Smith of 11th (Service) Battalion the Rifle Brigade:

> I met O— in the firing trench and we proceeded to reconnoitre the position together. We had not gone far when we met a tall figure

---

[1]   In fact, Lt. Gen. Sir Aylmer Hunter-Weston never rose higher than the command of a corps.

wearing red and gold tabs, and a red band round his brass bound cap (not steel helmet) - it was our Brigadier. We stopped and saluted, and he replied with a pleasant smile and asked our names and which was the senior. Actually, our commissions dated from the same day, but I suppose I had longer experience in the ranks, and the Brigadier told me to accompany him round the line. All went well at first until he noticed a small piece of bacon lying on the floor of the trench near the entrance to a dug-out and commented on it somewhat harshly.

Then he got up on the fire step and I stood beside him, looking through the long grass in front. "Are you happy here?" he asked suddenly. I was rather surprised at the question, but replied "Yes, thank you, sir; as happy as one can expect to be under these circumstances." "I don't mean that," he shouted, "Look at all this long grass; it's a perfect death-trap; it will have to be cut to give you a field of vision." He walked on along the trench and I followed. Then we came across a very dirty rifle, and at the sight of this the Brigadier became really angry, and after informing me he would speak to our Colonel about it, he went on into "A" Company's part of the line. Some time later an officer from "A" Company came along and I asked him if he had seen the Brigadier. "Have I hell!" was his reply, and from what he told me causes for complaint had been found there also. I quite expected some trouble would be made at headquarters but, strangely enough, we heard no more about it.

During the Battle of the Somme, Stuart Cloete was also confronted by his brigadier in the front line:

We had what is called a fighting brigadier. His brigade was always ready for action. He was much decorated and later knighted. At one time he put me under arrest and nearly had me court-martialled. He came up the line after an attack. We had fought hard and I had mounted my sentries, checked my wire and posted my Lewis guns, and he wanted me to turn out my men to inspect their rifles. I refused. He said I was under arrest. At that time I was so tired that I did not care. We had been in action for two days, had taken all our objectives and were waiting to be relieved when he turned up. The men were lying exhausted in all sorts of positions on the firestep and floor of the trench. Only the sentries were alert.

I said: 'The men are done, sir. There are none in dugouts. They can stand-to in a minute. I've inspected their rifles. Everything is in order, sir.'
'Do you refuse?' he said.

'No, sir. Not if you will give me the order in writing.' Every officer is entitled to ask for an order in writing if he does not like the sound of it. To wake the men after what they had already been through would impair their efficiency. We had had a lot of casualties and were pretty thin on the ground.

'Consider yourself under arrest,' he said.

I said: 'Yes, sir.'

'By God, I'll have you court-martialled,' he said.'The men are filthy, unshaven - filthy.'

I said: 'We've lost a lot of men. We've been fighting two days, and if the men are dirty their rifles and loaded and clean. They are ready for action, sir.'

The men in the trenches generally kept an old sock over their rifle-bolts to keep them clean. He had even taken exception to this.

He said nothing more but went off. One thing about him was his guts. He was the only general I ever saw in the line. Nor did I ever see a staff officer. The front line was too dangerous and too dirty.

Nothwithstanding the complaints about their absence, the presence of 'brass hats' in the front line was not always regarded as an unalloyed asset:

One advantage I soon perceived in the front line was the absence of interference of higher functionaries. 'Brass hats' did not throng the trenches. One brigadier who came to see us, and was supposed not to love shell fire, had his visit abbreviated by the Sergeant-Major drawing the pin of a Mills bomb and covertly dropping it over the back of the trench. Another old gentleman, however, of the same rank and of benevolent and kindly mien, joined us one day in the support trenches, and having gone the round was with difficulty dissuaded by our Captain from walking over the top in broad daylight down to the front line! [Lt. F. Laird, Royal Dublin Fusiliers]

Charles Edmonds and a colleague had a certain amount of fun in discouraging their brigade staff from appearing in their part of the line:

A memorable day it was when two of us had drained a long communication trench called Fifth Avenue, penning the mud and water behind a temporary dam of clay, in a dead end - a grand game of mud pies for a boy on a spring morning. Then came news that the brigadier and his staff were coming up the trench. Now trenches wind in curious zigzags lest enemy guns should be able to rake them, shooting along them in a straight line from end to end. The brigadier, though only a few yards away, could see and know nothing of our doings round the corner. We broke down the dam, releasing a flood of liquid slime, knee deep, glutinous, stinking, which swept him away. No gilded staff officers appeared after that to interrupt our innocent ease in the front line.

There existed an altogether exceptional breed of senior officer who continued always to set an example of courage, concern for their men's welfare and well-being and commitment to effective prosecution of their duties. There can be few finer examples of such a man than Frank Maxwell, VC, CSI, DSO and bar. Coming from a military background, he was one of six brothers, all of whom held regular army comissions, in his case in the Indian Army. He first arrived in France in March 1916, where he was appointed to the command of the 12th (Service) Battalion, the Middlesex Regiment, which had been weakly led up to that point and was suffering from low morale after several unsuccessful operations. Maxwell transformed his new command and effected the captures of Trônes Wood (July 1916) and Thiepval (September 1916), where many others had failed (q.v.). After these successes, he was appointed to command the 27th Infantry Brigade, in the 9th Division.

The strength of Maxwell's character, and his concern for his men are revealed in his standing up to his divisional commander in the matter of their shelter and comfort:

> I went up to the trenches and waded about, slush up to my shins in the front trench, which made me very sorry for the poor men in it. Everything so absolutely beastly - trenches already knocked about by fire, falling in continually from the weather; no drainage at the bottom, so melted snow deep in it. No dug-outs, as these have (quite right) been forbidden to be used in the front line, and only wretched shelters of corrugated iron, under which those not on the parapet sit freezing with cold. No blankets allowed - for the Division beat me about them (and I ought incidentally to have been under arrest as well for gross disobedience of orders). But I haven't done with them yet.
>
> Anyway, I have got time by the forelock, and am fairly well on the way with comfortable and warm shelters for the men. Poor chaps, they are so cold they can't sleep at night, and as they have to slop about in the mud by day, their rest is nil. How they stick it I don't know - got to, I suppose. And it makes me most mutinous and insubordinate to have to deny blankets to them, because certain fatuous idiots going to bed in a bed, with probably half a dozen blankets on them and a snug room outside all that, ordain that Jock in the trenches will go too fast asleep if he has one blanket, so mustn't have it! It's not only beastly cruel but most dangerous, for a man must sleep or doze sometime, and if he can't get it properly he will sleep or doze, or be perfectly inalert when on sentry-go; and then he either has a court martial for other people's wise orders, or he lets the enemy in and gets scuppered along with a number of half-frozen creatures.
>
> As I told you, I strafed our Divisional Commander, and sent him away to see the Corps Commander again, but both were decided against the blanket, and when he came to tell me the result yesterday morning, I could have eaten him - and he jolly well could see it too. Anyway, I told

him I wasn't going to leave it at that, and that if he and the Corps
General cared to give orders which, in my considered opinion, directly
led to dangerous risk, I should protect myself by making the strongest
protest I could on paper, and sending it to him official, so that he could
enjoy all the responsibilty, which I absolutely decline to accept, of any
mishap. I expect I shall get fired out of this job before long. I find that I
see differently to too many people on too many things to be able to
conform to the ordinary military ethics of sitting down and obeying
them, as most certainly I should if I were a proper soldier man. But then
I'm not, and never shall be now, for at my age it is too late to change my
skin.

So far I have always managed to disobey rotten orders, or been able to
square their non-compliance; but I can't always excpect such luck,
especially as one gets up the ladder.

This willingness to challenge higher authority was not characteristic of
the way the British Army functioned. In operational matters, too, he on
at least one occasion on the Somme, refused to acquiesce in ill-judged
interference from above with his plans. Maxwell, a Brigadier-General
by the time he wrote the following extract to his wife, also strongly
believed in leading by example:

A very long and interesting day, from about nine till six, in the new line.
It is a long one with big distances, but full of interest, and all sorts of fun
possible, I think. Bosch very retiring, and I found myself peacocking
about outside our wire, in some places 200 to 300 yards in front,
examining our trenches from the enemy point of view! Though 300
yards distant from one part of the line, he is anything from 500 to 600
elsewhere, and behind a small crest line, the top of which, as proved
to-day, he doesn't or didn't to-day, even occupy with snipers.

Of course, it is all very well for me to do this sort of thing, as I have a
particular object in doing so; nor is it any harm for them to see that it
can be done, as they, as a whole, think that No Man's Land is a most
dangerous place, whereas one has to try and persuade them to think it is
not so, in order that at night they may go out in it for patrol work, and
for enterprises against the enemy. As I passed down the trenches the
sentries were peeping through their silly old periscopes as usual, and no
doubt they thought I was quite mad to get up on the parapet and go
through the wire. I didn't mind them thinking that, for the reasons given
above. But when on one occasion I had returned to the trench, and had
gone some way down it, and had occasion to look back, I confess I
thought they had learnt the lesson of No Man's Land being not so
dreadful as they thought a little too well, for what did I see but the
whole platoon swaggering about on top! Curious fellows for extremes,
aren't they? However, they were soon shouted back into their more

normal positions, but I doubt whether they will bother about the periscopes any more, and a good job too.

I hatched all sorts of little enterprises against the rubbish opposite, and came home fairly content, and extremely muddy, after the long day, only to find that orders had just arrived, moving me to another sector three or four miles away. However, there is nothing like change, and to-morrow I hope to go off and see the new line, which is of quite a different type and condition; and it doesn't sound so interesting as this seemed likely to be. It feels like three long days wasted (one before coming in and two since), but it isn't really, as it exercises one's brain, and mine gets extemely lazy if left inactive for even a short time...

Frank Maxwell was shot and killed by a sniper when in the front line on 21st October 1917, during the Third Battle of Ypres.

12
Allies

When British troops came into contact with their allies (both soldiers and civilians) at the front, relations were generally cordial. Those first encountered by the BEF were the French and Belgians, and not surprisingly there was a degree of mutual incomprehension both on grounds of language and of culture. History played its part too; some peasants in North-West France were at first deeply suspicious of the British - after all, the battlefield of Crécy was not far from the front, and they feared that the British were not going to leave at the end of the war.

Equally, the British troops were sometimes wary of the local peasantry, whom they could view as grasping profiteers, not appreciating the effect of the BEF and the war on their homes and livelihood. Throughout the war, extracting billets from unwilling civilians could be difficult. In the confusion of the March 1918 fighting, Arthur Behrend was sent to billet his artillery brigade:

> Early next morning the Colonel and the four battery commanders and I drove back toward the line. Doullens was packed; the New Zealand Division was detraining at the station. Doullens itself was recovering fast, and already shops were reopening and prices soaring; it was said that a French division would arrive shortly too.

> The Doullens-Acheux road was almost empty, and things seemed to be settling down splendidly. Marieux Château, the lovely home of IV Corps Headquarters, was a centre of reassuring activity. From Authie to Bus-les-Artois we drove through budding woods. Battalions of big New Zealanders resting by the roadside cursed us loudly as we spattered them with mud. Chinese were hard at work digging reserve lines - which were not used.

> Bus was full. Interpreters attached to the New Zealand Division were hurrying about with notebooks in their hands searching volubly for billets for Divisional Trench Mortars, for the divisional Supply Company, for the A.P.M., the C.R.E., Ordnance, and a dozen more. Officers were seeking sites for the Salvage Dump, for the Divisional Canteen, and for the Prisoner-of-War cage. The Château had just been taken over for Divisional Headquarters; it would not be easy to find a billet anywhere in Bus, and we drove on. At the Colincamps corner

stood a New Zealand military policeman as smart as if there wasn't a German within fifty miles.

"No," he said, "you can't go along the Colincamps road. The diggers have only just driven the Boche out and they're working forward to Mailly-Maillet now."

So we went to Bertrancourt instead, where the Colonel left me to find a billet for brigade headquarters and pushed on towards Beaussart with the others to look for battery positions. But Bertrancourt was hopelessly full of infantry and Maori pioneers and wagon lines, and I walked back through the mud to Bus and told the first interpreter I saw that we were the Heavy Artillery now attached to his Division and that we therefore must find a headquarters somewhere in Bus.

"No," he said, "Sorry, Eet is impossible, full up."
"But your Divisional Commander will be angry when he learns that the Heavy Artillery attached to his Division is unable to find a billet."
"Perhaps I will see what can be done. Let us try Billet No. 32."

But Billet No. 32 was too small and too dirty.

"No," I said firmly, "I cannot ask the commander of a Heavy Artillery Brigade to live in such a house."
"Is eet for the commander of a Heavy Artillery Brigade himself that you seek a billet?"
"Yes."
"Then I think Billet No. 91 will suit your General[1] admirably. Would you care for me to lead you there?"

Off we went together to Billet No. 91, a low and charming red-roofed house with a big garden in front, and there I made the acquaintance of Monsieur, a nice old schoolmaster, of Mathilde his shrewish wife, and of Jeanette their graceful and pretty daughter.

"Yes," I told the interpreter, "this will suit us perfectly, and the General will be very pleased. I should like that big room for his bedroom, and, if it would not inconvenience Madame, that small room beside it for the office and mess. And also the cellar for the telephone exchange."
"No, no!" protested Madame. "The cellar is impossible - the cider and the potatoes!"
"*Ça ne fait rien, Mathilde,*" interposed Monsieur gently.

But Madame was adamant - until the interpreter had spoken rapidly to her for several minutes about *La France* and *réquisitions* and such like.

---

[1]   Behrend's CO was actually a Lt. Col.

Monsieur stood silent and nodded approvingly, while Jeanette winked at me and smiled and pouted and danced on her toes.

Occasionally, such mistrust ran deeper still, as a meeting with one Flemish civilian in November 1914 illustrates:

> We were badly taken in the other day. We had taken up a position close to a farm, and were using the latter as a nest. Towards evening a little old woman came in and sat down by the fire, and began to weep bitterly. We are always suspicious of civilians, but she looked so harmless, and all our attempts seemed only to make her shake her head and weep the more, and we took pity on her and allowed her to stay. Next morning she went away. I was away from the Battery all day, and returning at night, I was regaled with tales of a nightmare howitzer, which had rained projectiles on the Battery varying in weight from five hundredweight to ten tons...
>
> One thing I had almost forgotten to tell you: as a result of the episode of the old woman in the farm-house, the men have all got spy-fever. The next morning when one of them was out getting straw, an officer with a somewhat Teutonic moustache, and not absolutely correctly dressed, came up and asked who he was, what he was doing, and where his Battery was? The man came in and reported this to the sergeant-major; he promptly sent out a file of men to arrest the spy; they returned in triumph bringing with them a much enraged commanding officer of the neighbouring infantry regiment. [Major Francis Graham]

However, the fighting troops were generally on good terms with one another:

> What a very polite people are the French!
>
> The other day a French General sent a note asking us to turn on to a battery which was worrying his infantry. We could not see a battery, but we turned out my section and blazed into the blue, by way of encouragement. Next morning we got an effusive note of thanks for our 'wonderfully effective fire' which had 'completely annihilated' the German battery! [Major Francis Graham]

As well as courtesy, French hospitality lubricated the mechanism of liaison with the British. Having recently come into the line next to French units, Lt.Col. Neil Fraser-Tytler, commanding an artillery battery, paid a visit to his opposite number:

> On the 7th I had promised to take Capt. Armstrong over to lunch with the French and make their acquaintance, but I couldn't get off till late, having to wait all the morning for General Leckie, who didn't turn up. However, in spite of the delay, when I galloped over to Cappy I found

thirty-six oysters waiting for me, with the usual cheery crowd of French gunners round the table.

The oysters were followed by pâte de fois gras, veal and chicken mousse, a young roast pig, and Rumpelmayer's chocolate cake, washed down with Graves, some excellent Pontet Canet and champagne, then eau de vie, a very good cigar and perfect coffee.

The extra luxuries were accounted for by one of the staff having just returned from Paris leave.

After a most hilarious lunch, though I personally felt like an inflated frog, we mustered energy enough to stroll over and see a friend of mine, Captain Vieux, at his battery near the Chateau.

We took possession of one of his guns and fired it off with great rapidity - an international gun detachment of officers! and then I persuaded the whole party to come over to our side and see our happy home. After so large a lunch I had no desire to ride or walk, so we got hold of a battered old car which used to belong to the Chateau and Vieux, Dubois, Armstrong and I drove in triumph in it to Susanne. No vehicles are supposed to go beyond the turn in daylight, but as I said before we had "dejuened" extremely well, so ignoring the road-blocking sentry, we charged down the road, in full sight of the Huns across the river, the old car clanging like a smithy shop and bucking over the crump holes in the road with asthmatic grunts from every cylinder.

Fraser-Tytler was also shown around the French front line:

On the 28th Wilson and I had an interesting day in the French front line, with Commandant Lotte and his staff. Meeting them at the footbridge across the river at Eclusier, we first went up to a Battalion H.Q. about 1,000 yards behind the French front line, and spent some time with the Infantry C.O. in his dug-out, looking at the maps and drinking the inevitable "eau de vie." From there we went on to the famous Bois de Vaches, which has been changing hands repeatedly for the last three weeks... The whole wood is a criss-cross of trenches or connected shell holes, no regular system of trenches having been evolved. In its place we find merely frenzied scratchings wherever each side happen to find themselves at dawn. The French fire trenches are packed with men, very different from the solitude of our front line, but one must remember that they have no protecting wire up yet.

The infantry in the line were Colonials and had all seen active service in Cochin China. They were a tough but rather dirty-looking lot, and altogether the front line was in a very messy state, and as they had had a bit of a show at dawn one realized the truth of the saying: "It isn't what the eye sees but what the feet walk upon that matters." An absurd feeling, of course, as though the poor devils could feel one walking over them! They were a cold-blooded crowd. I noticed one Boche half-buried in the parapet and the men using his feet to hang their water bottles on!

Conditions in French trenches were commented on unfavourably by others too:

Most disconcerting, perhaps, was the sanitary accommodation, built, I concluded, for more robust races. A large pit, covered by a few boards, had been dug in - yes, actually in - a firebay. 'FEUILLES' read a laconic notice board; but the nose had compassed the exact translation of those leaves ten yards before one reached it. To cover this noisome plague breeder was No. 2's first task, undertaken with alacrity by the occupants of the adjoining posts. [Guy Chapman]

Britain's other principal ally in the fighting on the Western Front was America. Although she joined the war in April 1917, it took time for the USA to gear up for action - as it had for Britain - and troops did not arrive in France in significant numbers until a year later. Despite their initial inexperience, they proved to be a decisive factor in the outcome of the war, not least for their effect on Allied morale:

The war, now in its fifth summer, was ending, but we were not yet conscious of it. We and the French and the Germans were equally war-weary, and each of us knew only too well the meaning of the words 'scraping the bottom of the barrel.' ... Apart from [the Americans'] capacity to give as well as take severe casualties, their very presence - and in such numbers - knocked what stuffing was left out of the Germans and put fresh heart into the French and ourselves. No one in the line could fail to observe that from August onwards the Germans, though still tough and brave, were no longer the fighters they had been.

At brigade headquarters we met our first Americans during the early part of the summer, two or three quiet and earnest men quite unlike the boastful types Americans were generally believed to be. They were gunner officers, sent to learn how we did things and to profit from our experience, and if at the beginning of their visit they may have thought there was little we could teach them they quickly saw their mistake. [Arthur Behrend]

As 'green' troops, the Americans had one or two obstacles to overcome when dealing with their allies:

We occupied the front line trenches ETHEL and EMMA and support NINE ELMS when a detachment of Yankees was sent up to learn something about trench warfare. They arrived laden with all sorts of labour-saving devices such as a combined spoon, knife, fork (suitable for toasting or stabbing at food in the usual way), tin opener and tooth-pick. They had not been warned that the Londoners had been recruited from the Hackney and East End of London and when their tour of instruction ended, they left lighter as regards equipment but heavy at heart.

When Londoners suffered a casualty while doing a tour in a fairly quiet sector, their dead pal's body was laid in a recess in the trench to await removal in the evening by stretcher bearers to the MO's dressing stations and thence probably in a returning-empty ration-limber to rear HQ for burial; but not so a Yankee casualty for his pals deemed the open at the back of a trench to be a more suitable place for disposal of a corpse pending removal.

A feature of American hygiene which we endeavoured to teach the Yanks was unsuitable for trench warfare was the doctrine apparently taught at their Military schools that a really noisy and well-burdened expectoration was a sign of military efficiency and disdain for the enemy. We had to impress on them that in normal trench warfare, the trench was to Tommy his breakfast, dinner, tea, supper and sitting room, and it would require more than a Hoover to clean a trench floor after Yank occupation. Pails were accordingly placed at strategic points over which notices printed clearly by our Pioneers, made this request "Dammit, man, if you must spit, spit into this."

The American Officer accompanying the men, made haste on arrival for his dugout, accompanied by his assistant, one Johnny Haig, and there remained unseen for the tour; his assistant became a casualty. [Lt. Col. E.P. Cawston]

A smaller and less well-known contribution to the Allied cause was that of Portugal, which entered the war in 1916 and sent an army corps to the Western Front. To experienced British troops, their approach to trench warfare seemed rather eccentric:

Next door to us were our gallant allies, the Portuguese, who held a sector extending for several miles, nearly to Armentières.

For several reasons they were not the most convenient of neighbours, however gallant as allies.

Our C.O. lost no time in making the acquaintance of the C.O. of their nearest battalion, and to do so, had to go what appeared to be about two miles back from the front line. When he got there he was offered some very good port, and discovered in the course of conversation their method of occupying their line, which was original, to say the least. Their best behaved men they used to keep in support, less satisfactory men held the front trench, and their worst villains were sent on patrols. This method did not lend itself to loyal co-operation, and there was always a risk that their defence would break under pressure.

Some fool had given them four Stokes Guns (a quick-firing trench mortar which could get as many as eight shells in the air at once), and the officer in charge of these was like a child with a new toy, always wanting to use it. He would bring them out just after lunch, at a time when all good soldiers value a little repose, and spray these confounded shells all over the neighbourhood. Some of them, sooner or later, would fall in the enemy's lines, and the old Boche, naturally indignant at such untimely disturbance, would get to work with his heavy minnies, not on the Portuguese trenches, but on ours, which were a better target.

But with us the chief reason for their unpopularity was their vicious habit of firing Verey lights in the middle of our nightly patrols. so in order to put an end to this practice, we arranged for a Portuguese Sergeant to come and dwell just outside my company Headquarters for liaison purposes. He duly arrived. But as he spoke no English, and none of us knew Portuguese, his usefulness was strictly limited. On the evening of his arrival I was writing in my dug-out, when I heard one of my Sergeants speaking in the tone one uses to a deaf man in a thunderstorm. The sentence was evidently addressed to the Portuguese Sergeant.

English Sergeant: "Eh! Mossoo; nous patrolio to-nighto. Compree?"
Portuguese Sergeant (with great presence of mind): "Oui, Monsieur."
[Major R.T.Rees]

The BEF was joined in France - at different times - by contingents from the Empire. As early as 1914, an Indian corps disembarked at Marseilles, being transferred to the Middle East in November 1915, having been heavily engaged at Neuve Chapelle and the Second Battle of Ypres. The Canadian Expeditionary Force landed in France in February 1915, and reached corps strength later that year; Australia and New Zealand jointly contributed two 'Anzac' corps, which arrived in France from Gallipoli in 1916; South Africa also contributed a brigade in that year; and even Newfoundland (not then part of Canada) raised a regiment in 1914. Even before the Dominions had raised their own formations, not inconsiderable numbers of men made their own way to Britain to join the forces. In the 3rd King's Royal Rifle Corps, for instance, there was a completely Rhodesian Platoon, composed of colonials all keen to 'do their bit' who had paid for their passage together and enlisted together.

Colonial and Dominion troops enjoyed a considerable fighting reputation, based on their achievements, such as the Canadians at Vimy Ridge in 1917, the Australians at Poziéres in 1916 and the South Africans at Delville Wood, also in 1916. The Canadian and Anzac Corps, as formations, were held in increasingly high regard as the war went on. They seem to have owed their success partly to their homogeneity, partly to their working with the same corps staffs almost throughout and partly to the individual soldiers' fighting qualities. The latter were often attributed to the men's 'frontier spirit' and with that in mind, it is worth noting that 60% of the Canadians, for example, were first-generation emigrants from the UK.

The justifiable self-confidence of the colonials is reflected in the order issued to the 15th Battalion CEF prior to the attack on Vimy Ridge in April 1917, as related in the battalion's history:

> Lt. Eric Haldenly, the Adjutant, had issued the operation orders of the O.C. for the battle at the time when the battalions moved into the front line. They started with the simple and historic statement that: "The Canadian Corps will take Vimy Ridge."

That this self-confidence extended to all ranks is evident in Captain Dugdale's encounter with one Australian:

> Our company was quartered in a sunken road which led down to the canal bank, and on the other side the Australians held the line.
>
> We were now only about two miles from the Hindenburg line.
>
> I was on duty one lovely spring afternoon in this road, lying on the bank of the canal reading a book, when a shout from the other side startled me.
>
> "Say," called a man - an Australian soldier - "where does this path lead to?"
> "To Havrincourt Wood," I replied.
> "I'm going to have a look at it," he said.
> "Stop," I shouted. "There is a Bosche machine gun post in the corner; don't be a fool."
>
> The man had no equipment, just a rifle and a tin hat.
>
> "I shall be all right," he laughed. "I don't suppose the Bosche are there."
>
> It was nothing to do with us if he committed suicide.
>
> We watched his progress with much interest.
>
> Having lit a cigarette and slung his rifle over his shoulder he strolled off down the canal bank whistling. We could see him stop opposite the end of the wood and look over to our side. He then calmly proceeded to take his coat and boots off and swam to the other side. A series of splashes made it evident that he was throwing the machine gun post into the

canal. He swam back and put on his clothes. As he strolled up on his return he shouted to us:

"I chucked all their — goods into the canal. They won't half be wild when they come back to-night. So long."

Off he went as if he had been for a walk in the park.

Guy Chapman, however, noted that the Australians seemed to be rather in awe of their own feats:

> 'Your first job,' said Smith, 'is to sit down and compose stories for decorations. Have a drink and let your imagination rip.' During the last twelve months, it had become obvious that the award of decorations was chiefly a matter of penmanship. A barren statement of facts was invariably passed over. As someone had said, scanning the plethoric list in Army Orders of ribbons given to the Australians: 'With so many heroes, I can't think why the war is still going on.' There had been a wry jest about one colonel in the division, whose recommendation for a D.S.O. had been so florid that Corps had sent back to say that the leader of this counter-attack must have the V.C. and asked for the necessary corroborative evidence of eye-witnesses; which had not been forthcoming. Caution, as well as imagination, was therefore desirable.

One characteristic of Australian units was the informality of relations between officers and men, as compared to other units. While this was considered improper by the more traditional British Officer, Lt. Edwin Vaughan found this openness refreshing:

> Dawn was breaking as I plodded up the road, and where the road was bounded by banks 16 feet high, the dugouts showed signs of occupation. Suddenly I was challenged in an unmistakably colonial voice and in answer to my questions the sentry (an Australian) indicated the officers' dugout - a large shelter built into the bank with a table, chair and gas-gong outside. I opened the door quietly and saw an officer sitting at a table playing patience by the light of two candles, a whisky glass beside him.

> He looked up, and seeing me he spoke and acted simultaneously: 'Come in and sit down', and a fist shot out with a clean glass. He poured me a whisky as I unbuckled my equipment, and I liked the look of him. He was remarkably handsome, with very large blue eyes and silvery white curly hair. He had no collar or tie and his open tunic bore the Australian badge on the lapels.

> As I drank my whisky he told me that he was in command of that battery of Australian artillery and that he had been waiting up for me. I told him I had never heard of such an escort before, and could he tell me what it was and why. But he waved a brown hand at me.

'Tomorrow, sonny! Tomorrow. I'm dead tired, and you ought to be, so let's get to bed. Have you got your kit?' I told him 'No'. 'Oh, we'll soon fix that!' he replied and leaning back he yelled into what appeared to be an enormous grave which I had not noticed hitherto.

Two figures were squirming about and in response to his announcement of my arrival each handed up a blanket. I did not want to take them but he smothered my protests by wrapping them round my head and pushing me out of the door. Extricating myself, I followed him into a tin hut on the roadside where he lit a hurricane lamp and dragged the mattress from his bed onto the floor. Adding one of his own blankets, he ran out before I could argue and left me to settle in.

Waking up to a bright midday sun I lay looking at my untidy surroundings and wondering what the loud bangs were that I could hear. Only half awake, I thought they were the Australian guns, and that I ought to be escorting them! But as I jumped up I realised that they were crashes, not bangs - and uncomfortably near too!

I slipped on my tunic and went out into the road, bathed in dazzling sunlight. My side of the road was littered with evidence of troops' occupation - helmets, bully tins, buckets, wood, shell-cases etc; the other side was bare except for a military well and a large crowd of troops who were lying flat against the bank. The reason for this was obvious.

Behind us was a village of mingled red roofs and trees, which extended to the corner where we had parted from Ewing last night. And at this corner now was a large cloud of red dust into which shell after shell was falling with deadly regularity and precision. The chunks of shrapnel and brick were falling about me, so I did not stand still for long - I grabbed my tin hat and joined my platoon on the bank.

When I realised that it was only *my* fellows who were on that side of the road, and that the few Australian gunners who had worried to come out were sitting on their own side, smoking and watching the shelling, I felt quite ashamed, and returned to my bedroom to put on my puttees before going into their mess.

I found the skipper with his two subs, one very small and dark - black eyes, hair and 'toothbrush' - known as Garry, the other a silent, dull-looking chap called Jack. They greeted me very hospitably, and chipped me about the windiness of my troops. While I explained that they had not been subjected to shelling for some time, and would have to get used to it again, Garry fished out a gramophone and we listened to some cheery review records until a servant appeared with lunch. They were very familiar with this servant, and Christian names were freely interchanged.

During an excellent lunch I heard how some months before a party of 30 Boche had managed to get through our line to a battery of guns in this position. They had surprised and killed the gunners, spiked the guns and returned. They had been wiped out on trying to return through our posts, but ever since a platoon had been detailed to assist in defending the guns. The skipper pointed out to me a pile of shell boxes which he said contained a supply of shrapnel fused to burst at point blank, which he guaranteed would keep the Boche at 200 yards - if he ever did get so near again.

The shelling continued until 3 p.m., by which time we reckoned about 400 must have fallen. The troops had got used to them very early on and were walking about freely, but I noticed that they did not mix with the Australians; rather they acted on the popular mistrust and kept a wary eye on their belongings.

It is noteworthy that Vaughan's men kept their distance; the Australians also enjoyed a reputation for 'scrounging' as formidable as that for fighting.

New Zealanders appear to have come to a compromise between British and Australian ideas of propriety in terms of discipline and 'spit and polish'. Arthur Behrend found co-operation with them especially rewarding when working with the 'Kiwis' in 1918:

From April onwards, at any rate on our sector of the front, one was conscious of a prevailing spirit of profound thankfulness, almost of satisfaction, that the Germans were securely held. Of the two factors which contributed most to this happy feeling, the first was the daily evidence around us that now it was ourselves and not the Germans who were living and fighting in a green and wooded countryside hardly touched by the spoiling hand of war. The second and greater factor was our rapidly growing friendship with the New Zealand Division, with whom we now were working as closely as if we had been their own Divisional field artillery brigade.

We admired them more than any division we had previously met, and not only because we knew them better. They accepted us too, and in a matter of days they looked upon us as their private heavy artillery. Except when they were out of the line we were in daily contact with them till the end of the war - and with battalions and even companies as well as with their Divisional and Brigade headquarters. I cannot recall a single occasion when either side let the other down. For us, bearing in mind that Heavy Artillery Brigades were Corps troops, it was a novel and stimulating experience, and I have no doubt we shot all the better for it, for no words of mine can convey to the layman the feeling of heaven which an artilleryman knows when the Division he is supporting is a good one, and of all the good and very good Divisions of the British army I would rate the New Zealand Division high among the highest.

The men of all the nations represented in the line had a common experience which bound them together in a way that no-one back at home - they felt - could understand. London was only 90 miles from the front, and daily papers could be read in the line within 24 hours of publication, yet a huge gulf existed between the service and civilian experience. Attitudes to home are included here - with those to the Allies - since this divide was so great. When home on the leave they so craved when in the trenches, men yearned for the comradeship of the latter. Charles Edmonds was home on leave in early 1918:

> England was beastly in 1918; it was in the hands of the dismal and incompetent. Pessimism raged among those who knew nothing of the war; "défaistisme," the desire to stop the war at all costs, even by the admission of defeat, broke out among the faint-hearts; while those at home who still had the will to fight preferred to use the most disgusting means - to fight by lying propaganda, and by imitating the bad tradition of the German army which consistently made war against civilians. No wonder that a genuine and silent pacifism was rising in the breast of the war-weary populations. Envy, hatred, malice and all uncharitableness, fear and cruelty born of fear, seemed the dominant passions of the leaders of the nations in those days. Only in the trenches (on both sides of No Man's Land) were chivalry and sweet reasonableness to be found. How delightful was the comradeship of the trenches compared with the petty jealousy of a reserve battalion, where the staple conversation turned on the methods one's neighbours used to avoid being sent to France. In such a place the keen soldiers were inclined to form a coterie and affect a superior knowledge of world affairs. The temporaries waiting to go out with a draft of men to the trenches would despise the permanent staff, dug in, "embusqué" as the French said, in safe places in England; yet who knew in his heart which was the happier state: which "embusqé" would give his soul to go abroad, which of the others to stay at home?

> At first I was downright glad to have a dry bed and a whole skin, but unrest soon seized me. Boredom was succeeded by a longing to be "with the lads." I shrank from the trenches, and then pulled strings at the War Office to get sent back to them.

The apparent safety and high wages enjoyed by industrial workers at home, were regarded as a 'cushy number' as compared to the rigours of the front. Captain Gilbert Nobbs, whose account was published when the war was still in progress, perhaps expressed the feelings of many, albeit melodramatically:

Ammunition workers in England, and those who should be munition workers, come right over here; creep with us along the edge of Trones Wood [sic], and watch this amazing sight. You miners, you tramwaymen, you boilermakers! You, who would throw down your tools and strike, look upon this sight!

This is the voice of England. This is the stupendous effort which is protecting you. On your right, that dark, creepy, silent place is Trones Wood. Look across to your left, those sticks showing on the skyline, across the valley, were once High Wood. In those woods, churned up in the soil, lie the rotting bodies of your comrades, your brothers, your sons. They have sacrificed all; they have suffered untold deaths. The contrast between that thundering voice of England and the silent mystery of those woods causes a shudder. Bring out those strikers and let them get a glimpse of this and realize their danger, and the horrors which will come upon them, their wives, their children, their homes, if those guns fail... Throw down your tools, slacken your machinery, and High Wood and Trones Wood will become blacker still with the mutilated bodies of a thousand men. A penny an hour! You who are being coddled under the protection of these guns, what is your quarrel to this?

If those desperate fellows on the other side of the hill were to leave their tasks they would be called traitors. Yet when men in England, upon whom these fighters are dependent, and whose work is just as necessary for the success of the war, throw down their tools, they are only called strikers.

The crime is the same; the punishment should be the same.

A far more restrained Siegfried Sassoon commented on the self-satisfied indulgence of those at home:

They say the U-boat blockade will get worse and there will be a bad food-shortage in England in 1917. The sideboard in this Formby golf-club doesn't look like it yet; enormous cold joints and geese and turkeys and a sucking pig and God knows what, and old men with their noses in their plates guzzling for all they're worth.

Nevertheless, the importance of a link with home was strongly felt. From day to day, men eagerly anticipated the arrival of letters and provisions from home:

The parcels from Fortnum and Mason and the books arrived today. I do enjoy getting the parcels. They really seem to bring home nearer than anything else. One thing about this war is that it really does make one appreciate letters and parcels from home.

Now as to details. The fact is, anything is welcome, as, if we do not eat it ourselves, I give it to the men. However, if I make one or two points, you will quite understand that I am not in any way "looking a gift horse in the mouth," but just suggesting future improvements. The only thing as a matter of fact that I have to suggest is about the cake: I think the one you sent me before from A. and N. was better. It came in a tin, and was a fine rich one like plumpudding, and was in great request. However, if I just get about the same amount every week I shall do splendidly. It is much appreciated by every one in the Mess. Also, thank you very much for the cigarettes. They are very good indeed.

Really, there is no justification for having all these luxuries, as we are simply living a most unwarlike and idle life in a comfortable *château*; but we do like them (the luxuries) very much. Some of the others are getting bored with not having enough to do; so the books will come in very handy. [R. Cecil Hopkinson, RE]

Understandably, there was a tendency (not shared by all) to make light, when writing home, of the danger and discomfort attendant upon one's position at the Front:

On the day in question I had an exciting time up in the —shire's trenches. This regiment's day trenches are about one hundred yards behind their night trenches. Everything seemed quiet and the infantry were lying down, half asleep in the bottom of the trenches. Suddenly over the rise, about one hundred and fifty yards away, I saw a crowd of two hundred odd Germans running towards us. The infantry were up in a moment, but the beggars managed to get into their night trenches. There was a good deal of firing on both sides. I noticed a large smile on the faces of the infantry, and they began edging off towards an open space on the left. Suddenly, from this open space, they charged down on the Germans; 'twas a thrilling sight; almost at the same moment the gentlemen of the Landsturm remembered an important engagement, about half a mile nearer Berlin; however, the infantry cut into a few of them and shot down a good many as they ran.

The self-deprecation of 2nd Lieutenant Graham's description of his exploits on this occasion is evident, give that he was awarded the Distinguished Service Order for this action - a decoration not lightly given to junior combatant officers; the official citation for the award was as follows:

From *The Times* of January 1st, 1915.

The King has been pleased to approve of the appointment of the following officers to be Companions of the Distinguished Service Order, in recognition of their services with the Expeditionary force, specified below:

Second Lieutenant Francis Graham, 51st Battery, Royal Field Artillery.
When the officers of a party of the South Lancashire Regiment were
disabled, he took command, and succeeded in holding an important part
of our trenches until relief arrived, and drove out the enemy, who had
effected a footing, the situation being thus saved by his prompt action.

Consideration towards relatives at home was not confined to one's
own. One of the duties of officers was to write to the next of kin of
soldiers under their command who had been killed in action.
Inevitably, the grieving family wanted the fullest details, but even if the
officer were aware of the full circumstances of a man's death (which
was not always clear in the heat of battle) the gulf between him and the
bereaved family made it impossible to impart the full reality of the
event. It is not surprising that formulae such as 'he died instantly,' 'I
am sure he felt no pain' and 'he was shot through the heart' were relied
upon. This is not to say that this duty was taken lightly; many officers
felt considerable distress at performing this task:

> "There's a big party of reinforcements for the brigade just turned up, sir.
> There's no nominal roll with them. Will you keep them here tonight and
> post them to batteries in the morning?"
> "Yes, Sergeant-major. You might make out a nominal roll, and-"
>
> CRASH!
>
> God, what was that? We both ducked blindly. Huge splinters burst
> through the hut, travelling with incredible speed. Outside the branches
> were snapping off the trees as though torn down by a hurricane.
>
> For fifteen seconds almost complete silence reigned through the camp. It
> was broken only by the noise of falling stones and branches. Then a
> piteous chorus of moaning and shouting was heard, and the
> Sergeant-major ran to the door and looked out.
>
> "It hit the hut where I put the reinforcements," he said... The casualties
> inflicted by that one shell were high. Apart from fifteen killed and
> wounded, others were so completely blown to pieces that they could not
> be identified nor could the number be determined. Many weeks later we
> received a letter from a woman in England asking if we could give her
> any news about her son, from whom she had not heard since he sailed
> to France. She had written to the R.G.A. Base Depot and been referred to
> us; the Depot had told her that according to their records he had been
> despatched to our brigade on March 20 in company with a draft of 40
> other men. How could one adequately reply to her letter and tell her
> that her son was one of those blown to pieces?

13
The Germans

The Great War opened with a blast of anti-German propaganda which was sustained throughout; stories of babies being bayonetted, nuns being violated and civilians shot out of hand were rife. This reached such a pitch that the First Sea Lord in 1914, Prince Louis of Battenberg, was hounded out of office for possessing a German surname and even the royal family changed its name in 1917 from Saxe-Coburg-Gotha.

This wave of emotion was largely confined to the Home Front, the men in France and Flanders finding the stories of the popular press at some times laughable and at others, distasteful. Nevertheless, there was a wide spectrum of opinion in the BEF, ranging from outright hatred of the Germans as the aggressors in the war, to compassion for them as fellow sufferers - even comrades - in the front line. In some quarters they were viewed with contempt, as unwilling conscripts, compared to the British professionals and volunteers. This gradually gave way to an appreciation of their fighting qualities, but in September 1914 the views of one regular medical officer were forthright:

> Stories of French prisoners being pushed in front of the German troops, and the bodies of dead Germans being used by their comrades as protecting ramparts, were of constant occurrence. We came into this war with individual minds free of prejudice, but one incident upon another fanned the flame until now personal hatred was rapidly developing. One cannot shake hands with prisoners who have lost their honour.

> The difference between races in the bearing of suffering was most marked. Tommy Atkins accepted his troubles and pains (as he always has done) with either stoical dumbness or a joke. The Frenchman was patient and enduring beyond belief, always pathetically grateful and wonderfully brave. Men who can continue to be gallant within touch of a surgeon's knife are men to be respected. The German, on the other hand, never stood up if he could possibly lie down, whined, or shouted for attention unceasingly as if by right, and stood pain badly. We surgeons had not expected these traits of national character. Such, however, are the unbiased facts. The whole attitude of the German wounded is that of intense selfishness, that of British and French notably the reverse. Is that not, perhaps, the national attitude as well? [Lt. Col. F.A.Symons, RAMC]

Pte. (later Capt.) A.O.Pollard arrived at the front in November 1914 and shortly thereafter recorded his opinion of the enemy:

> Were the Germans braver than ourselves? Certainly not! The stories of Le Cateau and Landrecies told us that. Tales were rife of the German soldiery being driven forward to attack by officers stationed behind them with revolvers. Man to man we were infinitely superior; in armament, we were sadly inferior. Artillery, shells, machine-guns, number of men in the field, we were outnumbered at every point. The odds against us were overwhelming. Nothing but indomitable British pluck pulled us through at this period of the War.

Such views as those of Symons and Pollard would seem to have been by no means universal, in view of the famous Christmas truce of 1914. The following account by Capt. Sir Edward Hulse of events in his sector is typical of the kind of unofficial fraternisation which took place in most of the line. It reveals a very different attitude towards the enemy:

> Just returned to billets again, after the most extraordinary Christmas in the trenches you could possibly imagine. Words fail me completely in trying to describe it, but here it goes!
>
> On the 23rd we took over the trenches in the ordinary manner, relieving the Grenadiers, and during the 24th the usual firing took place, and sniping was pretty brisk. We stood to arms as usual at 6.30 a.m. on the 25th, and I noticed that there was not much shooting; this gradually died down, and by 8 a.m. there was no shooting at all, except for a few shots on our left (Border Regt.). At 8.30 a.m. I was looking out, and saw four Germans leave their trenches and come towards us; I told two of my men to go and meet them, unarmed (as the Germans were unarmed), and to see that they did not pass the halfway line. We were 350-400 yards apart at this point. My fellows were not very keen, not knowing what was up, so I went out alone, and met Barry, one of our ensigns, also coming out from another part of the line. By the time we got to them, they were ¾ of the way over, and much too near our barbed wire, so I moved them back. They were three private soldiers and a stretcher-bearer, and their spokesman started off by saying that he thought it only right to come over and wish us a happy Christmas, and trusted us implicitly to keep the truce. He came from Suffolk, where he had left his best girl and a 3½ h.p. motor-bike! He told me that he could not get a letter to the girl, and wanted to send one through me. I made him write out a postcard in front of me, in English, and I sent it off that night. I told him that she probably would not be a bit keen to see him again. We then entered on a long discussion on every sort of thing. I was dressed in an old stocking-cap and a man's overcoat, and they took me for a corporal, a thing which I did not discourage, as I had an eye to going as near their lines as possible... I asked them what orders they had

from their officers as to coming over to us, and they said none; they had just come over out of goodwill.

They protested that they had no feeling of enmity towards us at all, but that everything lay with their authorities, and that being soldiers they had to obey. I believe that they were speaking the truth when they said this, and that they never wished to fire a shot again. They said that unless directly ordered, they were not going to shoot again until we did... We talked about the ghastly wounds made by rifle bullets, and we both agreed that neither of us used dum-dum bullets, and that the wounds are solely inflicted by the high-velocity bullet with the sharp nose, at short range. We both agreed that it would be far better if we used the old South African round-nosed bullet, which makes a clean hole...

They think that our Press is to blame in working up feeling against them by publishing false "atrocity reports." I told them of various sweet little cases which I have seen for myself, and they told me of English prisoners whom they have seen with soft-nosed bullets, and lead bullets with notches cut in the nose; we had a heated, and at the same time, good-natured argument, and ended by hinting to each other that the other was lying!

I kept it up for half an hour, and then escorted them back as far as their barbed wire, having a jolly good look round all the time, and picking up various little bits of information which I had not had an opportunity of doing under fire! I left instructions with them that if any of them came out later they must not come over the half-way line, and appointed a ditch as the meeting place. We parted after an exchange of Albany cigarettes and German cigars, and I went straight to H.-qrs. to report.

On my return at 10 a.m. I was surprised to hear a hell of a din going on, and not a single man left in my trenches; they were completely denuded (against my orders), and nothing lived! I heard strains of *"Tipperary"* floating down the breeze swiftly followed by a tremendous burst of *"Deutschland Uber Alles,"* and as I got to my own Coy H.-qrs. dugout, I saw, to my amazement, not only a crowd of about 150 British and Germans at the half-way house which I had appointed opposite my lines, but six or seven such crowds, all the way down our lines, extending towards the 8th Division on our right. I bustled out and asked if there were any German officers in my crowd, and the noise died down (as this time I was myself in my own cap and badges of rank).

I found two, but had to talk to them through an interpreter, as they could neither talk English nor French... I explained to them that strict orders must be maintained as to meeting half-way, and everyone unarmed; and we both agreed not to fire until the other did, thereby creating a complete deadlock and armistice (if strictly observed)...

Meanwhile Scots and Huns were fraternising in the most genuine possible manner. Every sort of souvenir was exchanged, addresses given and received, photos of families shown, etc. One of our fellows offered a German a cigarette; the German said, "Virginian?" Our fellow said, "Aye, straight-cut": the German said, "No thanks, I only smoke Turkish!" (Sort of 10/- a 100 me!) It gave us all a good laugh.

A German N.C.O. with the Iron Cross, - gained, he told me, for conspicuous skill in sniping, - started his fellows off on some marching tune. When they had done I set the note for *"The boys of Bonnie Scotland, where the heather and the bluebells grow,"* and so we went on, singing everything from *"Good King Wenceslaus"* down to the ordinary Tommies' song, and ended up with *"Auld Lang Syne,"* which we all, English, Scots, Irish, Prussian, Wurtembergers, etc., joined in. It was absolutely astounding, and if I had seen it on a cinematograph film I should have sworn that it was faked!...

From foul rain and wet, the weather had cleared up the night before to a sharp frost, and it was a perfect day, everything white, and the silence seemed extraordinary, after the usual din. From all sides birds seemed to arrive, and we hardly ever see a bird generally. Later in the day I fed about 50 sparrows outside my dug-out, which shows how complete the silence and quiet was.

I must say that I was very much impressed with the whole scene, and also, as everyone else, astoundingly relieved by the quiet, and by being able to walk about freely. It is the first time, day or night, that we have heard no guns, or rifle-firing, since I left Havre and convalescence!

Just after we had finished *"Auld Lang Syne"* an old hare started up, and seeing so many of us about in an unwonted spot, did not know which way to go. I gave one loud "View Halloa," and one and all, British and Germans, rushed about giving chase, slipping up on the frozen plough, falling about, and after a hot two minutes we killed in the open, a German and one of our fellows falling together heavily upon the completely baffled hare. Shortly afterwards we saw four more hares, and killed one again; both were good heavy weight and had evidently been out between the two rows of trenches for the last two months, well-fed on the cabbage patches, etc., many of which are untouched on the "no man's land." The enemy kept one and we kept the other. It was now 11.30 a.m. and at this moment George Paynter arrived on the scene, with a hearty "Well, my lads, a Merry Christmas to you! This is d—d comic, isn't it?"... George told them that he thought it only right that we should show that we could desist from hostilities on a day which was so important in both countries; and he then said, "Well, my boys, I've brought you over something to celebrate this funny show with," and he produced from his pocket a large bottle of rum (not ration rum, but the proper stuff). One large shout went up, and the nasty little spokesman uncorked it, and in a heavy, ceremonious manner, drank our healths, in the name of his "camaraden"; the bottle was then passed on and polished off before you could say knife.

During the afternoon the same extraordinary scene was enacted between the lines, and one of the enemy told me that he was longing to get back to London: I assured him that "So was I." He said that he was sick of the war, and I told him that when the truce was ended, any of his friends would be welcome in our trenches, and would be well-received, fed, and given a free passage to the Isle of Man! Another coursing meeting took place, with no result, and at 4.30 p.m. we agreed to keep in our respective trenches, and told them that the truce was ended. They persisted, however, in saying that they were not going to fire, and as George had told us not to, unless they did, we prepared for a quiet night, but warned all sentries to be doubly on the alert.

During the day both sides had taken the opportunity of bringing up piles of wood, straw, etc., which is generally only brought up with difficulty under fire. We improved our dug-outs, roofed in new ones, and got a lot of very useful work done towards increasing our comfort. Directly it was dark, I got the whole of my Coy. on to improving and remaking our barbed-wire entanglements, all along my front, and had my scouts out in front of the working parties, to prevent any surprise; but not a shot was fired, and we finished off a real good obstacle unmolested.

On my left was the bit of ground over which we attacked on the 18th, and here the lines are only from 85 to 100 yards apart.

The Border Regiment were occupying this section on Christmas Day, and Giles Loder, our adjutant, went down there with a party that morning on hearing of the friendly demonstrations in front of my Coy., to see if he could come to an agreement about our dead, who were still lying out between the trenches. The trenches are so close at this point, that of course each side had to be far stricter. Well, he found an extremely pleasant and superior stamp of German officer, who arranged to bring all our dead to the half-way line. We took them over there, and buried 29 exactly half way between the two lines. Giles collected all personal effects, pay-books and identity discs, but was stopped by the Germans when he told some men to bring in the rifles; all rifles lying on their side of the half-way line they kept carefully!...

They apparently treated our prisoners well, and did all they could for our wounded. This officer kept on pointing to our dead and saying *"Les Braves, c'est bien dommage."*...

When George heard of it he went down to that section and talked to the nice officer and gave him a scarf. That same evening a German orderly came to the half-way line, and brought a pair of warm, woolly gloves as a present in return for George.

The same night the Borderers and we were engaged in putting up big trestle obstacles, with barbed wire all over them, and connecting them, and at this same point (namely, where we were only 85 yards apart) the Germans came out and sat on their parapet, and watched us doing it, although we had informed them that the truce was ended... Well, all was quiet, as I said, that night; and next morning, while I was having breakfast, one of my N.C.O.'s came and reported that the enemy were again coming over to talk. I had given full instructions, and none of my men were allowed out of the trenches to talk to the enemy. I had also told the N.C.O. of an advanced post which I have up a ditch, to go out with two men, unarmed; if any of the enemy came over, to see that they did not cross the half-way line, and to engage them in pleasant conversation. So I went out, and found the same lot as the day before; they told me again that they had no intention of firing, and wished the truce to continue. I had instructions not to fire till the enemy did; I told them; and so the same comic form of temporary truce continued on the 26th, and again at 4.30 p.m. I informed them that the truce was at an end. We had sent them over some plum-puddings[1], and they thanked us heartily for them and retired again, the only difference being that instead of all my men being out in the "no man's zone," one N.C.O. and two men only were allowed out, and the enemy therefore sent fewer. [Captain Sir Edward Hamilton Westrowe Hulse, Bart., Scots Guards]

The festive spirit did not, however, prevail everywhere:

Your letters reached me as I was spending Christmas Day [1914], sitting very cold on the top of a haystack, looking for Germans. There was one German who was sending out little messages of peace and goodwill to all men, especially those on my stack; to put the matter in a nutshell, he was trying to shoot me, that was a nasty thing to do on Christmas Day, was it not? Just to show there was no ill feeling we fired a few shells into the trenches occupied by him and his friends, so I hope he is dead. [Francis Graham]

The 1914 truce came as a surprise to all concerned, and met with considerable disapproval from above. Nevertheless, in 1915, the weather put a temporary stop to the fighting:

The second Christmas of the Great War there was no repetition of the extraordinary truce which took place in several parts of the line on

---

1   Not, it is safe to assume, the trench mortar projectiles of that name.

Christmas Day, 1914. The High Command took care of that. Orders were issued that there was to be no fraternising with the enemy, and 'orders is orders'. As a matter of fact, in our part of the line, as it became light, several Germans called out 'A Happy Christmas, Tommy,' and our men replied with 'A Happy Christmas Fritz.' At one point they commenced to climb out of their trenches, but a few rounds fired high over their heads sent them back again. Seasonable greetings, however, were exchanged between friend and foe throughout the day, and as far as possible 'a good time was had by all!'

Two nights later Sergeant S— and I took one of the guns and mounted it on the parados of the front line trench. Our usual machine-gun emplacement had fallen in, together with most of the parapet, and the trenches were half-full of mud and water. It rained in torrents, and we obtained what shelter we could by crouching under our waterproof sheets. Small parties of our men patrolled the line just in front of our barbed wire, and the enemy did the same thing. Neither side fired on the other; the weather had stopped the fighting for the time being.
[H.Raymond Smith, 1/8th Worcesters]

At other times of year, a certain amount of communication across No-Man's-Land went on, as Anthony Eden discovered when his New Army division went into the line near Ypres:

...a party of officers and N.C.O.s was detailed for a spell in the trenches with the seasoned Scottish Division, then holding that section of the front. This was to be the first stage in our relief of the renowned Ninth Division.

The Germans, however, had other ideas and some useful intelligence reports. A night or two after our advanced details had begun to learn their way about, the enemy put down a short but intense bombardment of our forward areas followed by a raiding party, some of who broke into our front line.

Fortunately the relief had not yet got under way, and the raiders were soon killed, wounded or repulsed by a company of these formidable Scottish troops whose departure they had been so eager to celebrate. A signboard left behind was just a shade premature. It read, 'Farewell Jocks. Welcome to the Forty-first division.'

This battle of the notice boards continued for most of the summer and we did not always get the best of it. One displayed from our lines triumphantly announced the capture of Lemberg by the Russians with many thousands of prisoners. A few days later came the tit for tat: 'England expects that France and Russia will do her duty.'

Where the lines ran close to one another, oral communication sometimes occurred:

They wanted an officers' patrol to go out sometime, so Young and I went on after that and crawled down a hedge among mangold-wurzels, over lightly frozen ground that scrunched like grinding coffee. We got about 100 yards from their trenches, perhaps a bit less, and listened to them talking and working. I could not understand much, but I got a word every now and them. There were two sportsmen having a walk close in front of us talking sixty to the dozen - I think they were officers, but we heard nothing of any use. Most of the men were doing wire about 60 yards off us, and we could hear everything they did. After a bit, some blighter in our trenches fired, and the bullet ricochetted up close to us into the middle of this little party, but apparently did not hit them. They hated that, and when our fellows started shouting insults - the favourite one is 'Allyman Bully Beef!' Bang-bang-bang, off went the German rifles, and the machine gun joined in. Young rolled into the ditch pretty quick, into two feet of very cold water. I stopped where I was, and made a noise like a turnip. [2nd Lt. D.O.Barnett, 2nd Leinsters]

However, there were occasions when relations were more good-natured:

"Our learned friends opposite" at this time were a cheery crowd - the 33rd Bavarian Infantry. On one occasion later in the year - it was a frosty night - I heard a lot of laughing and shouting coming from a point just in front of their trench, and a big voice shouted across to us in English "Come on, Tommy; come on, Tommy! Where's your Major?" This he repeated several times, following each sally with a burst of deep-toned hearty laughter. Then there was another German who used to serenade us with tunes on a cornet. His favourite was "Love me, and the world is mine." He played beautifully, and in response to our hearty applause he would always oblige with an encore!

At times these Bavarians were relieved by a Saxon Division, who were equally friendly, if not more so. Only occasionally during our long tenure of these trenches were we opposed by Prussians. Our friends the enemy were kind enough to inform us of the unwelcome change. A voice shouted across from their trenches, "Look out, Tommy, the — Prussians are coming in to-morrow!" [H. Raymond Smith]

Good-natured relations could be taken to something of an extreme when the Germans in question had lived in this country before the war:

It is not to be wondered at that many a Fritz, who has lived amongst us for years, bears us far from bitter feelings. When a very green soldier, I was sent out at Armentieres [sic] to cover a party engaged in cutting down a patch of seeding chicory a few yards in front of our own wire. Being ordered to advance a hundred yards Fritzwards, I had paced but eighty odd, when, to my astonishment, I found myself securely entangled in wire of what was evidently an unlocated listening post. My rifle, wrenched from my hands, evidently collided with a screw stake, and a flare shot up *instanter*. Not fifteen yards away, sticking out from a hole sunk into the turf, were a rifle and the head and shoulders of a man. Of course I "froze" stiff. Seeing, however, no movement of the rifle, I began to think - thought such seemed impossible - that I was undiscovered. It was impossible. He had seen me plainly. Perhaps he was a sportsman, and scorned to wing a defenceless man. He laughed heartily, called out "Hallo, Johnny Bull, you silly old —," and sank into the earth. Yours truly likewise, plus rifle, but minus half a yard of tunic, and nearly a pair of pants. A very similar experience befell my friend a Captain of Canadian Infantry. Scouting alone in No Man's Land - a most unwise proceeding, by the way - he walked on to the levelled rifle of a sniper. Halting the Captain, the sniper ordered him to hands up and step back five paces. In the couple of minutes of conversation that ensued it appeared that my friend was in the hands of a Saxon, an Oxford graduate, and a man who - despite repeated requests not to be used on the British Front - had been sent against us. My friend was right-abouted and ordered to count fifty. At fifty-one he found himself alone and free. On the Roll of Honour of Oxford University is the name of a German who fell in defence of his fatherland. [Lt. M.Hastings, 52nd Battalion C.E.F.]

Notwithstanding such friendly interchanges, one is forcibly reminded by the following extracts that professional soldiers saw their job as that of killing the enemy:

We had a gorgeous killing yesterday. Macdonald saw 30 men go into a barn, which we had already accurately registered. We fired one salvo; one shell went right through the roof and blew out the ten-foot-high doors from inside. Several men ran out and many doubtless remained inside, as the shell must have burst right on top of them. We then tried the old trick of waiting for 15 minutes, which allows time for people to gather round the scene of a shelling, actuated by motives of curiosity or desire to help the wounded, after which we opened simultaneously with the 18-pdr. battery and fired fast for two minutes... One comes across only too many people who quite forget that the essence of war is to kill. They seem quite content to sit in their trench, or gun-pit, according to their profession, and grumble at being shelled; then when it is over make no attempt to take revenge. By hard thinking and hard work some new scheme can usually be devised, or a crafty plot hatched, to the end that a few more Huns may be wiped out. It often requires a lot of work, but the result, with any luck, justifies the trouble and risk taken. [Lt. Col. N. Fraser-Tytler, RFA]

In battle, where the objective was to occupy the German positions, prisoners were an inevitable concomitant of an attack, but, it seems, were not always permitted to become a hindrance to the advance.

Before an attack during Passchendaele, Hugh Quigley's CO made this plain in his pep-talk:

> "If the Hun shells too heavily, side-slip, but for God's sake don't go back. We have him by the short hairs, and it only remains for us to make a finished job. We had all had a fierce time punishing him and making him pay for those desecrations of human hearths and hearts; by the grace of God, we shall give him so much of his own hell that he will wish he had never created such misery. Do not shoot prisoners when such - that is, murder on his own lines; do not kill wounded if they are in desperate condition and helpless. If prisoners are in your way, you are allowed to dispose of them as you please. Not otherwise!"

The treatment of Germans who had surrendered was a controversial subject:

> R. and F. are such ripping fellows, and yet they look upon the "Bosch" as just so much unutterable vermin; they have no sort of pity or compunction for them; the more they kill the better. Once L. came into our mess, and he said in his boyish way, "And you know there was a rather rotten story about that raid last night" (it was a raid on the German trenches). "What was that?" said R. and F. "Why," said L., "they captured a German officer, and were taking him back to our lines, and he had his hands tied behind his back, and a chance bullet hit one of the men forming his escort, and so they turned on him and killed him."
>
> "I don't see anything rotten about that," said R. (and F. backed him up). "More Bosch you kill the better."
> "But," expostulated little L., "he was a *prisoner*; and it was only a stray bullet that hit his escort, and his hands were tied behind his back; and he could not defend himself; and they simply killed him just as he was."
> "And a damned good job too," says R. [2nd Lt. F.S.Snell, Royal Berkshire Regiment]

In the heat of battle, normal standards of conduct could easily be forgotten:

> ...we took a lot of prisoners in those trenches yesterday morning. Just as we got into their line, an officer came out of a dugout. He'd got one hand above his head, and a pair of field glasses in the other. He held the glasses out to S— you know, that ex-sailor with the Messina earthquake medal - and said, "Here you are, sergeant, I surrender." S— said, "Thank you, sir," and took the glasses with his left hand. At the same moment, he tucked the butt of his rifle under his arm and shot the officer straight through the head. What the hell ought I to do?'

He tore a withered blade of grass out of the ground and chewed it angrily, his eyes roving over the barren landscape. I thought hard for a minute.

'I don't see that you can do anything,' I answered slowly. 'What can you do? Besides, I don't see that S—'s really to blame. He must have been half mad with excitement by the time he got into that trench. I don't suppose he ever thought what he was doing. If you start a man killing, you can't turn him off again like an engine. After all, he is a good man. He was probably half off his head.'
'It wasn't only him. Another did exactly the same thing.'
'Anyhow, it's too late to do anything now. Suppose you ought to have shot both on the spot. The best thing now is to forget it.'
'I dare say you're right.' [Guy Chapman]

Understandably, anyone (on either side) who surrendered was apprehensive regarding the treatment he might receive. During the March 1918 German offensive, Lt. Frank Laird, wounded, with his position overrun and capture inevitable, found himself reassuring one of his men:

It was now dusk and things had quieted down for a space. The machine-gun fire and shelling had passed on behind us and our own people had not commenced to throw much over. I have no idea how long we lay around, face down to the ground, but it cannot have been long before the young fellow beside me interrupted my reflections by saying he saw the Boche coming along, and asking me did I think they would bayonet the wounded. I said "Not at all," but I did not feel quite so sure as I made out. However, our anxiety was soon relieved as a couple of them arrived, carrying very light equipment so far as I could see, pulled me up and took my revolver but none of my personal belongings. I pointed out that I was wounded and they whistled up a couple of stretcher bearers, who tied me up and set me on my feet, when I found I was able to walk with assistance.

What might perhaps be viewed as a striking example of gratitude for his survival was exhibited by one German officer during Passchendaele:

I found some of our men closely guarding two very dirty Germans. They both stood to attention; they were bare-headed.

The tallest man addressed me.

"I Must apologise, Sir, for my very dirty and unkempt appearance," he said in perfect English. "Your intense bombardment for the last three days has made shaving and washing impossible."

I was so astonished that I made no reply. I had not realised he was an officer.

The Colonel gave orders that he should be brought inside, so that he could cross-examine him on the dispositions of the enemy.

The German officer, standing strictly to attention, listened to him respectfully, but declined to answer any questions.

The General interviewed him at brigade headquarters with the same results. He was then sent down the line under escort with about fifty other prisoners, eventually arriving at Essex Farm, where they halted.

Our German officer calmly walked up to one of our medical officers:

"Excuse me, Sir" he said, "at your brigade headquarters I saw a large number of wounded. Would you like me to lead my men back there to act as stretcher bearers for you?"

The medical officer was of course surprised, but thankfully accepted the offer of this gallant German officer. [Dugdale]

It appears that, except during combat, each side often felt compassion for the other; they had, after all, more in common with one another than with their families at home:

Another funny thing happened yesterday. I had sent out a patrol to a hedge between the lines to investigate a suspected sniper's lair. They went out at 2 a.m., and I was in the front line about 3.30 a.m. to see them come in. They would come in in daylight. Suddenly a sentry said: "There is some one coming in on the right." I saw a man walking upright towards our trenches waving his cap over his head. It was rather hazy and I thought at first that he was coming in. The men were awfully funny and were calling out to him: "Come on, mate, it's all right. Are you hungry?" I spoke to him when he was still in the wire in my best German: *"Sprechen sie Englisch?"* He said, *"Nein, ich spreche frenzosischen."* He spoke very good French. He came in and was disarmed. I asked him what Regiment, and to my surprise he said *"La Garde"*. I expected to hear that he belonged to one or other of the Regiments that we knew are opposite us. He belonged to the Prussian Guard. He deserted in a fit of pique evidently, as he had been hit by his lieutenant. He left his rifle behind, but was wearing his equipment and bayonet and dagger. He was very young, but a fine, well-set-up chap, and extremely pleasant.

The men loved him and called him "Ginger." They gave him chocolate and made a great fuss over him. Isn't the British Tommy a weird person? He fraternised with "Ginger," who was certainly a very nice boy. He was evidently of a superior class and well educated. His French was perfect. To hear the men calling him "Mate" and fraternising with him made one feel the fatuity of war. [Capt. L.W.Crouch, Bucks. Battalion]

After all, the dead are all equal:

I wandered through the cemetery here to-day, where very many have been buried in the last few months. Among others, Guy Leach and [Major William La T.] Congreve. What a record! V.C., D.S.O., M.C., and Legion of Honour, and within an ace of becoming a Brigadier at 25. Incredible! But what really caught my interest most was a forgotten, uncared for patch beneath which were buried 5 or 6 Germans who had died in hospital. Poor Fritz Kolner of the 2nd Grenadier Regiment: I can pity him almost as much as John Macdonald of the Clyde R.G.A., who lies a few feet off. It is impossible to blame the individual for the sins of the nation, even though the nation is merely a collection of individuals. That is why all wars are so hateful. Those at the top make them and profit by them, but the rank and file, who bear the burden of it all, what do they get? [Capt. H. Dundas, Scots Guards, January 1917. Killed in action, 27th September 1918]

14
Offensive Operations - The Somme

The Somme offensive was initially proposed by the French, with the British assigned the subsidiary rôle of drawing the German reserves to the north of the River Somme, after which the French would attack to the south. However, this did not suit the commander of the BEF, Sir Douglas Haig, who proposed simultaneous offensives of equal weight. The French agreed to this, but then were overtaken by events, as the Germans launched their great attack at Verdun. This left them with insufficient men to make a large contribution to the Somme offensive and so the major rôle fell to the British. The task of conducting the attack fell to Sir Henry Rawlinson's Fourth Army. Rawlinson favoured a limited attack after a lengthy bombardment, to gain the enemy's first line of defences only; this was because he lacked the artillery firepower (in terms both of quantity and accuracy) to ensure that the German defences further back could be adequately suppressed and felt that the training of his troops was insufficient to ensure that formations would maintain cohesion in order to resist counter-attack if a deep advance were undertaken. Furthermore, he felt that no breakthrough was possible, so the aim was really to kill as many Germans as possible, and to that end, a small advance was as good as a large one. However, Haig disagreed. His view was that a breakthrough was undoubtedly possible, and so the attack should aim to capture the German second line (at this stage, there were only two) in addition to the first. Then cavalry (omitted altogether from Rawlinson's plan) could come forward to exploit the infantry's success. Furthermore, he felt that surprise would be forfeited if the bombardment were longer than a few hours, and so told Rawlinson that he was wrong to rely on anything more lengthy - even though the latter had told him that he simply did not have enough guns for a hurricane bombardment. Rawlinson capitulated, and amended his plan to include the seizure of the German second line, even though this considerably reduced the density of shelling of the first line and so risked not gaining it in the first place. On one point he did, however, stand his ground - the length of the bombardment - and Haig finally conceded that he was correct. And so the plan fell between two stools; the bombardment would be long enough to ensure that there would be no element of surprise, and not dense enough to destroy the German defences. Furthermore, by the time the attack took place, the Germans had constructed a third line of defence. The 'big push' was to go forward on a 20,000-yard front, from

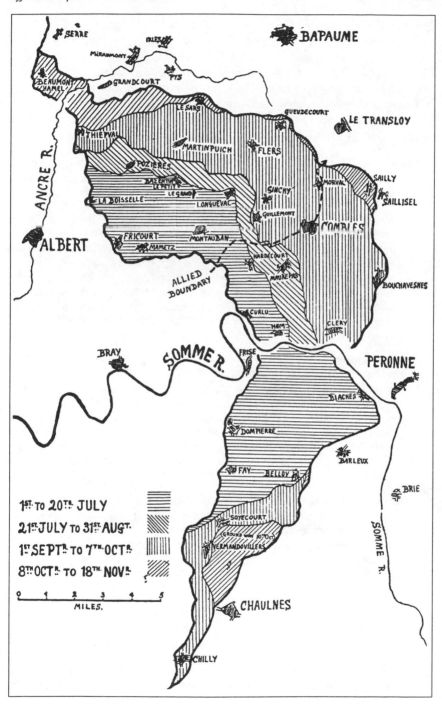

the fortified village of Serre in the north to Montauban in the south. Contrary to popular belief, the infantry were not all explicitly instructed to cross No-Man's-Land in line and at walking pace. In fact, Rawlinson abdicated responsibility for such matters and left it to corps or even divisional commanders to decide how their men should advance. Some advocated slow moving waves, but by no means all.

The attack was preceded by months of careful preparation. One artillery officer wrote home of the activity on the southern flank:

> Before this letter is posted the great attack will have been launched, so I am able at last to describe some of the hectic preparations that have occupied us all this month...
>
> As I mentioned before, the French have taken over the small sector between Maricourt and the Somme, which our battery and two 18-pdr. batteries formerly covered. To-day there are no less than 424 French guns and Howitzers packed into the little salient, and as we have increased our guns in nearly the same proportion, you can imagine the congestion of batteries in this valley. From Maricourt back to Susanne, all along the bottom of the Valley, row after row of batteries, and often brigades, can be seen, in lines one behind the other about 200 yards apart.
>
> The whole of May and the first half of June was spent in frenzied efforts to be ready. It was literally a race against time, and I don't think the people at home realize the stupendous preparations that a 'show' entails. The whole face of the country has to be altered, and altered, if possible, without the Hun spotting it. New roads everywhere, frequently of solid timber to take heavy traffic in wet weather; new trenches all over the place - some of the new communication trenches running back as far as three to four miles owing to the great depth of the salient we are in.
>
> Then in suitable localities behind the front line, trenches had to be dug to provide assembly places for Brigades forming the second wave of the attack. These positions consist of a labyrinth of trenches 10 to 12 feet deep, roofed with wire netting and grass to escape aerial observation; besides all this the country is covered with a network of telephone trenches, deep narrow slits with about 20 cables in each.
>
> When one is looking down from Maricourt towards Susanne the valley resembles one vast circus, with hundreds of motor-lorries, carts, timber wagons, caterpillars dragging big guns, convoys of trench store wagons going to forward dumps, often hundreds of the French trench mortar bomb carts - curious little vehicles like one-horse sulkies - and strings of anything up to 300 pack mules or horses bearing French S.A.A. All this in a place where four months ago not a single G.S. wagon was to be seen in daylight.

The traffic certainly is extraordinary, and our wagons often take six hours to do the seven-mile journey from the wagon line to the guns.

France ought really to be enlarged for this type of fighting. There honestly is not room for all the different kinds of dumps of engineers' stores, food and ammunition, and particularly trench mortar bombs. The latter especially take up a lot of ground, and as it is quite impossible to get the thousands of aerial torpedo bombs under any sort of cover, so they have just got to take their chance in the open. Each of the French battery positions looks like a busy anthill, as about 150 French Territorials are allotted to help each of their batteries to get dug in. I wish we could occasionally get infantry help like that for ourselves. [Lt. Col. N.Fraser-Tytler, D/151 Battery RGA]

Lt. Col. Fraser Tytler's letter provides a good example of the almost universal optimism preceding the 'Big Push,' and initial reports from the front line seemed to bear this out. But almost invariably these proved to be false and by late morning it had become apparent that the initial attack had been a bloody failure. In those places where the German lines had been breached, success was all too brief and the attacking infantry either repulsed with heavy loss or cut off and surrounded to be killed or captured later. Another artillery officer, in his front line observation post, recorded what he heard and saw that morning:

At zero I looked out of the O.P. The din had quietened a little. What I saw made me cry out, so that the others, telephonists and all, ran up to me. It was smoke and gas. For a mile stretching away from me, the trench was belching forth dense columns of white, greenish, and orange smoke. It rose curling and twisting, blotting everything from view, and then swept, a solid rampart, over the German lines. For more than an hour this continued, and I could see nothing. Sometimes the smoke was streaked with a scarlet star as a shell burst among it, and sometimes a smoke candle would be hurled high into the air, spluttering and making a cloud of its own far above the rest. It seemed impossible that men could withstand this awful onslaught - even if it were only smoke. And yet a machine gun played steadily all the time from the German front line. What fighters they are! He swept the O.P., cutting twigs from above our heads, and splashing mud out of our sandbags. Somewhere to the right of that smoke the Infantry were advancing. I could see nothing. Reports and rumours came dancing down the wires.

"Our Infantry have taken the front line without resistance."
"Prisoners are coming in."
"Enemy giving themselves up in hundreds."
"Infantry have crossed the Serre Ridge."
"Beaumont Hamel is ours."

"More prisoners reported."

This continued until 11.30 when the smoke cleared, and I looked out upon the invisible battle! Far as I could see not a soldier could be seen, not a movement of any sort. Could it be that we held those trenches. Had we captured Serre? Once the village had been hidden by thick trees and hedges, now it stood bare and shattered, the trees leafless, as though a comb had been dragged through them.

The Germans were shelling their own trenches, that was all the sign of change I noticed.

I tried to observe while F— ranged on hostile batteries, but the smoke was too confusing, and flying pieces and bullets made it a difficult matter. In the afternoon the Germans launched a counter attack immediately opposite our O.P., but unfortunately invisible to us. Their shelling was heavy and accurate. Our O.P. swayed perilously, our wires were cut in four places, within 100 yards of the O.P.; a linesman of D/241 mended them, and I have mentioned him for distinction. We sat in the dug-out waiting and calculating.

The captain from O.P.F. had a clear view of the counter attack and switched the LX on it. In fact the LX and one other battery stopped the attack. Unfortunately I could see nothing, as I had to watch another point from which attacks had been expected.

The Infantry were cut to pieces, they came running back between the lines; Germans stood on their parapets and shot them down. H— and his men left soon after, but I stayed to register the guns on to — Valley in case of a counter attack in that direction. Then about 6.30 I came away.

I met an Infantry officer. He was grey in the face and had not shaved.
"Well," he said, "what do you think of it?".
"Seems all right."
"Um, we got to their third line and were driven back; we are barely holding our own front line - we're - we're wiped out - General's a broken man."
"But Gommecourt?"
"Lost."
"Another Loos," I said.

"Looks it." He turned away.

I felt tired suddenly. The few yards home were miles.

The world was full of stretchers and white faces, and fools who gibbered about the great advance. [Lt. A. C. Stephen MC]

However, the picture was not as black everywhere. On the southern flank of the attack, the initial objectives were both taken and held, though the possibilities of a breakthrough and the capture of key positions which later took months and many lives to gain, were lost:

> The 1st of July opened with a glorious though very misty morning. Dense belts of fog were hanging in the valleys, and only the tops of the hills were to be seen. After an early breakfast at 4.30 a.m. and a final inspection of the guns, I went up to the O.P., and by six o'clock the other three battery commanders and their F.O.O.'s had also turned up, and the party for the great spectacle was complete.
>
> All night long the bombardment had continued, but at 6.25 a.m. the final intense bombardment started. Until 7.15 a.m. observation was practically impossible owing to the eddies of mist, rising smoke, flashes of bursting shells, and all one could see was the blurred outline of some miles of what appeared to be volcanoes in eruption. At 7.20 a.m. rows of steel helmets and the glitter of bayonets were to be seen all along the front line. At 7.25 a.m., the scaling ladders having been placed in position, a steady stream of men flowed over the parapet, and waited in the tall grass till all were there and then formed up; at 7.30 a.m. the flag fell and they were off, the mist lifting just enough to show the long line of divisions attacking: on our right the 39th French division; in front of us our 30th division; on our left the 18th.
>
> The line advanced steadily, scarcely meeting any opposition in the first three lines of trenches. Every point was reached at scheduled time, so the automatic artillery barrage was always just in front of the infantry. At 9 o'clock we could see our flags waving in the trench behind German's Wood, and by 8.20 the formidable Glatz Redoubt was captured, an advance of 700 yards with very little loss. This redoubt had been submitted to a terrific bombardment, and the infantry reported that the maze of strong points, machine-gun emplacements, etc., had all been swept away, and that the trenches were crammed with dead. By 8.40 a.m. we had captured Casement Trench, and from there a dense smoke barrage was created with a view to hiding the advance of the second wave (90th Brigade), their objective being Montauban village. They went across in perfect formation up to Glatz Redoubt; there they made a short pause, and then continued the attack and captured the whole village of Montauban by 10 a.m., establishing our line on the north side of the village, overlooking Caterpillar Valley.
>
> Between 10 and 12 noon there was a lull in the operations, and then came the capture of the Briquetterie, preceded by half an hour's intense bombardment. During all this time the country was dotted with little parties of prisoners, each with an escort of two men - one Tommy behind to whip up the laggards, while the one in front was usually

surrounded by a crowd of prisoners, all eager to show him the quickest
way back to safety and food in our lines!

After the mist lifted the light for observing was perfect. There was no
Hun shelling, and gradually people emerged from their tunnels and sat
on the top of the shafts till it felt quite like a 'point to point' crowd. On
the whole we had a very delightful day, with nothing to do except send
numerous reports through to Head-Quarters and observe the
stupendous spectacle before us. There was nothing to do as regards
controlling my Battery's fire, and any fresh targets were dealt with by
one officer, who sat all day in a dug-out by himself, with map board and
battery watch before him. All orders were written on slips and sent by
runners to each gun. Another officer was with the guns, while the third
remained with me ready to go forward if necessary, and also to
supervise the visual signalling arrangements in case our cable was
broken.

In the afternoon the Hun shelling increased slightly, but he appeared to
be completely demoralized, and, for the moment shaken out of his wits.

The night was troubled by constant futile Hun attacks, so we fired
practically all the time. I went to the O.P. at 3 a.m. and found things
were then quiet. Later I was relieved by one of the subalterns, but before
returning to breakfast I could not resist taking an hour's holiday and
running down to the old German front line. There is a wonderful
fascination in walking on ground lately shelled by one's own guns. In
this case, however, scarcely a trace of the outline of the trenches was left.
I could have picked up numerous souvenirs, but as they are always
heavy to carry and invariably get lost sooner or later, I refrained.

By this time the Hun was again shelling rather severely, so as I didn't
wish to become a casualty while joy-riding, I hurried back to the Battery
and a most enjoyable breakfast. [Lt. Col. N. Fraser-Tytler]

Notwithstanding this limited success, the attack as a whole had failed.
Despite the duration of the barrage (eight days), it had failed to cut all
the German barbed wire, destroy their dugouts (many of which were 20
feet deep) and to knock out their artillery and machine-guns, both of
which played havoc with the attacking - and later retreating - infantry.
Some battalions were virtually wiped out between their 'jumping-off
points' and the British front line ahead of them.

Those troops who broke into or got anywhere near the German
defences were soon pinned down at the mercy of the German fire,
unable to go forward or, perhaps more menacingly, to retreat. The
losses on this first day amounted to some 57,470, of whom 19,240 were
killed - the worst in the history of the British army on a single day.

Where the assault had been successful, the artillery preparation had been more effective - assisted by French guns - and generalship more imaginative, as in the 18th Division, which was ordered by its commander, Sir Ivor Maxse, to lie out in No-Man's-Land prior to the initial assault and so rush the German trenches before their surviving defenders had had time to emerge from their dugouts.

Over the coming months a pattern of attacks developed in order to win those prizes which had lain so temptingly open on 1st July. The fighting which ensued was continuous and bloody, for pushing the Germans back was slow work and the combat often at close quarters. The war poet Siegfried Sassoon served on the Somme with 1st Battalion, Royal Welch Fusiliers. Notwithstanding his later anti-war views he was a keen and conscientious front-line officer.

On Tuesday night (July 4) we struggled up to Mametz and on to Bottom Wood in awful mud. I sat with C. Company in a reserve trench till we were sent for (about 2.30 a.m.) to reinforce. This order was cancelled before we got there, but I went on to see what was happening (and got cursed considerably by the Colonel for doing so!). It was beginning to be daylight. I crossed from Bottom Wood, by the way they had attacked, and found our D. Company had got there all right, but things seemed in rather a muddle, especially on the right, where B. did no good - got lost or machine-gunned - and A. had gone up and saved the situation. The Companies advanced at 12.45 a.m. after a short bombardment by our guns. They had to cross five hundred yards of open ground and occupy Quadrangle Trench (a half-finished work the Germans were said to be holding lightly). There seems to have been a working-party there digging, but they cleared off without showing fight (except for a little bombing). Our attack was quite unexpected.

When I got there, morning was just getting grey; the trench taken had some wire in front, but was quite shallow and roughly dug. On the right loomed Mametz Wood - in front open country, a Bosche trench about five hundred yards away. Our men were firing a good deal at Bosches they couldn't see, and were rather excited, mostly.

The enemy were bombing up a communication-trench from the wood. The Royal Irish had attacked on our right and failed to get into the enemy trenches (Strip Trench and Wood Trench). We got a bombing-post established on our right where the Quadrangle Trench came to a sudden end. The Germans had fled, leaving their packs, rifles, bombs etc on the edge of the trench. Several of them were lying face downwards in the mud. We began digging the trench deeper, but the men were rather beat. After daylight the enemy sniped a lot from the wood, and we had five men killed and several wounded (C.D. Morgan got hit in the leg - not badly). I went across from our bombing-post to

where Wood Trench ended, as there was a Bosche sniper: the others
fired at the parapet, so they didn't see me coming. When I got there I
chucked four Mills bombs into their trench and to my surprise fifty or
sixty (I counted eighty-five packs left on the firestep) ran away like hell
into Mametz Wood. Our Lewis-gun was on them all the way and I think
they suffered. (Ask someone else about this show!) We had got the
Quadrangle Trench well held by mid-day - no counter-attacks, only a
little bombing (and the damned snipers playing hell).[1]

While numerous small attacks and raids such as Sassoon describes took
up a great part of the Somme fighting, in order to capture strongpoints
which had resisted such attempts, large-scale assaults inevitably had to
be undertaken. The Germans had a tendency to occupy woods as
strongpoints - the trees offering excellent concealment for them - and so
such attacks were frequently characterised by 'wood fighting.' One
especially hard nut to crack was Trônes Wood, which was finally taken
on 14th July by men of Maxse's 18th Division. As ever, careful artillery
preparation was an essential precursor to the infantry assault:

In my last letter I described the first round of desperate fighting for
Trônes Wood on the 8th and 9th. There were endless attacks and
counter-attacks; bombardments and counter-bombardments by night
and day until the morning of the 13th, when there was a lull before the
final struggle that night.

I forget how many times the centre of the wood changed hands, but we
never quite lost our hold of the southern end. The wood used to show
up as a dense compact mass on the skyline, but after the appalling
shelling it has got it is now only a tortured collection of stumps. The
hostile gun-fire has been gaining in severity each day; every night we
have tear gas and incendiary shells all round the village, and by day
heavy shells of every calibre, even up to three 17-inch...

No observing was possible for days, as all the skyline was in our hands,
and our only target the middle of Trônes Wood, so we used to go
forward by turns to study the Hun second line. On the 11th I sent
Wilson and Macdonald to see if it would be possible to establish an O.P.
in the north end of Bernafay Wood. They had a tough day. It took them
three hours to reach even the middle of the wood, hampered as they

---

1   For this exploit Sassoon was recommended for a further
     decoration, but the award was disallowed since the attack as a
     whole was a failure.

were by incessant shell-fire, the heavy going and the impossible tangle of broken tree stumps.

While working their way up a sap, they noticed a movement in a pile of about thirty bodies - chiefly Hun - and found one of the Manchesters, wounded in five places, who had been lying in that charnel house for three days and nights. The journey back to the south side of the wood, the search for stretcher bearers and the return journey to the wounded man, took another five hours' hard labour. On their arrival they found that the sap had been hit twice again by shells, and a tree had also fallen across the man, but luckily without crushing him. He was quite cheery and thanked them. Good luck to him! It was by that time so late that Wilson and Macdonald had to return without reaching their objective.

The morning of Thursday, the 13th, saw a pause in our firing, a lull before the great attack on the second system of enemy trenches, though before this attack could be launched Trônes Wood had to be taken. At 5 p.m., with redoubled fury, we commenced shelling the centre and north end of Trônes Wood. We continued bombarding the zone beyond the Wood until 1 a.m., but the enemy attempted no counter-attack. Soon after midnight we got orders that at 3.25 a.m. the 18th Division were to attack and capture the second line, and that the preparatory bombardment was to last for five minutes only. Accordingly, 3.20 a.m., the whole world broke into gun-fire. It was a stupendous spectacle - the darkness lit by thousands of gun flashes - the flicker of countless bursting shells along the northern skyline, followed a few minutes later by a succession of frantic S.O.S. rockets and the glare of burning Hun ammunition dumps. Our fire continued at a rapid rate till 10.30 a.m., when we got news of the capture of the objective, and soon after, on the skyline west of Montauban, we could see the silhouettes of cavalry and horse artillery moving forward, a thrilling sight after the weary round of trench warfare. [Lt. Col. N.Fraser-Tytler]

The infantry attack on this occasion was entrusted to Lt. Col. Frank Maxwell VC, under whose command were his own battalion, the 12th Middlesex, and the 6th Northants. In a letter to his wife he described the fighting in a characteristically dispassionate manner:

But from 11 p.m. onwards kept busy for an attack on the Trônes Wood, which had been taken (more or less), lost and retaken, about three times or four. Finally, it had to be taken, and kept at all costs, for certain military reasons, which are now in progress, and the Northants and my regiment, under myself, were ordered to do it. Not a pleasant or easy job to take on, and be warned for at 2 a.m., and get across the open before daylight to edge of the wood, or be Maxim gunned out of existence. My regiment was to lead, but had already been scattered by various orders, so when I reached the starting point there were but two companies, so I had to put the Northamptons in front, and not wait for my people. We

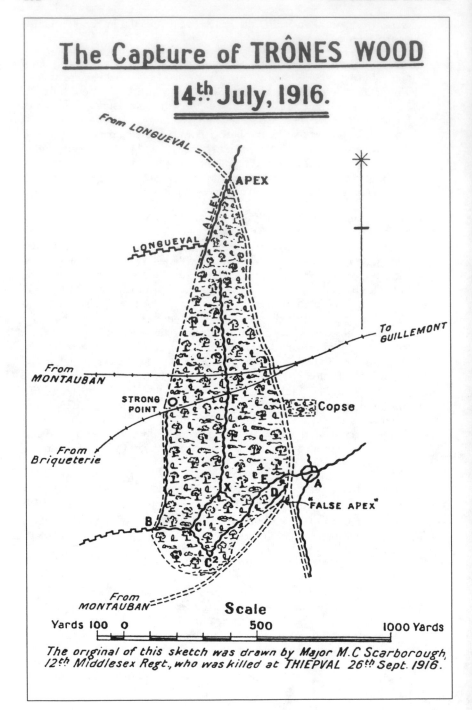

The Capture of TRÔNES WOOD
14th July, 1916.

The original of this sketch was drawn by Major M.C Scarborough, 12th Middlesex Regt., who was killed at THIEPVAL 26th Sept. 1916.

crossed just as dawn was breaking the half-mile of open to the wood, passing through a very thick enemy barrage of shell. (The edge of the wood we were aiming for was held by a battalion that had managed to stay in at the last attack.) We got over wonderfully well, and only one or two parties were blown away, which is wonderful. Men were very good and steady. On arrival at wood, my orders were for the battalion to halt on edge and reform; but the C.O. got muddled and didn't do this, and, consequently, hadn't a dog's chance of doing anything, except be killed just in the same way as other regiments had been for the same fault. Fortunately, I stopped mine inside, and kept them in hand; then waited for reports to come back from Northants. None came, nor could come, as they were soon lost and broken up into small bodies, playing just the game the G.'s like, for it let them play their old game of firing at them from sideways and behind. Realising after a time that it was a case of another regiment gone for nothing, I had to beat round and get at the situation, and collect its remains, and with my own began to form a line clean across the wood, in the way I always meant to. To talk of a 'wood' is to talk rot. It was the most dreadful tangle of dense trees and undergrowth imaginable, with deep yawning broken trenches criss-crossing about it; every tree broken off at top or bottom and branches cut away, so that the floor of the wood was almost an impenetrable tangle of timber, trenches, under growth, etc., blown to pieces by British and German heavy guns for a week.

Never was anything so perfectly dreadful to look at - at least, I couldn't dream of anything worse - particularly with its dreadful addition of corpses and wounded men - many lying there for days and days. (Our doctor found one to-day who had no food or water for five days.)

Well, I formed a line with fragments of Northants and two companies of my own, under a job lot of about five very young officers, all the rest being *hors de combat*.

After infinite difficulty, I got it shaped in the right direction, and then began the advance, very, very, slowly. Men nearly all much shaken by the clamour and din of shell-fire, and nervy and jumpy about advancing in such a tangle of debris and trenches, etc. I had meant only to organise and start the line, and then get back to my loathsome ditch, back near the edge of the wood where we had entered, so as to be in communication by runners with the Brigade and world outside. It is a fundamental principle that commanders of any sort should not play about, but keep in touch with the Higher Authorities behind. But though old enough soldier to realise this, and the wrath of my seniors for disregarding it, I immediately found that without my being there the thing would collapse in a few minutes. Sounds vain, perhaps, but there is nothing of vanity about it really. So off I went with the line, leading it, pulling it on, keeping its direction, keeping it from its hopeless (and humanly natural) desire to get into a single file behind me, instead of a long line either side. Soon I made them advance with fixed bayonets, and ordered them, by way of encouraging themselves, to fire ahead of them into the tangle of all the way. This was a good move, and gave them confidence, and so we went on with constant halts to adjust the line. After slow progress in this way, my left came on a hornet's nest, and I halted the line and went for it with the left portion. A curtain may be drawn over this, and all that need be said was that many Germans ceased to live, and we took a machine-gun. Then on again, and then again, what I had hoped for. The Germans couldn't face a long line offering no scattered groups to be killed, and they began to bolt, first back, then, as the wood became narrow, they bolted out to the sides, and with rifle and automatic guns we slew them. Right up to the very top this went on, and I could have had a much bigger bag, except that I did not want to show my people out of the wood, or too much out, for fear of letting the German artillery know how we had progressed, and so enable them to plaster the wood *pari passu* with our advance. So far they had only laid it on thick, strong, and deadly in the belt we had left behind. However, many we let go for this reason, we slew or picked up later.

And, finally, the job was done, and I was thankful, for I thought we should never, never get through with it.

The difficulties of this type of fighting, and especially of communication were described by Lt. Col. Fraser-Tytler:

One heard on all sides that it was impossible to keep a line going to Trônes Wood, but unobserved shooting is very dull, and often, I fear, very ineffective, so accordingly, early next day, Sunday, the 16th, I started off with four of our best signallers, my intention being to relay the line up Faviere Valley, so as to secure, if possible, observation from the Trônes Wood front line.

After about six hours' hard work we got a line carefully laid to our most advanced point, and then began one of the most amusing twenty-four hours I have ever spent. You know that when hunting one sometimes feels there will be a good run, so this day I felt we were going to have good luck and a successful kill. My first act was to locate a new enemy trench, very shallow and full of Huns; I sent down the map reference to the battery, telling them to engage it and if possible not to hit me, as I was lying out in a shell-hole in front of our line, and the target was barely 150 yards further on.

A really good 'target' is only too often wasted, being merely frightened away instead of destroyed, so in order not to alarm the Hun I registered the trench with the minimum number of shells, and then, having informed Group, I also registered the 18-pdr. batteries of our brigade. It was a rather ticklish job shooting other people's batteries so close to our lines. That done I phoned the officer at the guns to arrange a zero hour in five minutes' time, and then speedily crawled into a safer hole to watch the last act of the drama.

The trench meanwhile was as crowded as ever with quite unsuspicious Boches. Then down came the curtain. It was glorious to hear the shells of four batteries all at 'gun-fire', swooping down close over one's head and to see the havoc they were making in the trench, a great portion of which we enfiladed. That wonderful story in the 'Green Curve' came to my mind, and after four minutes of 'gunfire' I ran down to the guns, "It is enough." That diversion over, I registered my own guns and the 18-pdrs. on the other good spots, leaving one 18-pdr. from each battery to tickle up the trench with occasional rounds. While all this was going on, the news of my shoot appeared to have caused a mild panic at Divisional H.Q., as according to their information my target was in British hands. Endless questions began to come down the phone as to whether I was quite certain they were Germans. I replied that as their principal pastime had been sniping at my head (until I pasted them), I had strong reasons for believing them to be the enemy.

The afternoon was a busy one, as Group sent down a mass of targets for me to register the different batteries on. Owing to the incessant Hun shelling, communication was difficult, and during the idle intervals while the wire was being repaired, I was able to move about and examine the country. How different it all is from the neat, orderly manner of fighting in pukka trench warfare. From a flank, during one of my explorations, I spotted some Huns in a trench leading directly into our front line: no one had noticed its junction with our trench, as the entrance was blocked with debris. The Hun also seemed unaware that his front door was open, and I joined the infantry in a most successful and amusing bombing stunt up the trench, establishing a blocking post half-way along it. During another tour I met a most energetic infantry brigadier, and we spent an enjoyable hour crawling round together.

Towards evening the rain came down in torrents, but I managed to borrow an overcoat from the body of a fairly clean-looking Hun officer who was lying near. The sunken road (our front line), leading below Maltz Horn Farm to the S.E. corner of Trônes Wood is literally paved with dead Huns.

While this confused wood-fighting was taking place, the pressure on the Germans was maintained elsewhere by more conventional set-piece attacks. On July 16th, the 1/5th Royal Warwicks were involved in a renewed attempt to capture Ovillers - one of the numerous objectives of 1st July which the British had failed to take on that day.

The briefing by the Royal Warwicks CO for the attack was attended by Charles Edmonds:

In the evening Bickersteth and I were summoned to headquarters and I began to feel afraid again. We were the last to come, and found the C.O. already poring over a map, and talking to the ring of officers clustered round, their faces alone illumined by the light of a candle on the dugout table.

"Is that everyone, Heywood?" asked the C.O.
"Yes, sir."
"Right. We're going to do a little attack to-night. Our objective is the cross-roads behind Ovillers. Better look at it on my map - it's the best. Can you see, Suckling? Right. We've got to get there at 1 a.m. It'll be difficult. Jumping-off place is a line drawn from point 66 at right angles to the main road." He talked on as quietly as if he were giving operation orders for manoeuvres.

I could hardly listen. A tremendous sense of realisation came over me - I hardly know if it were fear or excitement. I knew just what to do. Attacks I was familiar with, but they were attacks over known ground against imaginary enemies. Fighting I knew, but it was fighting dream battles with visionary foes. That had been a favourite game since I had played at 'fighting Boers' in the nursery. For the very first time I thought what it meant, to struggle for life with a man of equal wit and training. Not all the strain of six months' trench warfare, of the ordeal of July 1st, of the last two days of preparation, had told me what was the meaning of war, the 'ultima ratio.' In a dream I heard, and in a dream I wrote notes of the plan. The battalion would form here in two waves, would wheel half-left here, would march by this line on the left and would extend and assault here. Our right was guarded by the 17th battalion: from the left the Irish would converge and join us. B company would take the left front.

Edmonds vividly recalled how difficult negotiating trench systems and the debris of previous attacks in order to reach the start position could become at night:

But that walk became a nightmare. I was at the tail of the company, which moved for hours through broken trenches in single file. Just before me the two Lewis-gun teams stumbled along hopelessly overloaded with guns and clumsy ammunition-buckets, swearing and tripping over broken ground and trailing wire. Presently we climbed out of the trench and hurried over a grassy slope that had been little shelled, where there was a light railway. Now and then we passed salvaged equipment and once or twice a corpse lying sprawled by the way. The battalion was already straggling out in the effort to reach that hopeless rendezvous in time. It became harder and harder to keep up the pace with these tired and heavy-laden men. Then we came out on a road that ran along the top of a spur. The high bank on its further side was honeycombed with little shelters dug in the mud, where snoring figures slept huddled under muddy groundsheets. Though the night was clear there was a suspicion of damp drizzle in the air. I rushed forward to try to halt the front of the column for a moment. Bickersteth was nowhere to be found. I pressed on again, but only at the centre of A company could I find an officer, Evers, a subaltern I knew well. He thought vaguely that the company commanders had gone ahead to find the way. At the head of the battalion there was no officer. I ordered them to halt.

"Gone ahead, sir," said a voice, "told us to follow on, and I think we're lost, sir."
"Hell!" said I. "Haven't they left an officer at the head of the column?"
"I dunno, sir," sad the voice as if it were quite resigned to its fate and very tired of me. "There's a guide somewheres, sir."

At last I found him, a bewildered private of another regiment, roped in to lead us to Point 66 on the Bapaume Road. He knew nothing: he was waiting for the officer to come back. As we waited for the rear to come up, I asked him about his regiment, and was told a pathetic story of how they had been sent over the top by accident at Contalmaison, and badly cut up because the orderly with the cancelling message never came in time. Then he told me of my cousin in his regiment whom I had not seen since 1914, and how to find his camp at Bécourt.

Soon the situation straightened out and the column moved on. As I dropped back to my place I sent Evers, who was my junior, to take the head of his company with the guide. So the weary march continued through dark winding ways. Climbing over obstacles, squeezing past narrow places, stumbling over fallen wires and débris, passing now and again shrouded bundles by the way that sometimes turned with a wary stare, or woke cursing, and sometimes lay still with death. At one point we came out on the main road, wide and clear and empty, flanked with shattered trees, and then went down again into the longest trench of all where the few occupants were men of the 17th battalion. Here, though we never knew it, we were right among the enemy and in danger of counter-attack from almost any side. This, Sickle Trench, was a long curving line that led in the direction of Ovillers from the furthest point of our advanced line.

The pace was now quicker than ever; the companies in rear had dropped right out of hearing, and I was feeling desperate, when suddenly I came, round a traverse, face to face with Thorne of D company, who was pushing and lifting the last man before me, gun, ammunition and all, out on to the parapet.

The troops having finally assembled at their starting positions, Edmonds experienced going forward into the unknown:

We were "over the top." We went on in the dark, breaking now and then into the double. The exhilaration of that rush of men was wonderful.

The two first waves, barely fifteen yards apart, bunched until the sections were almost shoulder to shoulder. The bayonets gleamed in the flashes of the barrage that crashed in front of us. It seemed unbelievable that this torrent of men could sweep upon the enemy unseen.

Down the hill. On. On.

Not a shot was fired.

Now, where the ground sloped up again over broken ground the ranks were breaking and we bunched together.

Someone cried "Extend" and the men threw themselves forward, running now over shell-holes ever closer together. I was no more afraid than if it were all a game. Only where the village was looming up, a black line of ruins and hedges against the dark sky, I glanced nervously, looking for the opening of that flanking machine gun fire. Surely they must have seen us.

The ground was now torn and furrowed, ploughed into powdery chaos by the bombardment. A battered trench could only just be distinguished in the general ruin.

We broke into a charge and someone behind me tried to cheer. We silenced him, but still no sign came from the enemy.

Over the empty trench, and on. So much for the first objective.

We struggled over mound and crater of spongy soil and reached the road. No sign from the enemy.

Beyond was a high bank, and over that I could see the Verey lights go up from the next German line. But the road was now filled with crowds of panting men. Where was my objective? The cross-roads were blasted out of existence. If that flattened ditch over which I had jumped was my trench, then heaven help us when the machine-guns fired down from the village on our left.

"Get your sections in hand," I shout to every N.C.O. I can see, "and keep quiet, for God's sake." Now to find Bickersteth. I rush madly about in the road and find no officer but Wells - vague and flurried.

"What are we to do?" whispers he, clutching me.

"Go on!"
"No, we've gone far enough."
"Can't stop here," say I.

Then the expected happened. Crack, crack, crack, went the Boche machine-gun, shooting uneasily at this noise from a strange direction, shooting wildly, but showing he had heard us.

I thought frenziedly. Bickersteth must be hit or lost. Had we gone too far or not far enough? The soldier's motto: "When in doubt go forward." At least we could not stay here and be shot down in the cutting. In this supreme moment I was inspired. More and more men crowded on to the road, and half a dozen orders and warnings were bandied about. I drew my revolver and scrambled up the bank.

"Come on lads," I shouted, "over the top."

For one ghastly moment I stood there alone.

It seemed that I was lifted out of myself, and something in me that was cynical and cowardly looked down in a detached way at this capering little figure posing and shouting unrepeatable heroics at the men below. Through the cracking of the machine-gun, and the banging of the barrage, at last I made myself heard.

"Forward!" and we'll have the next trench, too."

Then I became aware of a short little fat man standing beside me brandishing a rifle and bayonet. With a common impulse we turned and ran on towards the enemy.

"Who are you?" I shouted. "I can't see you."
"Don't cher know me, sir?" he said; "I'm the serjeant-major's batman."
"Good man," said I, "I'll remember you for this."

As we raced across the short fifty yards of grass a trickle of men and then a rush followed us over the bank. Before us we felt vaguely that there was commotion in the enemy's trench and the Verey lights went up no more.

We were now in the barrage which had seemed to go before us across the valley. I reached the edge of the trench wondering vaguely what I should do if I found a German bayonet-man poised in it to catch me as I jumped.

But the bay was empty, and I landed on the firm floor of the trench just as a shell burst with a metallic bang ten or fifteen yards on my right. This was as good fun as playing soldiers in the garden at home. In a minute there were twenty or thirty men behind me, shouting and laughing as they skylarked round the traverses.

Of course there was no officer or N.C.O handy. I began to think I was winning the Battle of the Somme alone. Then behind me I noticed the grey head of Corporal Turner, who always reminded me of Baloo in the 'The Jungle Book.'

"I've got my six men here," he said rather plaintively.

"We can't go for that machine-gun over there, sir. It's miles away. The Colonel told me to stick to you, sir, if we couldn't get at it."
"Good for C company," I shouted, "you're the only section that has stuck together. Take your men down the trench as far as you can to the left and make a bomb-stop and hold that side."
"Right oh, sir," and he went.

Then I rushed along to the right, the way the garrison had retired, but there was no N.C.O. to send to that flank. I put Griffin, an old hand whom I knew to have a head on his shoulders, in charge of two or three men to block the trench by cutting a firing position in a big traverse. Then I went back to my point of entry. The trench was deep and wide, with sheer sides and a firm floor of clay. The traverses were seven or eight feet high and ten feet thick.

I found Serjeant Broad then, an old ginger-whiskered fellow, who had served in the regular army.

"Well, serjeant," I said, "you are the only one here who has been over the plonk before. What do you think of things?"
"Well, sir," he answered deferentially. "I think you're doin' very well, sir. But what about these here dugouts?"

There was a dugout shaft right before us.

"Will I throw a bomb down, sir?"
"No," said I, feeling full of beans, "I'm going down to have a look. Don't let anyone throw a bomb down after me."

The serjeant didn't approve, but I called to Lee, a smart-looking lad who was close by, and we started down the shaft. Lee giggled.

"Lee," said I, "have you got an electric torch?"
"No, sir, but I've got a match somewheres."

So I lit a match and held it well away from me. We crept down the stairway, I with a match and a revolver, he with a bayonet and the giggles.

The dugout opened to the left at the foot of some twenty steps. I slid my revolver muzzle round the corner, gingerly showing the light. Six inches from my hand was the corner of a table on which stood half a loaf of bread, some tinned meat - and there just by my hand an electric torch.

I grabbed it and illuminated the dugout.

Thank God there was no one there. It was bigger, cleaner and more comfortable than the one at La Boiselle, and consisted of a corridor about twenty feet long, joining two small square chambers from each of which a shaft led up to the trench. The walls were all panelled and lined with a double row of bunks, on which lay blankets, ruffled from recent use. A greatcoat or two hung on the walls, and (joy!) there were five 'pickelhaubes' lying about. Evidently the Boches had been suprised and run, leaving food, blankets and equipment behind. And no wonder, if they had heard the battalion yelling and swarming over their trenches from the rear.

Attacks, both large and small, continued throughout the summer as the Germans were gradually forced back. Their original third line of defence was finally taken on 15th September, the day on which tanks were used for the first time ever. One key position to fall on that day was the village of Ginchy. An officer of the Royal Irish Fusiliers wrote home to a relative:

> It was about 4 o'clock in the afternoon when we first learned that we should have to take part in the attack on Ginchy. Now, Auntie, you expect me to say at this point in my narrative that my heart leapt with joy at the news and that the men gave three rousing cheers, for that's the sort of thing you read in the papers. Well, even at the risk of making you feel ashamed of me, I will tell you the whole truth and confess that my heart sank within me when I heard the news. I had been over the top once already that week, and knew what it was to see men dropping dead all round me, to see men blown to bits, to see men writhing in pain, to see men running round and round gibbering, raving mad. Can you wonder therefore that I felt a sort of sickening dread of the horrors which I knew we should all have to go through? Frankly I was dismayed. But, Auntie, I know you will think the more of me when I tell you, on my conscience, that I went into action that afternoon, not with any hope of glory, but with the absolute certainty of death. How the others felt I don't exactly know, but I don't think I am far wrong when I say that their emotions were not far different from mine... As a famous Yankee general said, 'War is Hell,' and you have only got to be in the Somme one single day to know it...
>
> But to get on with the story. We were ordered to move up into the front line to reinforce the Royal Irish Rifles... The bombardment was now intense. Our shells bursting in the village of Ginchy made it belch forth smoke like a volcano. The Hun shells were bursting on the slope in front of us. The noise was deafening. I turned to my servant O'Brien, who has always been a cheery, optimistic soul, and said, "Well, O'Brien, how do you think we'll fare?" and his answer was for once not encouraging. "We'll never come out alive sir!" was his answer. Happily we both came out alive, but I never thought we should at the time.
>
> It was at this moment, just as we were debouching on to the scragged front line of trench that we beheld a scene which stirred and thrilled us to the bottommost depths of our souls. The great charge of the Irish Division had begun, and we had come up in the nick of time... Between

the outer fringe of Ginchy and the front line of our own trenches is No Man's Land, you behold a great host of yellow-coated men rise out of the earth and surge forward and upward in a torrent - not in extended order, as you might expect, but in one mass, - I almost said a compact mass. The only way I can describe the scene is to ask you to picture five or six columns of men marching uphill in fours, with about a hundred yards between each column. Now conceive those columns being gradually disorganised, some men going off to the right, and others to the left to avoid shell-holes. There seems to be no end to them. Just when you think the flood is subsiding, another wave comes surging up the beach towards Ginchy. We joined in on the left. There was no time for us any more than the others to get into extended order. We formed another stream, converging on the others at the summit. By this time we were all wildly excited. Our shouts and yells alone must have struck terror into the Huns, who were firing their machine-guns down the slope. But there was no wavering in the Irish host. We couldn't run. We advanced at a steady walking pace, stumbling here and there, but going ever onward and upward. That numbing dread had now left me completely. Like the others, I was intoxicated with the glory of it all. I can remember shouting and bawling to the men of my platoon, who were only too eager to go on. The Hun barrage had now been opened in earnest, and shells were falling here, there, and everywhere in No Man's Land. They were mostly dropping on our right, but they were coming nearer and nearer, as if a screen were being drawn across our front. I knew that it was a case of "now or never" and stumbled on feverishly. We managed to get through the barrage in the nick of time, for it closed behind us, and after that we had no shells to fear in front of us. I mention, merely as an interesting fact in psychology, how in a crisis of this sort one's mental faculties are sharpened. Instinct told us, when the shells were coming gradually closer, to crouch down in the holes until they had passed.

We were now well up to the Boche. We had to clamber over all manner of obstacles - fallen trees, beams, great mounds of brick and rubble, - in fact over the ruins of Ginchy. It seems like a nightmare to me now. I remember seeing comrades falling round me. My sense of hearing returned to me for I became conscious of a new sound; namely the continuous crackling of rifle-fire. I remember men lying in shell-holes holding out their arms and beseeching water. I remember men crawling about and coughing up blood, as they searched round for some place in which they could shelter until help could reach them. By this time all units were mixed up: but they were all Irishmen. They were cheering and cheering and cheering like mad. It was Hell let loose. There was a machine-gun playing on us near-by, and we all made for it. At this moment we caught our first sight of the Huns. They were in a trench of sorts, which ran in and out among the ruins. Some of them had their hands up. Others were kneeling and holding their arms out to us. Still others were running up and down the trench distractedly as if they didn't know which way to go, but as we got closer they went down on their knees too.

By this time we had penetrated the German front line, and were on the flat ground where the village once stood surrounded by a wood of fairly high trees... As I was clambering out of the front trench, I felt a sudden stab in my right thigh: I thought I had got a 'Blighty' but found it was only a graze from a bullet, and so went on... McGarry and I were the only two officers left in the company, so it was up to us to take charge. We could see the Huns hopping over the distant ridge like rabbits, and we had some difficulty in preventing our men from chasing them, for we had orders not to go too far. We got them - Irish Fusiliers, Inniskillings and Dublins - to dig in by linking up the shell-craters, and though the men were tired (some wanted to smoke and others to make tea) they worked with a will, and before long we had got a pretty decent trench outlined. [2nd Lt. A. C. Young, Royal Irish Fusiliers]

But the cost of the 'success' on that day was heavy. Anthony Eden was left out of the attack, since it had become the custom not to send all of a battalion into action, in order to provide a nucleus for its reconstruction in the event of heavy losses. His account of a roll-call bears out the wisdom of this policy:

The attack took place without further preparation and failed with heavy loss. Feversham was killed leading his riflemen and Honey, his adjutant, lost an eye. Oakley was wounded and his adjutant killed. There was soon no senior officer left in either battalion, and it says much for the subalterns that they were able to rally their units and dig in for the night without losing much ground. The Gird ridge was not captured for several weeks and only then after more hard fighting. It may be that from corps headquarters the depth of the Forty-first Division's advance raised hoped of a break-through, but the Gird ridge defences were much too strong for that without effective preliminary artillery bombardment. The methods of Messines 1917 had not yet been learnt on the Somme in 1916.

On the afternoon of September 16th came the roll-call, and my saddest hour with C Company. It would not have been so bad if we had not known each other so well, but after anything up to a year of living and training together, we were friends. It fell to me to call the roll. After each silence, and there were so many, I had to ask who had last seen Sergeant Carmichael or Rifleman Hunter, or whoever it might be, and enter what scraps of information we could gather.

As we finished I noticed Foljambe standing a few yards away and silently watching the scene.

Although the attack was deemed a success, it was not the breakthrough it could have been had it succeeded on 1st July. The Germans had had two months in which to construct new lines of defence behind their original three. And in response to more sophisticated artillery work on the part of the British (principally the development of the 'creeping' barrage, in which the attacking infantry walked behind a curtain of shellfire and so could get into the enemy's trenches before they could take up defensive positions) and heavier barrages, their defensive tactics had changed. Their front line now often consisted of shellholes containing part of the defending force, with machine gunners in between the front and second lines.

To neutralise a whole defensive area like this, rather than one trench line, required huge quantities and density of artillery and ammunition. This problem was exacerbated by differences amongst the British commanders. Haig, the commander-in-chief, continued to believe that the bombardment would have a shattering effect on the morale of an already shaken enemy, despite the evidence of 1st July. In consequence, he believed a breakthrough still possible. By contrast, Rawlinson still favoured attacks with limited objectives, which could then be held against counter-attack and used as bases for further attacks (the so-called 'bite and hold' approach). And it would seem that the 14th July and 15th September attacks bore out his view; after all, with limited objectives, there were fewer enemy positions to be assaulted, and so heavier artillery support could be provided. But - as before 1st July - Haig's view prevailed, and the campaign continued into the Autumn, despite worsening weather and a consequent increase in the army's worst enemy after the Germans - mud.

The by now almost customary combination of a few large- and numerous small-scale attacks went on. The most notable of these actions was the taking of the German redoubt at the village of Thiepval (which, again, had been an objective on the first day of battle). Once again, Frank Maxwell was involved in a successful operation. He wrote to his wife:

> We pushed off at 12.25 p.m. yesterday, over the most awful country that human being ever saw or dreamt of. July 1st was a playground compared to it, and the resistance small. I knew it would be, and I confess I hated the job from the first - which was only three days before we began it. So many attempts had been made, and so many failures, that one knew it could only be a tough thing to take on, and I hadn't personally any particular hopes of accomplishing it, more especially as the distance to be covered - nearly one mile - was enormous for these

attacks under any circumstances, and under the special one, of country absolutely torn with shell for three months, it was, I considered, an impossibility.

We accomplished three-quarters of it, and were extraordinarily lucky at that, and it seems to have surprised the Higher Command, which, at least, is something. But the price has been heavy - how heavy I don't know, as regards men, yet, but as regards officers I have, of the twenty who went over, nine killed, seven wounded, and four, including myself, untouched. Two other regiments, who came most of the way with us, lost heavily in officers, and a third engaged later suffered fairly heavily. I lost all my regimental staff, viz. three officers and regimental sergt.-major killed.

It was an extraordinarily difficult battle to fight, owing to every landmark, such as a map shows, being obliterated - absolutely and totally. The ground was, of course, the limit itself, and progress over it like nothing imaginable, the enemy quite determined to keep us out, as they had so many [times] before.

I will not describe the details of the battle - they would be very difficult to understand. Briefly, we worked up and up our long journey, but left untaken, on our left, a very strong place filled with machine guns and a determined garrison. This was a thorn in our side, indeed, and it defied all our efforts to take it till this morning, but not till it had done us in for a large number of casualties from first to last.

All the regiment spent its night out, of course, either in shell holes or (a very few) in dug-outs, either bombing or engaged with the enemy at close quarters. I had a safe place in a pile of ruins, which managed to ward off shells and all the other unpleasant things of modern battle. It was a busy night for me, though, and not unmixed with anxiety - in fact, very much to the contrary.

We have two tanks with us, but they failed us, as they only could fail in such country - both arrived on the scene behind us instead of level with us. One got 'ditched' hopelessly almost immediately, and left behind; the other was panting along boldly, but, trying to dodge wounded men, lost ground and fell behind, and finally got 'ditched' also. I wonder if any one has learnt one lesson about them, viz. that these monsters must precede troops and not follow. Nobody seems to have thought of the wounded men difficulty; some were, I fear, rolled over. The awful callousness of one about such things! I saw in a trench several men buried, three or four sticking out but unable to move - more, of course, underneath. But humanity has no place. I had my business on hand, and couldn't stay even one minute to give one of them a hand. If I saw any evil and wicked sights in Trônes, I saw more and varied ones yesterday and to-day.

Another view of the same battle was given by Lt. A. C. Steven, MC, RFA:

> ...Noon on the 26th found me at the O.P. with the Captain. Zero was at 12.35, and as yet the trenches were silent and motionless. Then suddenly, at the appointed minute, the slopes of Thiepval seemed to move with small brown figures, like a field alive with rabbits, and the guns swept down on Thiepval and the country to the right of it. At first the men advanced in disordered masses, but gradually taking their own time they opened out like a stage crowd falling into their allotted places. I could see the first wave walking towards Thiepval, and then a second wave sprang up and spread out behind them, then the last wave took shape and followed up in artillery formation; small bunches of men, with an interval between each bunch, or more often six men advancing in single file with a stretcher bearer in the rear. It was a wonderful sight. Never have I seen such a calm, methodical and perfectly ordered advance. The barrage was as perfect as it was terrible. The white smoke of shrapnel ran like a rampart along the trenches that were the first objective, as clear as though it were made of tape carefully placed and measured. Indeed, the barrier of white smoke, broken now and again by a black puff from an enemy gun, might have been as ermine fur with its little black tufts.
>
> From my vantage point I could even look over the barrage on to the trenches beyond, but it was hard even for a moment to drag one's eyes away from the little brown figures that were slowly but steadily drawing upon Thiepval. Sometimes a wave of men would dip and disappear into a trench only to emerge on the other side in perfect line again. Now they are into Thiepval! No, the line suddenly telescopes into a bunch and the bunch scurries to right or left, trying to evade a machine-gun in front, and then with a plunge the first wave, broken now into little groups, vanished amidst the ruined houses.
>
> Farther to the right, where the barrage had lifted, more brown figures streamed across the open. A black dog ran out of a dug-out to meet them; a man stooped down and fondled it. When they drew near to a line of chalk heaps I saw black masses emerge and march towards our lines. Prisoners were giving themselves up without a fight. Prisoners were pouring in from all sides, sometimes in black batches, guided by a brown figure and a shining bayonet, sometimes a single Boche would race, hands above head, panic-stricken till he reached our lines. Thiepval was now a closed book, though runners would sometimes emerge and dash stumbling to our trenches. The Boche retaliation was feeble and badly placed. His barrage fell behind all our men, and very few shells had burst among them, and even then never did they cause a man to turn his head or swerve out of place - unless he fell. At this stage a tank crawled on to the scene and crept laboriously, like a great slug, towards Thiepval. It disappeared among the ruins, puffing smoke. Subsequently

it caught fire. Thiepval now became as stony and devoid of life, as it was before the attack.

Lt. Col. Fraser-Tytler, whose optimism was so notable on 1st July, was present during the entire Somme campaign. As the battle ended, he wrote of the appallingly difficult conditions then prevailing, as a consequence of four and a half months of heavy shelling, combined with the effects of bad weather since mid-August.

> The difference between peace soldiering and push-fighting is really vast! By peace soldiering I mean the days when we used to sit looking at each other from nice tidy trenches and shooting from well-kept gun-pits. The happy-go-lucky muddle that we live in here would horrify anyone well versed in the science of the latter sort of fighting, but if we didn't treat things in that spirit the ordinary individual would pretty soon become insane. There is, however, a wealth of comedy and tragedy in every moment here. Take for example the day before we marched out (the 15th). An officer of the Divisional Ammunition Column who was on the point of marching out, looked into our mess to say that he had been ordered to hand over to us two G.S. wagons and teams to help our move, as they themselves were moving empty. Profuse thanks and the request that the wagons should be sent at once to nestle in our horse lines for the night. The first wagon successfully negotiated the 250 yards stretch of mud to our lines. But the second, also empty, despite all the efforts of its team of twelve mules, managed to stick after the first thirty yards, and when once anything halts, it begins to sink at once. Much advice from onlookers was wafted across to our lines. At that moment a Hun 'plane loafed up, and having approached from our back areas, none of our 'Archies' had spotted it. The area round is littered with observation balloons, and when they are sitting on the ground the Hun loves throwing things at them. The third bomb came near us by mistake and killed the D.A.C. cook and three of the above-mentioned team of mules, or rather two were actually killed and the third lay down and died out of sheer cussedness. The poor cook we laid to rest not far from the scene of his labours, and the mules were decently interred by the simple process of standing on them until they had sunk out of sight in the roadway. Exit the Hun 'plane and the D.A.C., leaving the wagon to struggle for the next hour till it got half-way across, when it was finally brought into the fold by our water cart team of eight horses which came to its rescue.

In the four and a half months of fighting on the Somme, British casualties are estimated at 400,000; French 200,000 and German at 600,000. Any substantial increase in losses to the BEF would, it was felt, have unacceptably reduced its effectiveness in the projected offensives for 1917; this, more than the disappointing territorial gains and terrible weather and terrain led to the 'closing down' of the Somme offensive on 19th November 1916.

15
The Armistice

When the Armistice finally came into effect and fighting on the Western Front stopped at 11am on the 11th of November 1918, despite the celebrations at home, the overwhelming feeling of the soldiers at the Front was one of anti-climax. The diary of a junior officer, 2nd Lieutenant R.D.Reid of the 11th Somerset Light Infantry, gives the view of one man, and reflects the experience of others at the time. Recalling November 9th, Reid wrote: 'The C.O. called and I remember discussed the effects of an armistice, fearing there would be difficulty in controlling the men...'

When the time came, however, there was very little exuberance; the enormity of 'peace' was too much to grasp.

> 11/11/1918. I have written in my diary, made on the spot 'the greatest day in history and we know it not.' However extravagant the first phrase may be the second is certainly true. There are no celebrations. We were of course, almost certain that an armistice was coming. Chits were sent round to the companies about 10.30 am. I obtained the one which came to 'B' Company and have it still. The usual phrasing "Hostilities will cease at 11 am today 11.11.18 Troops to stand fast in their present positions." "For your information please." There was a parade and some sort of announcement made but no cheers raised. The occasion was too much for that. It was a curious physiological study of human nature too overcome with the significance of the good news to rejoice. The maffiking was left, as we saw afterwards, to those at home less in touch with realities.
>
> There was of course no fighting up to 11.00 unless it was a desultory anti-aircraft gun firing which we saw particularly clearly. How the day was spent I do not remember but one was never bored during this period. The atmosphere was too full of - romance since I can find no better word. I can remember going down to headquarters which was on the Pecq road and reading the notices there which showed how complete and abject was Germany's defeat. During the day the civilians belonging to the house next to our billet came back and attempted to clear up and even I believe to close the hole in the roof. It was a beautiful clear autumn day - nature had staged the end of Armageddon very well and appreciatively. Wade, captain and then O.C. 'D' Company, I believe, came to dinner with us and was provided with the one glass of whiskey remaining in the mess stores. Our rejoicing was therefore not hilarious. On walking 'home', alone, it suddenly dawned

upon me how deadly quiet everything was on this first night of peace. The everlasting din to which we had grown accustomed, had suddenly ceased; even the leaves were still. There was a slight frost. And so bed. To-morrow the sun rises over a new world. I, by the mercy of God have seen this, history's most tremendous occasion, save one, arrive and pass.

Desmond Young also felt no exhilaration, although his morning was enlivened by the appearance of one of our allies:

For the first time we marched in silence; a half-hearted song died quickly away. Perhaps for most of us there were too many memories - and too many ghosts. Then we caught up with a Portuguese battalion, straggling all over the road. As I went forward, a fat, bearded Portuguese colonel, in bright yellow field boots, made me an impassioned oration and, from the back of his charger, attempted to kiss me on both cheeks. As both Dolly and I drew rapidly away, there was a ripple of laughter in the leading company.

However, some individuals and units found themselves, although equally impressed with the occasion, able to celebrate in a more uninhibited manner:

On the 11th a telegram was brought to me before breakfast, while I was in bed, that hostilities would cease at "11 hours."

The news was so overwhelming that I could not absorb it, and I am inclined to think now that, because there had been no anticipation, we lost at first the fine savour of it. I could not understand - until two of my officers started to ring the bell of the village church. The day became a smiling dream. I found myself walking up and down the village street, stopping everybody I met and saying -

"Do you realise that in one hour the war will be over?"

At 11 A.M. I stood opposite the church and exclaimed in a loud voice to nobody in particular - "Gentlemen, the war is now over - absolutely!"

The company, naturally enough, had begun already to celebrate the occasion with appropriate rites, and its steadiness on parade, when before lunch the General came round to make a little speech, was truly remarkable. Only one officer in the rear was humming a little ditty to himself, and only one man interrupted the speech by a faint "hear! hear!" Salutes at the conclusion of the parade were superb...

We had a cold lunch, but one faithful mess waiter served us nobly with a set face. The two cooks with arms around each other's waists were strolling up and down outside the window. I think they must have been singing.

In the afternoon we went for a long walk - the news had come too early in the day. We returned a little refreshed. At night there was a bonfire; but I cannot do better that quote from the vivid narrative of one of my most trusted officers:-

"November 11th was a great day - and a greater night. the dreariness and loneliness of the place vanished suddenly on the receipt of the news of the enemy's capitulation. Would we not soon all be back in Blighty? The thought came like champagne to our thirsting souls. Imagination responded promptly. The bareness of officers [sic] billets vanished before visions of cosy sofas and arm-chairs, carpeted floors and clean-sheeted beds. Better still, faces of those we longed to see, especially of those we longed to kiss, came to us. Their owners moved amidst the pictured cosiness, sat in those arm-chairs, shared their sofas... What a picture after the gritty holes and cramping caves of earth covered ammunition boxes in the Cérisy Valley, or the stuffy, fly-ridden dilapidation of billets in Fouilloy! And it was the same with the men. No doubt their visions were as fair. The delight of these things shone in every one's faces. Unwonted cheerfulness was general. Every one smiled.

"And at night every one cheered. A way must be found to give free and full expression to bounding spirits. A huge bonfire was decided upon... At twenty hours the massed logs that had been heaped on top of the fallen masonry were saturated with petrol, a match was thrown, and a sheet of flame shot up. A war of cheering followed. Songs burst forth. Every one sung who could or thought he could. The rest shouted. It didn't matter - noise was the thing. Half an hour later the officers joined the shouting throng. The din grew louder. Some one shouted Speech!... Next the Adjutant, and in turn every other officer was called. Reversing the order, the officers then called upon the sergeant-major and senior N.C.O.'s. Finally, the 'other ranks' vociferously sang of the officers, 'For they are jolly good fellows,' and the officers in similar fashion paid compliments to the men. By this time the flames had died down. Flickering light and shadow replaced the ruddy glow, and slowly the crowd broke up. But for hours yet a small group of enthusiastic maffickers sat around the dying embers. [Major W.H.L.Watson]

Pte. A.S.Dolden found it hard to believe that peace had actually arrived:

Folks at home apparently went frantic with joy and excitement. It seemed to be taken for granted that the war had finished, although an armistice in the strict sense of the word is only a truce. That we fellows did not conduct ourselves like a crowd of maniacs, as many at home seemed to have done, was no doubt due to the fact that we looked upon the armistice merely as a truce - a temporary cessation of hostilities. We had faced the Germans for many weary months, and knew by experience that they were fighters, by no means to be despised.

He also noted what may seem to be a callous act qiven that the ammunition in question was bound to land somewhere:

> About 10.55am on Armistice Day, our artillery began to open fire on the Germans, and for five minutes every battery on the whole of our front was sending over salvo after salvo. The air was rent with the whining and shrieking of shells as they hurtled over our heads. All this, or course, sounded very much like permanent peace! However, when 11am arrived the noise began to die down and a comparative calm prevailed. I discovered later that the final five minutes burst of firing was not due to any war-like spirit on the part of the artillery, but to the fact that every shell not used had to be carried about; empty shell cases were of course, dumped. When the 'Cease Fire' order was sounded the artillery, stout hearted fellows, did not want to be bothered with live shells that would have to be carried, so they adopted the perfectly legitimate method of disposing of them in action. My utmost sympathy went out to the Germans, poor devils; it was rough luck on them when the war was practically over, for many must have passed over the the Great Beyond in that final burst of fire.

Few would now doubt that the seeds of the Second World War were sown in the First. Within months of the Armistice the reality of German defeat in the field was being denied in that country and blamed on civilians and especially politician.s Leslie Yorath Sanders, who was killed in the Great War, prophetically wrote in February 1917:

> The campaign that is opening now, it seems to me, will be the bloodiest in history... Then, as the mud of winter once more renders the arena too slippery for the combatants to remain at grips, there will come the lull of exhaustion. both sides will be exhausted, *but the Bosche far more, and with far less material for recruitment.* In the years that follow, I imagine, there can never again be the same intensity of effort there will be this summer; but though the Allies grow absolutely weaker, yet relatively they will grow stronger and stronger until at last, if only their will to win remains, they can overwhelm the Bosche in hopeless ruin.

> There's the rub! - if their will to win continues. For in this case "they" does not mean their armies, it means their civilian populations. The war has hardly touched England yet. If English people want to win this war, they must be prepared for things scarcely dreamed of as yet - for starvation rations; for unremitting labour of man, woman and child; for death in every home in the land. These things may not come, but unless they are faced and accepted in spirit, we cannot truly win.

> I dread beyond most things a peace brought about by any other cause than military victory. The Bosche knows as well as we that our ultimate victory is certain. If he staves it off, in whatever way - *even by granting our terms* - it is a victory for him. Our own terms, and those at the point

of the sword - then and then only will he be cured of his love of the sword. I shall be sorry if he is starved into submission. That would give him a leg to stand on. "It wasn't our army's fault: it was our cursed populace, that didn't know how to take up a hole in their belts." And so our son's sons get the job to do again, and the blood of those who have perished up to now is betrayed.

"The War that will end War?" Perhaps. And may be not.

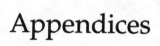

Appendices

Appendix 1 - Glossary

Alleyman/Alleman - Slang for German; from the French *allemand*.

ANZAC - Australia and New Zealand Army Corps; eventually there were two.

APM - Assistant Provost Marshal; a senior Military Policeman

Archie - Slang for an anti-aircraft gun and its shellbursts.

ASC - Army Service Corps; known to the troops in the front line as 'Ally Sloper's Cavalry,' after a comic character in a pre-war paper. Responsible for transport in rear areas, they were viewed as having a safe and comfortable life, and hardly regarded as soldiers at all by the front line troops.

Battery - A group of six guns or howitzers.

BGGS - Brigadier-General, General Staff. The most senior staff officer in a corps; also present in the staffs of higher formations.

Blighty - Slang for Britain. Derived from the Hindi *bilaik*, meaning 'home.'

Boche/Bosche - Slang for the Germans. Derived from the French *alboche*, which seems to be itself derived from a combination of *Allemands* and *tête de boche*, the latter meaning a 'bad lot.'

BQMS - Battery Quartermaster Sergeant; NCO responsible for an artillery battery's logistical affairs.

Buzzer - Device used for sending messages in morse code over the field telegraph.

CCS - Casualty Clearing Station; buildings or tents behind the lines where wounded were operated on and classified according to the the severity of their wounds.

Chatting - Removing lice from one's clothes.

CO - Commanding Officer.

Concertina Wire - a non-barbed type of wire which would coil around someone if they were to touch it.

CQMS - Company Quartermaster Sergeant. As BQMS, but for an infantry company.

CRE - Commander Royal Engineers; the senior engineer officer attached to a formation.

Crump - A 5.9-inch or heavier German shell (or its explosion). The black smoke produced also led to their being called 'coal-boxes' or 'Jack Johnsons,' after the famous black boxer of the day.

CSM - Company Sergeant Major.

CT - Communication Trench; a trench not facing the enemy lines and used for movement between, for example, the front and support trenches.

DCM - Distinguished Conduct Medal; gallantry award for other ranks, ranking above the MM (q.v) and immediately below the VC (q.v.). Its first connotation to many old soldiers, however, was 'District Court Martial.'

Dixie - Large iron pot for boiling and carrying food or tea.

DSO - Distinguished Service Order; an award for commissioned officers. Awarded either for gallantry in action or, controversially, to officers in the rear echelons for conscientious performance of their duties. See Chapter 11.

Duckboard - A construction of wood, consisting of two narrow planks about eight feet long with horizontal slats nailed across them. Intended for flooring trenches or making paths across boggy ground, but sometimes used for firewood or roofing dugouts (q.v.).

Dugout/Dug-out - Term for various types of shelter, ranging from a hole scraped in the side of a trench ('cubby-hole') to a deep dugout, ten or more feet underground and possibly walled with wood and provided with sleeping accomodation and electric light. Captured German dugouts, if not badly damaged, were viewed as most luxurious.

Enfilade - To fire down a trench or at a row of men lengthways, rather than crossways. A particularly lethal way of firing, since it is much less likely that bullets or shells will fall short or over their target. In addition, the target itself is denser - a row of 50 men, one deep, is equivalent to a column of 50 when enfiladed.

Firestep - The trenches, in order to provide protection, were usually deeper than a man's height. In order for sentries or troops at 'stand to' (q.v.) to be able to fire upon an enemy, the front wall of the trench had a raised portion for them to stand on. This was the firestep.

Flying Pig - A type of trench mortar bomb.

FOO - Forward Observation Officer for artillery batteries - see Chapter 4.

GHQ - General Headquarters; the headquarters of the Commander in Chief.

GS Wagon - General Service Wagon; standard horse- or mule-drawn cart used for transporting supplies etc.

GSO1 - General Staff Officer, grade one.

HAC - The Honourable Artillery Company, the oldest Territorial unit in the army. It was composed of both infantry and gunners in the Great War.

Hate - A bombardment, especially in the context of 'morning hate' for a regular event. Refers to the German *Hymn of Hate*, which was composed at the start of the war.

HQ - Headquarters.

Hun - Slang for the Germans; from a remark made by the Kaiser in 1900, when he exhorted troops departing for China to carry themselves like Attila's huns of old. The expression was swiftly capitalised upon by the British Press when war broke out.

Jock - Slang for Scottish soldier.

Kultur - German word for 'culture.' As a comparatively young state, Germany was before the war very proud of her cultural achievements. The term is usually used in this book sarcastically, the Germans' shelling and destruction of historic towns having appalled a world not yet used to the devastating effects of modern warfare.

Mafficking - To celebrate; derived from the riotous scenes across the country when the news of the Relief of Mafeking came through, during the Boer War.

MC - Military Cross; gallantry award for warrant officers (q.v.) and commissioned officers of the rank of major and below.

Minenwerfer/Minnie - German trench mortar.

MM - Military Medal; gallantry award for other ranks.

MO - Medical Officer.

NCO - Non-commissioned Officer, such as a corporal or sergeant.

OC - Officer Commanding.

OP - Observation Post.

ORs - Other ranks; soldiers who are not officers, including NCOs but not warrant officers.

Pickelhaube - German helmet with a spike on top, superseded during the war by the 'coalscuttle' helmet. A very popular souvenir.

Pipsqueak - Small-calibre German artillery piece; sometimes used synonymously with 'whizzbang' (q.v.).

Plugstreet Wood- Army rendition of Ploegsteert Wood, near Ypres. Flemish place-names caused the soldiers considerable difficulty, to the extent that one village, also near Ypres, was referred to as 'the place with the unpronounceable name.'

RE - Royal Engineers.

Register - Technical term used by gunners, meaning to locate a target by means of each gun in a battery firing ranging rounds. A FOO (q.v.) would inform the battery of what adjustments to their range etc. were required in order to hit the target.

RFA - Royal Field Artillery.

RFC - Royal Flying Corps; became the RAF on 1st April 1918.

RGA - Royal Garrison Artillery; used heavier guns than the RFA.

RSM - Regimental Sergeant-Major.

SAA - Small Arms Ammunition, i.e. for rifles, pistols and machine-guns.

Stand To - Period when troops in the front line were required to man the firestep (q.v.) of their trench, fully armed, in case of enemy attack. Routinely done at dawn and nightfall every day.

Strafe - Punishment, either verbal or in the form of enemy fire. Later became specific to attack from aircraft.

Stick Bomb - Type of German hand grenade with a wooden handle, so that it could be thrown further.

Toc 1,2,3,4 - The code names of 90th Brigade RGA's four batteries.

Toffee Apples - Slang for early trench mortar bombs, which were round and mounted on a stick. Also known as 'plum-puddings.'

Traverse - The trenches were not straight ditches, since this would have made them far too vulnerable to enfilade fire (q.v.). Instead, they periodically had traverses built in. These were protrusions of earth or sandbags into the trench, giving trench lines a crenellated appearance when viewed from the air. They also had the function of limiting the effects of shells, mortar bombs, etc. when they landed in the trench.

Verey Light - A type of flare, fired from a brass pistol and used to illuminate No-Man's-Land at night, or for signalling purposes.

VC - Victoria Cross; the highest gallantry award in the British armed forces, which could be won by any rank.

WO - Warrant Officer; senior level of NCOs, such as RSM or Battalion QMS.

Whizzbang - A type of shell fired by a small artillery piece. The name is derived from their sound and effect, since they tended only to be heard immediately before their arrival.

Appendix 2 - The Structure of the BEF

The BEF expanded from 125,000 men in 1914 to nearly five million by the end of the war, organised at various times into four or five Armies. This appendix is designed to describe the structure of a 'typical' Army and to explain which formations were commanded by which ranks of soldier. The figures given for the number of men in a given formation are theoretical; units were rarely, if ever, at full strength.

An Army itself was commanded by a full General (the Commander in Chief being a Field-Marshal). The next formation down was the corps, of which an Army would usually have three or four; they tended to be moved between Armies as required. A corps was commanded by a Lieutenant General. Corps HQ had attached to it a number of officers and men for staff work, and also field and heavy artillery, for attachment to divisions (q.v.) in action as the corps commander saw fit. Arthur Behrend's brigade (in artillery terms, a collection of four batteries) of heavy artillery was a corps unit.

Below corps came the division (commanded by a Major General), of which a corps would usually have two or more. The division was the most important fighting unit in the army. It consisted of about 19,000 men - 12,000 infantry, 4,000 artillery and the rest medical, supply, HQ and support troops. Its artillery consisted of about five batteries, and it also had 24 machine-guns. Like corps within Armies, divisions could be moved between corps, with the notable exceptions of the Canadian and ANZAC corps, which always kept the same divisions; it has been suggested that this was a major contribution to their efficiency.

A division was composed of three infantry brigades, commanded by Brigadier Generals; brigades were almost always permanently assigned to their division, and the men's loyalty to their division was second only to that to their regiment. Brigades were subdivided into four battalions (three after manpower shortage forced a reorganisation in early 1918), each of about 1000 men. A battalion was commanded by a Lieutenant Colonel or a Major and was further divided into four companies of about 200 men, under Captains. These each consisted of four platoons, under Lieutenants, and each of them comprised four sections of ten men commanded by sergeants.

Bibliography

Bibliography

The editor and publishers gratefully acknowledge the following source works.

Primary sources

An Appreciation and some letters of the late 2nd Lt. T.B. Stowell, MC, who fell in action in France, Nov. 17th 1917. Liverpool, Lee & Nightingale, Printers. nd.

Behrend (Arthur) *As From Kemmel Hill: An Adjutant in France and Flanders 1917 & 1918.* Eyre & Spottiswoode. 1963. Copyright 1963 by Arthur Behrend, reproduced by kind permission of Methuen London incorporating Eyre & Spottiswoode.

Buckley (Francis) *Q.6.A. and other places: Recollections of 1916, 1917, 1918.* Spottiswoode. 1920.

Cawston (Lt.Col. E.P.) *Personal Reminiscences of Incidents in the Kaiser War.* Kent & Sussex Writers Conclave. 1968.

Chapman (Guy) *A Passionate Prodigality.* Buchan & Enright. 1985. Copyright by The Estate of Guy Chapman, 1933, 1965, 1985. Reproduced by kind permission of A.D.Peters & Co. Literary Agency.

Clapham (H.S.) *Mud and Khaki: The Memories of an Incomplete Soldier.* Hutchinson. 1930.

Cloete (Stuart) *A Victorian Son: An Autobiography.* Collins. 1972. Copyright by Stuart Cloete 1972, extracts reproduced by kind permission of Mrs M.E.Cloete and Shelley Power Literary Agency.

Crouch (Capt. L.W.) *Letters from the Front from...* Printed for private circulation. 1917.

Crutchley (C.E.) Ed. *Machine Gunner 1914-1918: Personal Experiences of the MGC.* 2nd Ed. (revised and enlarged). Bailey Bros. 1975. Reproduced by kind permission.

Denis Oliver Barnett: In Happy Memory... His Letters from France and Flanders, October 1914-August 1915. Privately published. 1915.

Dolden (A.Stuart) *Cannon Fodder: An Infantryman's Life on the Western Front 1914-1918.* Blandford Press. 1980. Copyright by Blandford Press, 1980. Extracts reproduced by kind permission of Cassell Plc.

Dugdale (Capt. Geoffrey) *"Langemarck" and "Cambrai": A War Narrative 1914-18.* Shrewsbury. 1932.

['E.A.F.'] *Vermelles: Notes on the Western Front by a Chaplain.* Scottish Chronicle. 1918.

Eden (Sir Anthony) *Another World 1897-1917.* Allen Lane. 1976.

Edmonds (C.) [Pseud. for Charles Carrington] *A Subaltern's War.* Davies. 1930.

Essays, Poems, Letters by Bernard Pitt, M.A. Francis Edwards. 1917.

Foot (S.) *Three Lives.* Heinemann. 1934.

Fraser-Tytler (Lt.Col. N.) *Field Guns in France.* Hutchinson. 1922.

Gibbs (Sir Philip) *Realities of War.* Heinemann. 1920.

Graham (Major Francis) *Letters from the Front August 1914-March 1918.* The Harrow School Bookshop. nd.

Hart-Davis (Rupert) Ed. *Siegfried Sassoon Diaries 1915-1918.* Faber & Faber. 1983. Copyright by George Sassoon, 1983, extracts reproduced by kind permission of Faber and Faber Ltd.

Henry Dundas, Scots Guards, A Memoir. Blackwood. 1921.

Housman (L.) Ed: *War Letters of Fallen Englishmen.* Gollancz. 1930.

In Memoriam Harold Parry, Second Lieutenant, K.R.R.C. Privately published. nd.

Laird (Frank M.) *Personal Experiences of the Great War (An Unfinished Manuscript).* Dublin, Eason & Son. nd.

Leslie Yorath Sanders, 'A Soldier of England.' J.Maxwell & Son, Dumfries. 1920.

Letters Home from John Savill Tatham. Privately published. nd.

Maxwell (Mrs Charlotte) *Frank Maxwell, Brig.-General, V.C., C.S.I., D.S.O.: A Memoir and Some Letters.* Murray. 1921.

Memoir of Captain Geoffrey Grenside Bowen, MC, The Lancashire Fusiliers. Privately published. nd.

Nobbs (Captain Gilbert) *Englishman Kamerad! Right of the British Line.* Heinemann. 1918.

Pollard (Capt. A.O.) *Fire-Eater: The Memoirs of a VC.* Hutchinson. 1932.

Quigley (Hugh) *Passchendaele and the Somme: A Diary of 1917.* Methuen. 1928.

R. Cecil Hopkinson, Lt., R.E.: Memoir and Letters. Cambridge University Press (privately published). 1918.

Rees (Major R.T.) *A Schoolmaster at War.* Haycock Press. nd.

Sansom (A.J.) *Letters from France written between June 1915-July 1917, Edited by His Wife, Ivy.* Melrose. nd.

Smith (Capt. H. Raymond) *A Soldier's Diary: Sidelights on the Great War 1914-1918.* Evesham: The "Journal" Press. 1940.

[Symons (Lt.Col.F.A.)] 'Royal Field Leech' *The Tale of a Casualty Clearing Station.* Blackwood. 1917.

220 Hot Blood and Cold Steel

Vaughan (E.C.) *Some Desperate Glory: The Diary of a Young Officer, 1917.*
Leo Cooper. 1981. Copyright by C.E.C.Vaughan & P.J.M.Vaughan, 1981,
extracts reproduced by kind permission of Leo Cooper Ltd.

Watson (Major W.H.L.) *A Company of Tanks.* Blackwood. 1920.
Wheatley (Denis) *The Time Has Come... Officer and Temporary Gentleman
1914-1919.* Hutchinson. 1978. Copyright by Denis Wheatley Ltd. 1978.
Extracts reproduced by kind permission.

Young (Desmond) *Try Anything Twice.* Hamish Hamilton. 1963.
Copyright by Desmond Young. 1963

Secondary sources and suggestions for further reading

Barnett (Correlli) The Swordbearers: Studies in Supreme Command in
the First World War. Eyre and Spottiswoode. 1963.

Barrie (Alexander) *War Underground. The Tunnellers of the Great War.*
Tom Donovan. 1988.

Baynes (John) *Morale: A Study of Men and Courage: The Second Scottish
Rifles at the Battle of Neuve Chapelle 1915.* Cassell. 1967.

Beckett (Ian F. W.) and Simpson (Keith) eds. *A Nation in Arms.* Tom
Donovan. 1990.

Bidwell (Shelford) and Graham (Dominick) *Fire-Power: British Army
Weapons and Theories of War, 1904-45.* Allen and Unwin. 1982.

Cooper (Bryan) *The Ironclads of Cambrai.* Pan Books. 1970.

Essame (H.) *The Battle for Europe 1918.* Batsford. 1972.

Farrar-Hockley (A. H.) *The Somme.* Batsford. 1964.

Liddell Hart (B. H.) *The Real War 1914-1918.* Faber and Faber. 1930.

Middlebrook (Martin) *The First Day on the Somme.* Allen Lane. 1971.

Nicholson (Col. W.N.) *Behind the Lines: An Account of Administrative Staffwork in the British Army 1914-1918.* Strong Oak Press/Tom Donovan. 1989.

Prior (Robin) and Wilson (Trevor) *Command on the Western Front.* Blackwell. 1992.

Terraine (John) *Douglas Haig: The Educated Soldier.* Hutchinson. 1963.

Terraine (John) *To Win a War: 1918, the year of victory.* Sidgwick and Jackson. 1978.

Travers (Tim) *How the War was Won. Command and Technology in the British Army on the Western Front 1917-1918.* Routledge. 1992.

Travers (Tim) *The Killing Ground: The British Army, the Western Front and the Emergence of Modern Warfare 1900-1918.* Allen and Unwin. 1987.

Tuchman (Barbara) *The Guns of August.* Macmillan. 1962.

Williams (Jeffrey) *Byng of Vimy: General and Governor General.* Leo Cooper/Secker and Warburg. 1983.

Woolf (Leon) *In Flanders Fields: The 1917 Campaign.* Longmans, Green. 1960.

Index